Houghton Mifflin Harcourt

CALIFORNIA
MATH
Expressions
Common Core

Dr. Karen C. Fuson

GRADE
4

Volume 1

This material is based upon work supported by the
National Science Foundation
under Grant Numbers
ESI-9816320, REC-9806020, and RED-935373.

Any opinions, findings, and conclusions, or recommendations expressed in this material
are those of the author and do not necessarily reflect the views of the National Science Foundation.

VOLUME 1 CONTENTS

UNIT 1 Place Value and Multidigit Addition and Subtraction

UNIT 2 Multiplication with Whole Numbers

UNIT 3 Division with Whole Numbers

UNIT 4 Equations and Word Problems

STUDENT RESOURCES

© Houghton Mifflin Harcourt Publishing Company

Family Letter

Content Overview

Dear Family,

Your child is learning math in an innovative program called *Math Expressions*. In Unit 1, your child will use place value drawings and charts to understand that the value of each place is 10 times greater than the value of the place to its right. This understanding is essential when comparing, rounding, or adding multidigit numbers. *Math Expressions* encourages children to think about "making new groups" to help them understand place values.

We call the method below "New Groups Above". The numbers that represent the new groups are written above the problem.

1. Add the ones:

5 + 7 = 12 ones
12 = 2 ones + 10 ones,
and 10 ones = 1 new ten.

$$\begin{array}{r} \overset{1}{5,1\,7\,5} \\ +\;3,9\,6\,7 \\ \hline 2 \end{array}$$

2. Add the tens:

1 + 7 + 6 = 14 tens
14 = 4 tens + 10 tens,
and 10 tens = 1 new hundred.

$$\begin{array}{r} \overset{1\;1}{5,1\,7\,5} \\ +\;3,9\,6\,7 \\ \hline 4\,2 \end{array}$$

3. Add the hundreds:

1 + 1 + 9 = 11 hundreds
11 = 1 hundred + 10 hundreds,
and 10 hundreds = 1 new thousand.

$$\begin{array}{r} \overset{1\;1\;1}{5,1\,7\,5} \\ +\;3,9\,6\,7 \\ \hline 1\,4\,2 \end{array}$$

4. Add the thousands:

1 + 5 + 3 = 9 thousands

$$\begin{array}{r} \overset{1\;1\;1}{5,1\,7\,5} \\ +\;3,9\,6\,7 \\ \hline 9,1\,4\,2 \end{array}$$

We call the following method "New Groups Below." The steps are the same, but the new groups are written below the addends.

It is easier to see the totals for each column (12 and 14) and adding is easier because you add the two numbers you see and then add the 1.

1.
$$\begin{array}{r} 5,1\,7\,5 \\ +\;3,9\,6\,7 \\ \hline 2 \end{array}$$

2.
$$\begin{array}{r} 5,1\,7\,5 \\ +\;3,9\,6\,7 \\ \hline 4\,2 \end{array}$$

3.
$$\begin{array}{r} 5,1\,7\,5 \\ +\;3,9\,6\,7 \\ \hline 1\,4\,2 \end{array}$$

4.
$$\begin{array}{r} 5,1\,7\,5 \\ +\;3,9\,6\,7 \\ \hline 9,1\,4\,2 \end{array}$$

It is important that your child maintains his or her home practice with basic multiplication and division.

Sincerely,
Your child's teacher

 CA CC

Unit 1 addresses the following standards from the *Common Core State Standards for Mathematics with California Additions:* **4.NBT.1, 4.NBT.2, 4.NBT.3, 4.NBT.4, 4.MD.2** and all Mathematical Practices.

© Houghton Mifflin Harcourt Publishing Company

Estimada familia,

Su niño está aprendiendo matemáticas mediante el programa *Math Expressions*. En la Unidad 1, se usarán dibujos y tablas de valor posicional para comprender que el valor de cada lugar es 10 veces mayor que el valor del lugar a su derecha. Comprender esto es esencial para comparar, redondear o sumar números de varios dígitos. *Math Expressions* enseña a pensar en "formar grupos nuevos" para comprender los valores posicionales.

Este método se llama "Grupos nuevos arriba". Los números que representan los grupos nuevos se escriben arriba del problema:

1. Suma las unidades:

5 + 7 = 12 unidades
12 = 2 unidades + 10 unidades,
y 10 unidades = 1 nueva decena.

$$\begin{array}{r} ^{1} \\ 5,175 \\ +\ 3,967 \\ \hline 2 \end{array}$$

2. Suma las decenas:

1 + 7 + 6 = 14 decenas
14 = 4 decenas + 10 decenas,
y 10 decenas = 1 nueva centena.

$$\begin{array}{r} ^{1\ 1} \\ 5,175 \\ +\ 3,967 \\ \hline 42 \end{array}$$

3. Suma las centenas:

1 + 1 + 9 = 11 centenas
11 = 1 centenas + 10 centenas,
y 10 centenas = 1 nuevo millar.

$$\begin{array}{r} ^{1\ \ 1\ 1} \\ 5,175 \\ +\ 3,967 \\ \hline 142 \end{array}$$

4. Suma los millares:

1 + 5 + 3 = 9 millares

$$\begin{array}{r} ^{1\ \ 1\ 1} \\ 5,175 \\ +\ 3,967 \\ \hline 9,142 \end{array}$$

Este método se llama "Grupos nuevos abajo". Los pasos son iguales, pero los nuevos grupos se escriben abajo de los sumandos:

Es más fácil ver los totales de cada columna (12 y 14) y es más fácil sumar porque sumas los dos números que ves, y luego sumas 1.

1.
$$\begin{array}{r} 5,175 \\ +\ 3,967 \\ \hline 2 \end{array}$$

2.
$$\begin{array}{r} 5,175 \\ +\ 3,967 \\ \hline 42 \end{array}$$

3.
$$\begin{array}{r} 5,175 \\ +\ 3,967 \\ \hline 142 \end{array}$$

4.
$$\begin{array}{r} 5,175 \\ +\ 3,967 \\ \hline 9,142 \end{array}$$

Es importante que su niño siga practicando las multiplicaciones y divisiones básicas en casa.

Atentamente,
El maestro de su niño

CA CC

En la Unidad 1 se aplican los siguientes estándares auxiliares, contenidos en los *Estándares estatales comunes de matemáticas con adiciones para California:* **4.NBT.1, 4.NBT.2, 4.NBT.3, 4.NBT.4, 4.MD.2** y todos los de prácticas matemáticas.

Name _____ **Date** _____

CA CC Content Standards 4.NBT.1
Mathematical Practices MP.2, MP.5, MP.7

▶ Model Hundreds

You can represent numbers by making **place value drawings** on a **dot array**.

1. What number does this drawing show? _____
   Explain your thinking.

   _____

   _____

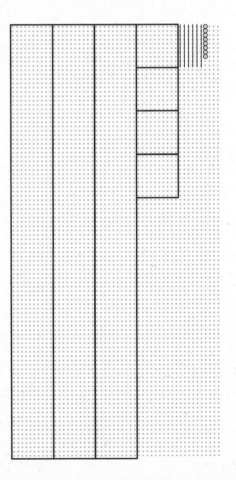

▶ Model Thousands

Discuss this place value drawing. Write the number of each.

2. ones: _____

3. quick tens: _____

4. hundred boxes: _____

5. thousand bars: _____

6. How many hundred boxes could we draw inside each thousand bar? Explain.

   _____

   _____

7. What number does this drawing show?

Name _____ Date _____

► Model Greater Numbers

Place value can also be shown without using a dot array.

8. What number does this drawing represent?
Explain your thinking.

_____

_____

_____

_____

What would the drawing represent if it had:

9. 3 more hundred boxes? _____

10. 0 hundred boxes? _____

11. 2 fewer quick tens? _____

12. 2 more quick tens? _____

13. 0 quick tens? _____

14. 5 fewer ones? _____

15. 0 ones? _____

16. 4 more thousand bars? _____

17. On your MathBoard, make a place value drawing for a different number that has the digits 1, 2, 7, and 9.

18. Explain how your drawing is similar to and different from the drawing for 1,279.

_____

_____

► Practice with Place Value Drawings

Make a place value drawing for each number, using ones, quick tens, and hundred boxes.

19. 6

20. 3

21. 603

22. 300

23. 63

24. 32

25. 325

26. 285

27. 109

28. 573

Name _____ Date _____

► Practice Modeling Thousands

Make a place value drawing for each number, using ones, quick tens, hundred boxes, and thousand bars.

29. 2,596   30. 3,045

► **Whole Number Secret Code Cards**

1,000	100	10	1
1,000	100	10	1
2,000	200	20	2
2,000	200	20	2
3,000	300	30	3
3,000	300	30	3
4,000	400	40	4
4,000	400	40	4
5,000	500	50	5
5,000	500	50	5
6,000	600	60	6
6,000	600	60	6
7,000	700	70	7
7,000	700	70	7
8,000	800	80	8
8,000	800	80	8
9,000	900	90	9
9,000	900	90	9

▶ Whole Number Secret Code Cards

one	ten (teen) (one ten)	one hundred	one thousand
two	twenty (two tens)	two hundred	two thousand
three	thirty (three tens)	three hundred	three thousand
four	forty (four tens)	four hundred	four thousand
five	fifty (five tens)	five hundred	five thousand
six	sixty (six tens)	six hundred	six thousand
seven	seventy (seven tens)	seven hundred	seven thousand
eight	eighty (eight tens)	eight hundred	eight thousand
nine	ninety (nine tens)	nine hundred	nine thousand

Whole Number Secret Code Cards

► The Place Value Chart

Discuss the patterns you see in the Place Value Poster below.

× 10 (Greater)

Thousands	Hundreds	Tens	ONES
1,000.	100.	10.	1.
$\frac{1{,}000}{1}$	$\frac{100}{1}$	$\frac{10}{1}$	$\frac{1}{1}$
$1,000.00	$100.00	$10.00	$1

Use your Whole Number Secret Code Cards to make numbers on the frame.

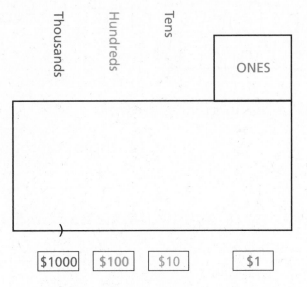

Thousands   Hundreds   Tens   ONES

| $1000 | $100 | $10 | | $1 |

► **Write Numbers Using Expanded Form**

Standard form: 8,562

Word form: eight thousand, five hundred sixty-two

Expanded form: 8,000 + 500 + 60 + 2

Read and write each number in expanded form.

1. 73 _70+3_

2. 108 _100+8_

3. 5,621 _5,000+600+20+1_

4. 4,350 _4,000+300+50_

5. 8,083 _8,000+80+3_

6. 1,006 _1,006+6_

Read and write each number in standard form.

7. 40 + 3 _43_

8. 200 + 60 + 1 _261_

9. 900 + 5 _905_

10. 1,000 + 70 + 9 _1,079_

11. 5,000 + 30 _5,030_

12. 9,000 + 800 + 4 _9,804_

Read and write each number in word form.

13. 400 + 40 + 1 _four fourty one_

14. 1,000 + 50 _one thousand fifty_

Read and write each number in standard form.

15. thirty-five

_____

16. three hundred five

_____

17. six thousand, eight

_____

18. six thousand, one hundred eight

_____

Write the value of the underlined digit.

19. 7<u>5</u>6 _____

20. <u>4</u>,851 _____

21. 6,<u>5</u>07 _____

Place Value Patterns

Name

Date

CA CC Content Standards **4.NBT.2, 4.NBT.3**
Mathematical Practices **MP.2**

▶ Summarize Rounding Rules

Use these rounding frames as a visual aid when rounding
to the nearest 10, 100, 1,000.

Nearest 10	Nearest 100	Nearest 1,000
100	1,000	10,000
90	900	9,000
80	800	8,000
70	700	7,000
60	600	6,000
50	500	5,000
40	400	4,000
30	300	3,000
20	200	2,000
10	100	1,000

Round to the nearest ten.

1. 87 _____

2. 16 _____

3. 171 _____

4. 2,165 _____

5. 5,114 _____

6. 3,098 _____

Round to the nearest hundred.

7. 734 _____

8. 363 _____

9. 178 _____

10. 6,249 _____

11. 8,251 _____

12. 8,992 _____

Round to the nearest thousand.

13. 1,275 _____

14. 8,655 _____

15. 5,482 _____

16. 3,804 _____

17. 1,501 _____

18. 9,702 _____

Name _Mia_

Date _____

VOCABULARY
greater than >
less than <

▶ Compare Numbers

Discuss the problem below.

Jim has 24 trading cards and Hattie has 42 trading cards.
Who has more trading cards? How do you know?

Draw a place value model for each problem.
Write > (greater than), < (less than), or = to make
each statement true.

19. 26 (<) 29   **20.** 44 (>) 34   **21.** 26 (<) 62

Compare using >, <, or =.

22. 74 (<) 77   **23.** 85 (>) 58   **24.** 126 (<) 162

25. 253 (>) 235   **26.** 620 (>) 602   **27.** 825 (>) 528

28. 478 (<) 488   **29.** 3,294 (<) 3,924   **30.** 8,925 (<) 9,825

31. 6,706 (<) 6,760   **32.** 4,106 (>) 4,016   **33.** 1,997 (>) 1,799

34. 9,172 (=) 9,712   **35.** 5,296 (=) 5,269   **36.** 7,684 (=) 7,684

▶ Discuss and Summarize

Patterns to Millions

Hundred Millions	Ten Millions	Millions	Hundred Thousands	Ten Thousands	Thousands	Hundreds	Tens	Ones
100,000,000	10,000,000	1,000,000	100,000	10,000	1,000	100	10	1
millions			*thousands*			*[ones]*		

The Patterns to Millions chart shows that each digit in the number has a place value name. When we read a number, we do not say the place value name. We say the group name.

We say the word *million* after the digits in the millions group.

We say the word *thousand* after the digits in the thousands group.

We do not say the word *ones* after the digits in the ones group.

To read greater numbers, say each group of digits as if they were in the hundreds, tens, and ones places and then add the special name for that group.

▶ Read Numbers

Use your Whole Number Secret Code cards to make the groups of digits as shown below. Put them in the spaces on the Reading Millions Frame below to read them.

28,374   123,456   458,726   654,321   92,148   789,321

Reading Millions Frame

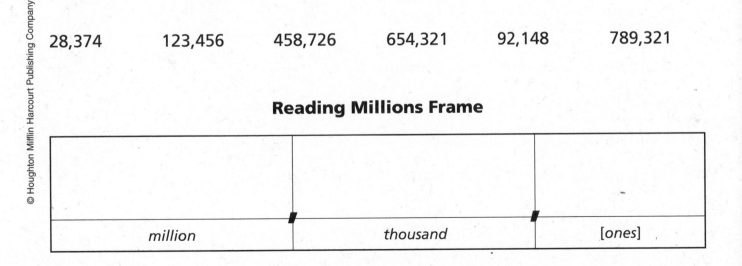

million	*thousand*	*[ones]*

© Houghton Mifflin Harcourt Publishing Company

► Read and Write Expanded Form

Read and write each number in expanded form.

1. 32,568 _30,000 + 2000 + 500 + 60 + 8_

2. 820,149 _800,000 + 20000 + 100 + 40 + 9_

3. 405,763 _400,000 + 5,000 + 700 + 60 + 3_

4. 703,070 _700,000 + 3,000 + 70_

Read and write each number in standard form.

5. 20,000 + 4,000 + 800 + 10 + 7 _24,817_

6. 700,000 + 50,000 + 3,000 + 200 + 90 + 6 _753,296_

7. 300,000 + 3,000 + 10 + 9 _303,19_

8. 800,000 + 40,000 + 400 + 80 _840,480_

Read and write each number in word form.

9. 90,000 + 7,000 + 300 + 20 + 4 _ninty thousand seven thousand three hundrad twenty four_

10. 600,000 + 30,000 + 4,000 + 700 + 30 _trety thousand four thousand six hundrad thousand_

11. 200,000 + 3,000 + 80 + 6 _____

12. 500,000 + 20,000 + 400 + 1 _____

Read and write each number in standard form.

13. seventy-eight thousand, one hundred five _____

14. one million _____

15. five hundred sixty-three thousand, fifty-two _____

► Compare Greater Numbers

Discuss the problem below.

A stadium hosted both a concert and a sporting event.
The concert had 101,835 people in attendance. The sporting
event had 101,538 people in attendance. Which event had
more people in attendance? How do you know?

Compare. Write >, <, or = to make each statement true.

1. 12,563 $>$ 11,987

2. 14,615 $<$ 15,651

3. 23,487 $<$ 28,734

4. 83,342 $>$ 80,423

5. 79,131 $>$ 79,113

6. 126,348 $<$ 162,634

7. 705,126 $=$ 705,126

8. 532,834 $>$ 532,843

9. 647,313 $>$ 647,310

10. 198,593 $>$ 98,593

11. 75,621 $<$ 705,126

12. 1,000,000 $>$ 100,000

► Greatest Place Value

Round to the nearest ten thousand.

13. 25,987 _26,000_   14. 13,738 _14,000_   15. 48,333 _48,000_

16. 84,562 _85,000_   17. 92,132 _92,000_   18. 99,141 _99,000_

Round to the nearest hundred thousand.

19. 531,987 _5 0,000_   20. 701,828 _700,00 0_

21. 670,019 _670,000_   22. 249,845 _200,000_

23. 390,101 _400,000_   24. 999,999 _1,000,000_

▶ Round to Any Place

Solve.

25. Write a number that changes to 310,000 when it is rounded. To what place was your number rounded?

_____

26. Write a number that changes to 901,400 when it is rounded. To what place was your number rounded?

_____

27. Write a number that changes to 800,000 when it is rounded. To what place was your number rounded?

_____

28. Write a number that changes to 122,000 when it is rounded. To what place was your number rounded?

_____

29. What is 395,101 rounded to the nearest:

   a. ten? _____

   b. hundred? _____

   c. thousand? _____

   d. ten thousand? _____

   e. hundred thousand? _____

30. What is 958,069 rounded to the nearest:

   a. ten? _____

   b. hundred? _____

   c. thousand? _____

   d. ten thousand? _____

   e. hundred thousand? _____

> **VOCABULARY**
> groups

▶ Discuss Different Methods

Discuss how each addition method can be used to add
4-digit numbers.

$5,879 + 6,754$

1. New Groups Above Method

Step 1	Step 2	Step 3	Step 4
¹	¹¹	¹ ¹¹	¹ ¹ ¹
5,879	5,879	5,879	5,879
+ 6,754	+ 6,754	+ 6,754	+ 6,754
3	33	633	12,633

2. New Groups Below Method

Step 1	Step 2	Step 3	Step 4
5,879	5,879	5,879	5,879
+ 6,754	+ 6,754	+ 6,754	+ 6,754
₁	₁₁	₁ ₁₁	₁ ₁ ₁
3	33	633	12,633

3. Show Subtotals Method (Right-to-Left)

Step 1	Step 2	Step 3	Step 4	Step 5
5,879	5,879	5,879	5,879	5,879
+ 6,754	+ 6,754	+ 6,754	+ 6,754	+ 6,754
13	13	13	13	13
	120	120	120	120
		1,500	1,500	1,500
			11,000	+ 11,000
				12,633

▶ PATH to FLUENCY **Practice**

4.   908
     + 653

5.   692
     + 543

6.   5,362
     + 3,746

7.   3,786
     + 6,335

© Houghton Mifflin Harcourt Publishing Company

► **Practice (continued)**

8.   2,782
    + 5,246

9.   6,293
    + 3,862

10.   3,729
    + 4,541

11.   8,196
    + 3,865

12.   7,862
    + 2,839

13.   2,764
    + 6,648

14.   4,825
    + 2,467

15.   5,364
    + 4,754

► Addition and Money

Think about how to solve this problem.

Carlos is saving money to buy a skateboard. He saved $27 one week and $14 the next week. How much did Carlos save altogether?

Solve each problem.

16. Robyn's grandmother gave her $38 for her birthday and her uncle gave her $25. How much did Robyn get altogether?

_____

17. A parent-teacher club sold baked goods to raise money for the school. They collected $268 on Friday and $479 on Saturday. How much did they collect altogether?

_____

► Analyze Different Methods

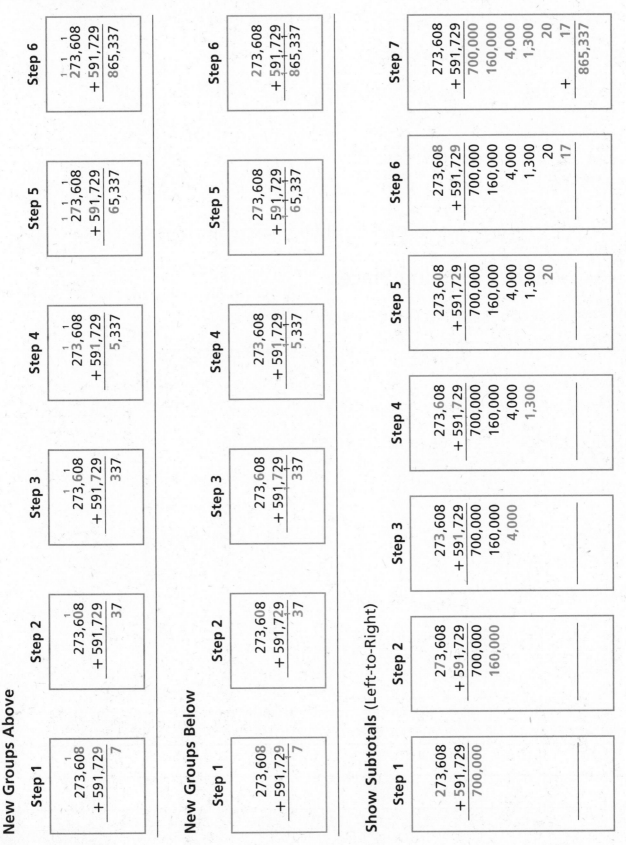

New Groups Above

Step 1	Step 2	Step 3	Step 4	Step 5	Step 6
273,608 + 591,729 7	273,608 + 591,729 37	273,608 + 591,729 337	273,608 + 591,729 5,337	273,608 + 591,729 65,337	273,608 + 591,729 865,337

New Groups Below

Step 1	Step 2	Step 3	Step 4	Step 5	Step 6
273,608 + 591,729 7	273,608 + 591,729 37	273,608 + 591,729 337	273,608 + 591,729 5,337	273,608 + 591,729 65,337	273,608 + 591,729 865,337

Show Subtotals (Left-to-Right)

Step 1	Step 2	Step 3	Step 4	Step 5	Step 6	Step 7
273,608 + 591,729 700,000	273,608 + 591,729 700,000 160,000	273,608 + 591,729 700,000 160,000 4,000	273,608 + 591,729 700,000 160,000 4,000 1,300	273,608 + 591,729 700,000 160,000 4,000 1,300 20	273,608 + 591,729 700,000 160,000 4,000 1,300 20 17	273,608 + 591,729 700,000 160,000 4,000 1,300 20 + 17 865,337

VOCABULARY
digit

► Find the Mistake

When you add, it is important that you add **digits** in like places.

Look at the these addition exercises.

43,629 + 5,807   1,468 + 327,509   470,952 + 4,306

$$
\begin{array}{r}
43,629 \\
+\ 5,807 \\
\hline
101,699
\end{array}
\qquad
\begin{array}{r}
1,468 \\
+\ 327,509 \\
\hline
474,309
\end{array}
\qquad
\begin{array}{r}
470,952 \\
+\ 4,306 \\
\hline
901,552
\end{array}
$$

1. Discuss the mistake that appears in all three exercises above.

► PATH to FLUENCY Practice Aligning Places

Copy each exercise, aligning places correctly. Then add.

2. 2,647 + 38

3. 156 + 83,291

4. 4,389 + 49,706

5. 135,826 + 2,927

6. 347,092 + 6,739

7. 15,231 + 697,084

8. Write an addition word problem that has an answer of $43,568.

_____

_____

_____

_____

Name _____ Date _____

CA CC Content Standards 4.OA.3, 4.NBT.3, 4.NBT.4
Mathematical Practices MP.1, MP.2, MP.6

► Use Estimation

You can use rounding to estimate a total. Then you can adjust your estimated total to find the exact total.

The best-selling fruits at Joy's Fruit Shack are peaches and bananas. During one month Joy sold 397 peaches and 412 bananas.

1. *About* how many peaches and bananas did she sell in all?

   _____

2. *Exactly* how many peaches and bananas did she sell?

   _____

Estimate. Then adjust your estimate to find the exact answer.

3. $89 + 28$ 4. $153 + 98$

5. $1,297 + 802$ 6. $1,066 + 45,104$

Solve.   *Show your work.*

Tomás has $100. He wants to buy a $38 camera. He also wants to buy a $49 CD player and 2 CDs that are on sale 2 for $8.

7. How can Tomás figure out whether he has enough money for all four items? Does he have enough?

   _____

   _____

▶ Use Estimation (continued)

Solve.   *Show your work.*

Students at Washington Middle School collected
1,598 cans during the first month of their aluminum
drive. During the second month of the drive, they
collected 2,006 cans.

8. About how many cans did the students collect in all?

   _____

9. Exactly how many cans did the students collect in all?

   _____

▶ Look for "Easy" Combinations

You can sometimes find number combinations that make it
possible to add numbers mentally.

10. Add 243, 274, 252, and 231 vertically.

11. Explain how you can use number combinations to help
    you add the numbers.

    _____

    _____

    _____

▶ Share Solutions

Find the total. Add mentally if you can.

12.	13.	14.	15.	16.
8	46	35	348	147
4	21	29	516	182
6	+ 64	75	+ 492	108
+ 2		+ 61		+ 165

Family Letter

Content Overview

Dear Family,

Your child is now learning about subtraction. A common subtraction mistake is subtracting in the wrong direction. Children may think that they always subtract the smaller digit from the larger digit, but this is not true. To help children avoid this mistake, the *Math Expressions* program encourages children to "fix" numbers first and then subtract.

When one or more digits in the top number are smaller than the corresponding digits in the bottom number, fix the numbers by "ungrouping." For example, 1,634 − 158 is shown below:

1. We cannot subtract 8 ones from 4 ones. We get more ones by ungrouping 1 ten to make 10 ones.

We now have 14 ones and only 2 tens.

$$
\begin{array}{r}
2\,14 \\
1,6\,\cancel{3}\,\cancel{4} \\
-\;\;158 \\
\hline
\end{array}
$$

2. We cannot subtract 5 tens from 2 tens. We get more tens by ungrouping 1 hundred to make 10 tens.

We now have 12 tens and only 5 hundreds.

$$
\begin{array}{r}
12 \\
5\,\cancel{2}14 \\
1,\cancel{6}\,\cancel{3}\,\cancel{4} \\
-\;\;158 \\
\hline
\end{array}
$$

3. Now we can subtract:
1 − 0 = 1 thousand
5 − 1 = 4 hundreds
12 − 5 = 7 tens
14 − 8 = 6 ones

$$
\begin{array}{r}
12 \\
5\,\cancel{2}14 \\
1,\cancel{6}\,\cancel{3}\,\cancel{4} \\
-\;\;158 \\
\hline
1,476
\end{array}
$$

In the method above, the numbers are ungrouped from right to left, but students can also ungroup from left to right. Children can choose whichever way works best for them.

Your child should also continue to practice multiplication and division skills at home.

If you have any questions or comments, please call or write me.

Sincerely,
Your child's teacher

 CA CC

Unit 1 addresses the following standards from the *Common Core State Standards for Mathematics with California Additions*: **4.NBT.3, 4.NBT.4, 4.MD.2** and all Mathematical Practices.

© Houghton Mifflin Harcourt Publishing Company

Estimada familia:

Ahora su niño está aprendiendo a restar. Un error muy común al restar, es hacerlo en la dirección equivocada. Los niños pueden pensar que siempre se resta el dígito más pequeño del dígito más grande, pero no es verdad. Para ayudar a los niños a no cometer este error, el programa *Math Expressions* les propone "arreglar" los números primero y luego restar.

Cuando uno o más dígitos del número de arriba son más pequeños que los dígitos correspondientes del número de abajo, se arreglan los números "desagrupándolos". Por ejemplo, 1,634 − 158 se muestra abajo:

1. No podemos restar 8 unidades de 4 unidades. Obtenemos más unidades al desagrupar 1 decena para formar 10 unidades.

Ahora tenemos 14 unidades y solamente 2 decenas.

$$
\begin{array}{r}
\overset{\overset{2\ 14}{}}{1,6\,\cancel{3}\,\cancel{4}} \\
-\ \ 1\ 5\ 8 \\
\hline
\end{array}
$$

2. No podemos restar 5 decenas de 2 decenas. Obtenemos más decenas al desagrupar 1 centena para formar 10 decenas.

Ahora tenemos 12 decenas y solamente 5 centenas.

$$
\begin{array}{r}
\overset{\overset{12}{5\ \cancel{2}\ 14}}{1,\cancel{6}\,\cancel{3}\,\cancel{4}} \\
-\ \ 1\ 5\ 8 \\
\hline
\end{array}
$$

3. Ahora podemos restar:
$1 − 0 = 1$ millar
$5 − 1 = 4$ centenas
$12 − 5 = 7$ decenas
$14 − 8 = 6$ unidades

$$
\begin{array}{r}
\overset{\overset{12}{5\ \cancel{2}\ 14}}{1,\cancel{6}\,\cancel{3}\,\cancel{4}} \\
-\ \ 1\ 5\ 8 \\
\hline
1,4\ 7\ 6
\end{array}
$$

En el método de arriba se desagrupan los números de derecha a izquierda, pero también se pueden desagrupar de izquierda a derecha. Los niños pueden escoger la manera que les resulte más fácil.

Su niño también debe seguir practicando las destrezas de multiplicación y de división en casa.

Si tiene alguna pregunta, por favor comuníquese conmigo.

Atentamente,
El maestro de su niño

© Houghton Mifflin Harcourt Publishing Company

 CA CC

En la Unidad 1 se aplican los siguientes estándares auxiliares, contenidos en los *Estándares estatales comunes de matemáticas con adiciones para California*: **4.NBT.3, 4.NBT.4, 4.MD.2** y todos los de prácticas matemáticas.

▶ Discuss Ungrouping With Zeros

Look inside the magnifying glass and discuss each ungrouping step.

1. Ungroup step-by-step: *or*   **2.** Ungroup all at once:

▶ Decide When to Ungroup

3. Ungroup left-to-right: *or*   **4.** Ungroup right-to-left:

▶ Other Ungrouping Situations

5. When we have zeros and other digits on the top:

6. When we have the same digit on the top and bottom:

▶ PATH to FLUENCY **Practice**

Subtract. Show your new groups.

7.   634
     − 256

8.   800
     − 691

9.   9,462
      − 5,678

Subtract. Show your new groups.

10.	7,919	11.	8,502	12.	4,221
	− 3,846		− 3,749		− 2,805

13.	7,000	14.	4,650	15.	4,605
	− 572		− 2,793		− 1,711

16.	3,120	17.	6,082	18.	2,107
	− 38		− 95		− 428

19.	1,852	20.	3,692	21.	8,715
	− 964		− 2,704		− 6,742

22.	6,000	23.	7,400	24.	3,583
	− 4,351		− 1,215		− 1,794

Solve.

25. Jake has 647 pennies in his penny collection album. The album has space for 1,000 pennies. How many more pennies can Jake place in his album?

_____

26. A ship is making an 8,509-mile voyage. So far, it has sailed 2,957 miles. How many miles of the voyage remain?

_____

Name

Date

CA CC Content Standards **4.NBT.4**
Mathematical Practices **MP.1, MP.4**

▶ Relate Addition to Subtraction

Addition and subtraction are **inverse operations**.
Break-apart drawings help to show inverse relationships.

1. Write a word problem that requires adding 1,310
and 2,057.

_____

_____

_____

2. Write the **addends** and the sum in the break-apart
drawing.

3. Complete the two addition problems represented by
the break-apart drawing.

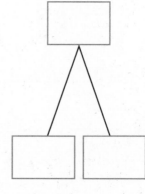

$$\begin{array}{r} 1{,}310 \\ +\underline{} \\ \hline 3{,}367 \end{array} \qquad \begin{array}{r} 2{,}057 \\ +\underline{} \\ \hline \underline{} \end{array}$$

4. Write a word problem that requires subtracting 1,310
from 3,367.

_____

_____

_____

5. Write two subtraction problems represented by the
break-apart drawing.

Name _____ Date _____

▶  **PATH to FLUENCY** **Practice**

Subtract. Then use addition to check the subtraction.
Show your work.

6. 1,900
  − 574

Check: _____

7. 1,800
  − 1,216

Check: _____

8. 5,192
  − 341

Check: _____

9. 6,350
  − 2,460

Check: _____

10. 7,523
   − 3,424

Check: _____

11. 2,000
   − 651

Check: _____

Solve.

12. In April, the zookeepers fed the penguins 4,620 fish.
    In May, they fed the penguins 5,068 fish. How many
    fish did they feed the penguins altogether?

    _____

13. The head keeper knew how many fish the penguins
    had been fed altogether, and she knew they had been
    fed 4,620 fish in April. Write a subtraction problem to
    show how the keeper could determine the number of
    fish the penguins had been fed in May.

    _____

Subtraction Undoes Addition

Name _____ **Date** _____

CA CC Content Standards **4.OA.3, 4.NBT.4**
Mathematical Practices **MP.1, MP.3, MP.6**

► Find and Correct Mistakes

Always check your work. Many mistakes can be easily fixed.

What is the mistake in each problem? How can you fix the mistake and find the correct answer?

1. 67,308 − 5,497

$$
\begin{array}{r}
\overset{\overset{12}{6\ \cancel{13}\ 10}}{6\,\cancel{7}\,\cancel{3}\,\cancel{0}\,8} \\
-\ 5{,}4\,9\,7 \\
\hline
1\,2{,}3\,3\,8
\end{array}
$$

2. 134,865 − 5,294

$$
\begin{array}{r}
1\,3\,4{,}8\,6\,5 \\
-\ \ \ \ 5{,}2\,9\,4 \\
\hline
1\,3\,1{,}6\,3\,1
\end{array}
$$

_____   _____

_____   _____

_____   _____

_____   _____

_____   _____

► Check Subtraction by "Adding Up"

"Add up" to find any places where there is a subtraction mistake. Discuss how each mistake might have been made and correct the subtraction if necessary.

3.
$$
\begin{array}{r}
163{,}406 \\
-\ 84{,}357 \\
\hline
79{,}159
\end{array}
$$

4.
$$
\begin{array}{r}
526{,}741 \\
-\ 139{,}268 \\
\hline
413{,}473
\end{array}
$$

5.
$$
\begin{array}{r}
1{,}000{,}000 \\
-\ 300{,}128 \\
\hline
600{,}872
\end{array}
$$

6.
$$
\begin{array}{r}
5{,}472{,}639 \\
-\ 2{,}375{,}841 \\
\hline
3{,}096{,}798
\end{array}
$$

7. Write and solve a subtraction problem with numbers in the hundred thousands.

_____

_____

Name _____ Date _____

▶ Estimate Differences

You can use estimation to decide if an answer is reasonable.

Dan did this subtraction: 8,196 − 5,980. His answer was 3,816. Discuss how using estimation can help you decide if his answer is correct.

Decide whether each answer is reasonable. Show your estimate.

8. 4,914 − 949 = 3,065

9. 52,022 − 29,571 = 22,451

_____   _____

_____   _____

Solve.

Show your work.

10. Bob has 3,226 marbles in his collection. Mia has 1,867 marbles. Bob says he has 2,359 more than Mia. Is Bob's answer reasonable? Show your estimate.

_____

11. Two towns have populations of 24,990 and 12,205. Gretchen says the difference is 12,785. Is Gretchen's answer reasonable? Show your estimate.

_____

12. Estimate to decide if the answer is reasonable. If it is not reasonable, describe the mistake and find the correct answer.

$$\begin{array}{r} 805,716 \\ -\ 290,905 \\ \hline 614,811 \end{array}$$

_____

_____

_____

▶ Discuss the Steps of the Problem

Sometimes you will need to work through more than one step to solve a problem. The steps can be shown in one or more equations.

1. In the morning, 19 students were working on a science project. In the afternoon, 3 students left and 7 more students came to work on the project. How many students were working on the project at the end of the day?

_____

2. Solve the problem again by finishing Anita's and Chad's methods. Then discuss what is alike and what is different about each method.

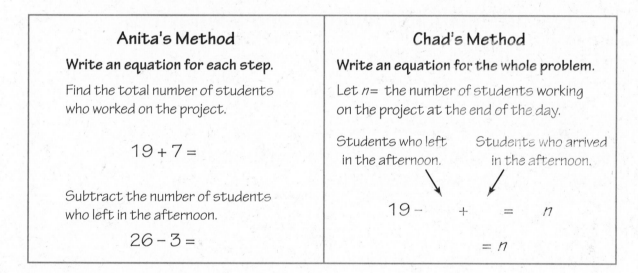

Anita's Method	**Chad's Method**
Write an equation for each step.	**Write an equation for the whole problem.**
Find the total number of students who worked on the project.	Let $n=$ the number of students working on the project at the end of the day.
$19 + 7 =$	Students who left in the afternoon. Students who arrived in the afternoon.
Subtract the number of students who left in the afternoon.	$19 - \quad + \quad = \quad n$
$26 - 3 =$	$= n$

3. Solve. Discuss the steps you used.

A team is scheduled to play 12 games. Of those games, 7 will be played at home. The other games are away games. How many fewer away games than home games will be played?

_____

_____

► **Share Solutions**

Solve each problem.   *Show your work.*

4. The school library has 288 science books. Altogether the library has 618 science and animal books. How many fewer science books than animal books does the library have?

_____

5. Olivia's stamp collection consists of 442 stamps. There are 131 butterfly stamps and 107 dolphin stamps in her collection. How many of Olivia's stamps are not of butterflies or dolphins?

_____

► (PATH to FLUENCY) **Practice Multidigit Addition and Subtraction**

6.   985
   − 792
   _____

7.   2,931
   + 8,563
   _____

8.   4,201
   + 9,979
   _____

9.   98,309
   − 48,659
   _____

10.   78,196
   − 14,587
   _____

11.   21,682
   + 95,436
   _____

12.   373,095
   + 185,543
   _____

13.   709,032
   − 239,125
   _____

14.   540,721
   + 375,699
   _____

Practice Addition and Subtraction

▶ **Discuss Problem Types**

Think of different types of problems for each exercise.
Write an equation for the problem then solve it.

1. $a + 278 = 747$ **2.** $b - 346 = 587$ **3.**   **4.**

747   b   933   747
/ \   / \   / \   ┌──────────┐
a   278   346   587   c   346   │   e   469 │

_____   _____   _____   _____

_____   _____   _____   _____

▶ (PATH to FLUENCY) **Share Solutions**

Write an equation for the problem then solve it.   *Show your work.*
Make a math drawing if you need to.

5. Of 800,000 species of insects, about 560,000 undergo
complete metamorphosis. How many species do not
undergo complete metamorphosis?

_____

_____

6. The Great Pyramid of Giza has about 2,000,000 stone
blocks. A replica has 1,900,000 fewer blocks. How many
blocks are in the replica?

_____

_____

7. Last year 439,508 people visited Fun Town. This is
46,739 fewer visitors than this year. How many people
visited Fun Town this year?

_____

_____

▶ ⬤ PATH to FLUENCY **Share Solutions (continued)**

8. At the end of a baseball game, there were 35,602 people in the stadium. There were 37,614 people in the stadium at the beginning of the game. How many people left before the game ended?

_____

_____

9. This year Pinnacle Publishing printed 64,924 more books than Premier Publishing. If Pinnacle printed 231,069 books, how many books did Premier print?

_____

_____

10. Mary drove her car 2,483 miles during a road trip. Now she has 86,445 miles on her car. How many miles did her car have before her trip?

_____

_____

11. The Elbe River in Europe is 1,170 km long. The Yellow River in China is 5,465 km long. How long are the two rivers altogether?

_____

_____

12. A bridge is 1,595 feet long. Each cable holding up the bridge is 1,983 feet longer than the bridge itself. How long is each cable?

_____

_____

Problem Solving With Greater Numbers

► Subtraction and Money

Sondra had $140 to spend on new clothes for school. She bought a shirt for $21. You can use a model to help you find out how much money she has left.

Sondra had _____ left.

Solve each problem. Use money if you need to.

Show your work.

13. Jason had $30. He gave $18 to his brother. How much money does Jason have left?

_____

14. Elana's coach had some money to spend on softball equipment. She spent $76 on bases. She has $174 left. How much did she have to start?

_____

15. The school science club raised $325. After buying equipment for an experiment they had $168 left. How much did they spend?

_____

16. Amy paid $575 for new furniture. Before buying it she had $813. How much did she have afterward?

_____

Name _____ **Date** _____

▶ Determine Reasonable Answers

Solve each problem. Check your answers using inverse operations.

17. Mrs. Washington has $265. She wants to buy shoes for $67 and dresses for $184. Does she have enough money? Explain your answer. _____

18. Terrell wants to run a total of 105 miles during the month. He ran a total of 87 miles during the first 3 weeks of the month. How much does he have to run in the 4th week to make his goal? _____

▶ What's the Error?

Dear Math Students,

My friend is taking a trip to Antarctica. He gave me $112 to buy him some clothes. I tried to buy a parka and two pairs of wool socks, but the clerk said I didn't have enough money. I added up the cost like this:

$98 + $12 = $110

Can you help me figure out what I did wrong?

Your friend,
Puzzled Penguin

Bill's Outdoor Wear

Pair of Wool socks	$12
Hat	$15
Mitten	$10
Parka	$98

19. Write a response to Puzzled Penguin.

_____

_____

Name _____ **Date** _____

CA CC Content Standards **4.NBT.3, 4.NBT.4**
Mathematical Practices **MP.1, MP.4**

► Math and Bridges

Bridges are structures that are built to get over obstacles like water, a valley, or roads. Bridges can be made of concrete, steel, or even tree roots. Engineers and designers do a lot of math to be sure a bridge will stand up to its use and the forces of nature that affect it.

Lengths of Bridges		
Bridge	**Length Over Water (ft)**	
Manchac Swamp Bridge, U.S.A.	121,440	
Hangzhou Bay Bridge, China	117,057	
Lake Pontchartrain Causeway, U.S.A.	125,664	
Jiaozhou Bay Bridge, China	139,392	

1. Use the data in the table above to make a bar graph.

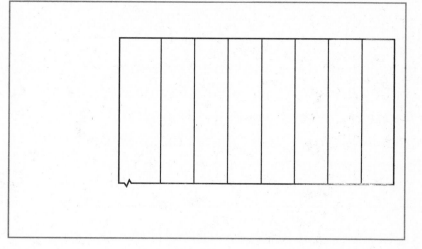

► Add and Subtract Greater Numbers

Lake Pontchartrain Causeway, U.S.A

For Exercises 2–5, use the data in the table on Student Book page 35.

Show your work.

2. How much longer is the Lake Pontchartrain Causeway than the Hangzhou Bay Bridge?

_____

3. What is the difference in length between the longest bridge and shortest bridge listed in the table?

_____

4. Liang's goal is to ride over the Hangzhou Bay Bridge and the Jiaozhou Bay Bridge. Tanya wants to ride over the Lake Pontchartrain Causeway and the Manchac Swamp Bridge. Who will travel the greater distance on the bridges? How many more feet will he or she travel?

_____

5. The Danyang-Kunshan Grand Bridge in China is the longest bridge over land and water in the world. It is 401,308 feet longer than the Jiaozhou Bay Bridge. How long is the Danyan-Kunshan Grand Bridge?

_____

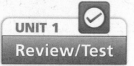
1. Anthony's family drives 659 miles from Miami to Atlanta. Then they drive another 247 miles to Nashville. How far does Anthony's family drive in all? Show your work.

2. A scientist measures 3,470 milliliters of water into a beaker. She pours 2,518 milliliters of the water in a solution. If the beaker can hold 5,000 milliliters, how much water is needed to fill the beaker? Show your work. Then show a way to check your answer.

3. Fill in the blank to show the number of hundreds.

   4,500 = _____ hundreds

   Explain how you know.

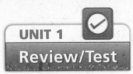

4. A mining truck is loaded with 147,265 kilograms of dirt. Another 129,416 kilograms of dirt is added. What is the total mass of the dirt in the mining truck? Show your work.

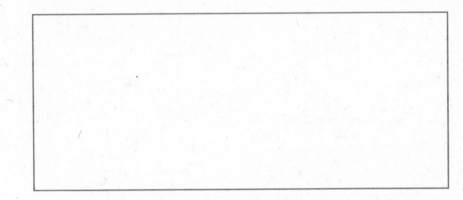

5. The downtown location of Mike's Bikes earned $179,456 last year. The store's riverside location earned $145,690. The store with the greater earnings gets an award. Which store gets the award? Show your work.

6. Select another form of 65,042. Mark all that apply.

Ⓐ $6 + 5 + 0 + 4 + 2$

Ⓑ sixty-five thousand, forty-two

Ⓒ $60,000 + 5,000 + 40 + 2$

Ⓓ six hundred fifty, forty-two

7. For numbers 7a–7e, choose Yes or No to tell if the number is rounded to the nearest thousand.

7a. 234,566
235,000   ○ Yes   ○ No

7b. 7,893
7,900   ○ Yes   ○ No

7c. 64,498
65,000   ○ Yes   ○ No

7d. 958,075
958,000   ○ Yes   ○ No

7e. 49,826
50,000   ○ Yes   ○ No

8. For numbers 8a–8e, choose True or False to describe the statement.

8a. $34,639 > 34,369$ ○ True   ○ False

8b. $2,709 = 2,790$ ○ True   ○ False

8c. $480,920 > 480,902$ ○ True   ○ False

8d. $259 < 261$ ○ True   ○ False

8e. $6,924 < 6,299$ ○ True   ○ False

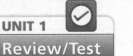
9. Make a place value drawing for 1,534.

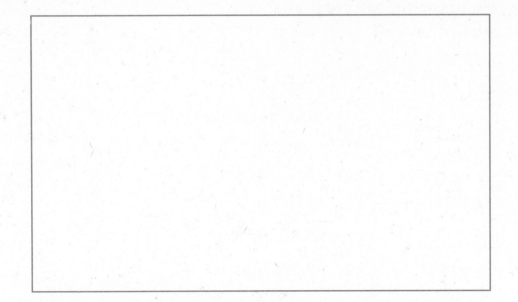

10. For numbers 10a–10e, write 685,203 rounded to the nearest place value.

10a. ten _____

10b. hundred _____

10c. thousand _____

10d. ten thousand _____

10e. hundred thousand _____

11. For numbers 11a–11d, find the sum or difference.

11a.
```
   4,379
 + 3,284
```

11c.
```
   389,416
 + 237,825
```

11b.
```
   57,340
 − 26,817
```

11d.
```
   648,939
 − 584,172
```

12. There were 2,683 books sold at a bookstore this year. There were 1,317 more books sold last year. How many books were sold last year? Write an equation for the problem then solve it. Show your work.

13. Wren added the numbers 1,376 and 6,275.

Part A

Write the addends and the sum in the break-apart drawing. Then complete the two addition problems represented by the break-apart drawing.

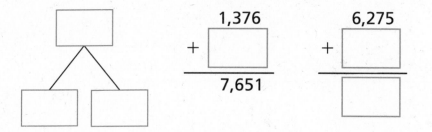

Part B

Write a word problem that requires subtracting 1,376 from 7,651.

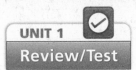
14. Last week there were two soccer games. There were 3,982 people at the first soccer game. There were 1,886 fewer people at the second soccer game than at the first soccer game.

Part A

How many people attended the soccer games last week? Show your work.

Part B

Explain how you found your answer.

15. Order the numbers from least to greatest by writing a number in each box.

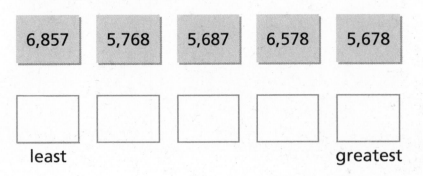

| 6,857 | 5,768 | 5,687 | 6,578 | 5,678 |

least   greatest

Family Letter

Content Overview

Dear Family,

In this unit, your child will be learning about the common multiplication method that most adults know. However, they will also explore ways to draw multiplication. *Math Expressions* uses area of rectangles to show multiplication.

	30	+	7
20	20 × 30 = 600		20 × 7 = 140
+			
4	4 × 30 = 120		4 × 7 = 28

Area Method:

$$20 \times 30 = 600$$
$$20 \times 7 = 140$$
$$4 \times 30 = 120$$
$$\underline{4 \times 7 = 28}$$
$$\text{Total} = 888$$

Shortcut Method:

$$\overset{\frac{1}{2}}{37}$$
$$\underline{\times\ 24}$$
$$148$$
$$\underline{74}$$
$$888$$

Area drawings help all students see multiplication. They also help students remember what numbers they need to multiply and what numbers make up the total.

Your child will also learn to find products involving single-digit numbers, tens, and hundreds by factoring the tens or hundreds. For example,

$$200 \times 30 = 2 \times 100 \times 3 \times 10$$
$$= 2 \times 3 \times 100 \times 10$$
$$= 6 \times 1{,}000 = 6{,}000$$

By observing the zeros patterns in products like these, your child will learn to do such multiplications mentally.

If your child is still not confident with single-digit multiplication and division, we urge you to set aside a few minutes every night for multiplication and division practice. In a few more weeks, the class will be doing multidigit division, so it is very important that your child be both fast and accurate with basic multiplication and division.

If you need practice materials, please contact me.

Sincerely,
Your child's teacher

CA CC

Unit 2 addresses the following standards from the *Common Core State Standards for Mathematics with California Additions*: **4.OA.3, 4.NBT.1, 4.NBT.2, 4.NBT.3, 4.NBT.5, 4.MD.2** and all Mathematical Practices.

Carta a la familia

Un vistazo general al contenido

Estimada familia:

En esta unidad, su niño estará aprendiendo el método de multiplicación común que la mayoría de los adultos conoce. Sin embargo, también explorará maneras de dibujar la multiplicación. Para mostrar la multiplicación, *Math Expressions* usa el método del área del rectángulo.

	30	+	7
20	20 × 30 = 600		20 × 7 = 140
+			
4	4 × 30 = 120		4 × 7 = 28

Método del área

$20 \times 30 = 600$
$20 \times 7 = 140$
$4 \times 30 = 120$
$4 \times 7 = 28$
Total = 888

Método más corto

$$\begin{array}{r} \overset{1}{}\overset{2}{} \\ 37 \\ \times\ 24 \\ \hline 148 \\ 74 \\ \hline 888 \end{array}$$

Los dibujos de área ayudan a los estudiantes a visualizar la multiplicación. También los ayuda a recordar cuáles números tienen que multiplicar y cuáles números forman el total.

Su niño también aprenderá a hallar productos relacionados con números de un solo dígito, con decenas y con centenas, factorizando las decenas o las centenas. Por ejemplo:

$$200 \times 30 = 2 \times 100 \times 3 \times 10$$
$$= 2 \times 3 \times 100 \times 10$$
$$= 6 \times 1{,}000 = 6{,}000$$

Al observar los patrones de ceros en productos como estos, su niño aprenderá a hacer dichas multiplicaciones mentalmente.

Si su niño todavía no domina la multiplicación y la división con números de un solo dígito, le sugerimos que dedique algunos minutos todas las noches para practicar la multiplicación y la división. Dentro de pocas semanas, la clase hará divisiones con números de varios dígitos, por eso es muy importante que su niño haga las operaciones básicas de multiplicación y de división de manera rápida y exacta.

Si necesita materiales para practicar, comuníquese conmigo.

Atentamente,
El maestro de su niño

© Houghton Mifflin Harcourt Publishing Company

 CA CC

En la Unidad 2 se aplican los siguientes estándares auxiliares, contendidos en los *Estándares estatales comunes de matemáticas con adiciones para California*: **4.OA.3, 4.NBT.1, 4.NBT.2, 4.NBT.3, 4.NBT.5, 4.MD.2** y todos los de prácticas matemáticas.

Name _____ **Date** _____

CA CC Content Standards **4.NBT.5**
Mathematical Practices **MP.5, MP.6, MP.8**

VOCABULARY
array
area

▶ Model a Product of Ones

The number of unit squares in an **array** of connected unit squares is the **area** of the rectangle formed by the squares. We sometimes just show the measurement of length and width.

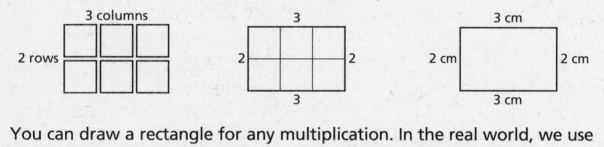

You can draw a rectangle for any multiplication. In the real world, we use multiplication for finding both sizes of arrays and areas of figures.

A 2 × 3 rectangle has 6 unit squares inside, so 2 × 3 = 6.

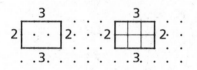

1. On your MathBoard, draw a 3 × 2 rectangle. How is the 3 × 2 rectangle similar to the 2 × 3 rectangle? How is it different?

_____

_____

_____

2. How do the areas of the 2 × 3 and 3 × 2 rectangles compare?

_____

_____

VOCABULARY
square units

► Factor the Tens to Multiply Ones and Tens

This 2 × 30 rectangle contains 2 groups of 30 unit squares.

```
                    30
1 |————————————————————————————————————| 1
+ |           1 × 30 = 30               | +
1 |           1 × 30 = 30               | 1
                    30
```

This 2 × 30 rectangle contains 3 groups of 20 unit squares.

```
30 =      10        +        10        +        10
2 |  · 2·×·10 = 20 ·  |  · 2·×·10 = 20 ·  |  · 2·×·10 = 20 ·  | 2
        10          +          10        +         10
```

This 2 × 30 rectangle contains 6 groups of 10 unit squares, so its area is 60 **square units**.

```
30 =      10        +        10        +        10
1 |  1 × 10 = 10  |  1 × 10 = 10  |  1 × 10 = 10  | 1
1 |  1 × 10 = 10  |  1 × 10 = 10  |  1 × 10 = 10  | 1
        10        +        10        +        10
```

3. How can we show this numerically? Complete the steps.

$$2 \times 30 = (2 \times 1) \times (\underline{\hspace{1cm}} \times 10)$$

$$= (\underline{\hspace{1cm}} \times \underline{\hspace{1cm}}) \times (1 \times 10)$$

$$= \underline{\hspace{1cm}} \times 10 = 60$$

4. On your MathBoard, draw a 30 × 2 rectangle and find its area.

_____

5. How is the 30 × 2 rectangle similar to the 2 × 30 rectangle? How is it different?

_____

_____

_____

_____

CA CC Content Standards 4.NBT.1, 4.NBT.5
Mathematical Practices MP.1, MP.2, MP.3, MP.4, MP.7, MP.8

▶ Use Place Value to Multiply

You have learned about the Base Ten Pattern in place value. This model shows how place value and multiplication are connected.

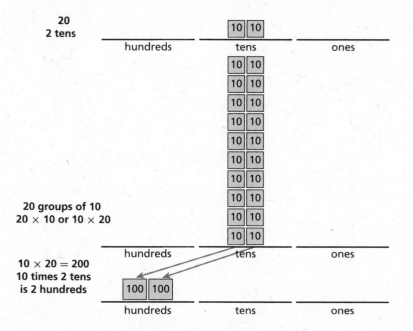

You can use properties to show the relationship between place value and multiplication.

Associative Property	$10 \times 20 = 10 \times (2 \times 10)$
	$= (10 \times 2) \times 10$
Commutative Property	$= (2 \times 10) \times 10$
Associative Property	$= 2 \times (10 \times 10)$
	$= 2 \times 100$
	$= 200$

1. Ten times any number of tens gives you that number of hundreds. Complete the steps to show 10 times 5 tens.

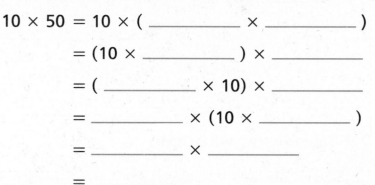

$10 \times 50 = 10 \times (\underline{\hspace{2cm}} \times \underline{\hspace{2cm}})$

$= (10 \times \underline{\hspace{2cm}}) \times \underline{\hspace{2cm}}$

$= (\underline{\hspace{2cm}} \times 10) \times \underline{\hspace{2cm}}$

$= \underline{\hspace{2cm}} \times (10 \times \underline{\hspace{2cm}})$

$= \underline{\hspace{2cm}} \times \underline{\hspace{2cm}}$

$= \underline{\hspace{2cm}}$

► Model a Product of Tens

Olivia wants to tile the top of a table. The table is 20 inches by 30 inches. Olivia needs to find the area of the table in square inches.

2. Find the area of this 20 × 30 rectangle by dividing it into 10-by-10 squares of 100.

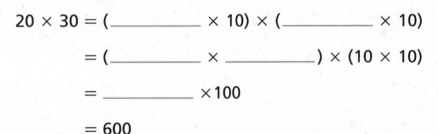

3. Each tile is a 1-inch square. How many tiles does Olivia need to cover the tabletop? _____

4. Each box of tiles contains 100 tiles. How many boxes of tiles does Olivia need to buy? _____

► Factor the Tens

5. Complete the steps to show your work in Exercise 2 numerically.

$$20 \times 30 = (\underline{\hspace{1.5cm}} \times 10) \times (\underline{\hspace{1.5cm}} \times 10)$$

$$= (\underline{\hspace{1.5cm}} \times \underline{\hspace{1.5cm}}) \times (10 \times 10)$$

$$= \underline{\hspace{1.5cm}} \times 100$$

$$= 600$$

6. Is it true that 20 × 30 = 30 × 20? Explain how you know.

_____

VOCABULARY
factor
product

▶ Look for Patterns

Multiplying greater numbers in your head is easier when you learn patterns of multiplication with tens.

Start with column A and look for the patterns used to get the expressions in each column. Copy and complete the table.

Table 1

	A	B	C	D
	2 × 3	2 × 1 × 3 × 1	6 × 1	6
1.	2 × 30	2 × 1 × 3 × 10	6 × 10	_____
2.	20 × 30	2 × 10 × 3 × 10	_____	_____

3. How are the expressions in column B different from the expressions in column A?

_____

_____

_____

4. In column C, we see that each expression can be written as a number times a place value. Which of these **factors** gives more information about the size of the **product?**

_____

5. Why is 6 the first digit of the products in column D?

_____

6. Why are there different numbers of zeros in the products in column D?

_____

_____

▶ Compare Tables

Copy and complete each table.

Table 2

A	B	C	D
6 × 3	6 × 1 × 3 × 1	18 × 1	18
7. 6 × 30	6 × 1 × 3 × 10	18 × 10	_____
8. 60 × 30	6 × 10 × 3 × 10	_____	_____

Table 3

A	B	C	D
5 × 8	5 × 1 × 8 × 1	40 × 1	40
9. 5 × 80	5 × 1 × 8 × 10	40 × 10	_____
10. 50 × 80	_____	_____	_____

11. Why do the products in Table 2 have more digits than the products in Table 1?

_____

_____

12. Why are there more zeros in the products in Table 3 than the products in Table 2?

_____

_____

Name _____   Date _____

CA CC Content Standards **4.NBT.2, 4.NBT.5, 4.MD.2**
Mathematical Practices **MP.1, MP.2, MP.3, MP.5, MP.6**

▶ Explore the Area Model

```
         20              +    6
  ┌──────────────────────┬─────────┐
  │ · · · · · · · · · · · │ · · · · │
4 │ · · · · · · · · · · · │ · · · · │
  │ · · · · · · · · · · · │ · · · · │
  └──────────────────────┴─────────┘
```

1. How many square units of area are there in the tens part of the drawing? _____

2. What multiplication equation gives the area of the tens part of the drawing? Write this equation in its rectangle.

   _____

3. How many square units of area are there in the ones part? _____

4. What multiplication equation gives the area of the ones part? Write this equation in its rectangle. _____

5. What is the total of the two areas? _____

6. How do you know that 104 is the correct product of 4 × 26?

   _____

7. Read problems A and B.

   A. Al's photo album has 26 pages. Each page has 4 photos. How many photos are in Al's album?

   B. Nick took 4 photos. Henri took 26 photos. How many more photos did Henri take than Nick?

   Which problem could you solve using the multiplication you just did? Explain why.

   _____

   _____

▶ Use Rectangles to Multiply

Draw a rectangle for each problem on your MathBoard.
Find the tens product, the ones product, and the total.

8. 3×28 9. 3×29 10. 5×30 11. 5×36

_____   _____   _____   _____

_____   _____   _____   _____

_____   _____   _____   _____

12. 4×38 13. 8×38 14. 4×28 15. 5×28

_____   _____   _____   _____

_____   _____   _____   _____

_____   _____   _____   _____

Solve each problem.   *Show your work.*

16. Maria's father planted 12 rows of tomatoes in his garden. Each row had 6 plants. How many tomato plants were in Maria's father's garden?

_____

17. A library subscribes to 67 magazines. Each month the library receives 3 copies of each magazine. How many magazines does the library receive each month?

_____

18. Complete this word problem. Then solve it.

_____ has _____ boxes of _____.

There are _____ _____ in each box.

How many _____ does _____

have altogether? _____

Name _____   Date _____

▶ Multiply One-Digit Dollar Amounts by Two-Digit Numbers

You can use your skills for multiplying a one-digit number by a two-digit number to multiply one-digit dollar amounts by two-digit numbers.

Find the exact cost. Give your answer in dollars.

Show your work.

19. A package of paper costs $2. If someone is purchasing 24 packages, how much will it cost?

_____

20. A box lunch can be purchased for $3. How much will 83 lunches cost?

_____

21. A movie ticket costs $8 per person. If 61 people go to the five o'clock show, how much money does the theater make for that show?

_____

22. A round-trip train ticket costs $4 per person. If 58 fourth-graders take a class trip to the city on the train, how much will the train tickets cost altogether?

_____

23. Admission to the zoo costs $5 per person. If a group of 72 students takes a trip to the zoo, how much will their tickets cost altogether?

_____

24. Sara earns $9 per hour as a cashier. How much does she earn in a 40-hour week?

_____

© Houghton Mifflin Harcourt Publishing Company

► Multiply Two-Digit Dollar Amounts by One-Digit Numbers

You can use your skills for multiplying a one-digit number by a two-digit number to multiply one-digit numbers by two-digit dollar amounts.

Find the exact cost. Give your answer in dollars.

Show your work.

25. A bike costs $53. If 2 bikes are purchased, how much will be the total cost?

_____

26. A store sells CDs for $14. If someone buys 7 of them, how much will they cost altogether?

_____

27. An amusement park entrance fee is $23 per person. If 4 friends go to the amusement park, how much will their tickets cost altogether?

_____

28. A hotel costs $72 per night. How much will it cost to stay 3 nights?

_____

29. An airplane ticket costs $87. How much will 6 tickets cost?

_____

30. Jorge earns $99 each week. He goes on vacation in 9 weeks. How much will he earn before his vacation?

_____

Model One-Digit by Two-Digit Multiplication

Name _____   Date _____

CA CC Content Standards **4.NBT.3, 4.NBT.5**
Mathematical Practices **MP.1, MP.2, MP.3, MP.6**

▶ Estimate Products

It is easier to **estimate** the product of a two-digit number and a one-digit number when you think about the two multiples of ten close to the two-digit number. This is shown in the drawings below.

1. In each drawing, find the rectangles that represent 4 × 70 and 4 × 60. These rectangles "frame" the rectangles for 4 × 68 and 4 × 63. Find the values of 4 × 70 and 4 × 60.

   4 × 70 = _____   4 × 60 = _____

2. Look at the rectangle that represents 4 × 68. Is 4 × 68 closer to 4 × 60 or to 4 × 70? So is 4 × 68 closer to 240 or 280?

   _____

3. Look at the rectangle that represents 4 × 63. Is 4 × 63 closer to 4 × 60 or to 4 × 70? Is 4 × 63 closer to 240 or 280?

   _____

4. Explain how to use **rounding** to estimate the product of a one-digit number and a two-digit number.

   _____

   _____

   _____

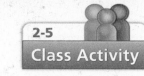

▶ **Practice Estimation**

Discuss how rounding and estimation could help solve these problems.

5. Keesha's school has 185 fourth-grade students. The library has 28 tables with 6 chairs at each table. Can all of the fourth-graders sit in the library at one time? How do you know?

_____

_____

_____

6. Ameena is printing the class newsletter. There are 8 pages in the newsletter, and she needs 74 copies. Each package of paper contains 90 sheets. How many packages of paper does she need to print the newsletter?

_____

_____

_____

Estimate each product. Then solve to check your estimate.

7. 3×52 _____

8. 7×48 _____

9. 9×27 _____

10. 8×34 _____

11. 8×35 _____

12. 5×22 _____

Estimate Products

VOCABULARY
Place Value Sections Method

▶ Use the Place Value Sections Method

You can use an area model to demonstrate the
Place Value Sections Method. This strategy is
used below for multiplying a one-digit number
by a two-digit number.

Complete the steps.

27 =	20	+	7	
5	5 × 20 = 100		5 × 7 = 35	5

$+ \underline{}$
$\overline{}$

Use the Place Value Sections Method to solve the problem.
Complete the steps.

1. The fourth-grade class is participating in a walk-a-thon.
   Each student will walk 8 laps around the track. There
   are 92 fourth-grade students. How many laps will the
   fourth-grade class walk?

   _____

92 =	90	+	2	
8	___ × ___ = ___		___ × ___ = ___	8

$+ \underline{}$
$\overline{}$

Draw an area model and use the Place Value Sections
Method to solve the problem.

2. A football coach is ordering 3 shirts for each football player.
   There are 54 players in the football program. How many
   shirts does the coach need to order for the entire program?

   _____

▶ Use the Expanded Notation Method

You can also use an area model to show how to use the **Expanded Notation Method**. Use the Expanded Notation Method to solve 5 × 27 below.

Complete the steps.

3.

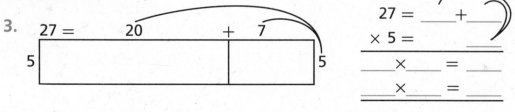

$27 =$ ____ + ____
$× 5 =$
____ × ____ = ____
____ × ____ = ____
____

Use the Expanded Notation Method to solve the problem. Complete the steps.

4. A farm stand sold 4 bushels of apples in one day. Each bushel of apples weighs 42 pounds. How many pounds of apples did the farm stand sell?

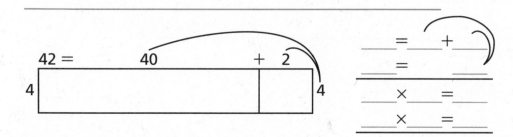

____ = ____ + ____
____ =
____ × ____ = ____
____ × ____ = ____
____

Draw an area model and use the Expanded Notation Method to solve the problem.

5. A marina needs to replace the boards on their pier. The pier is 7 feet by 39 feet. What is the area of the boards that need to be replaced?

_____

▶ Model the Distributive Property

You have used area models to help you multiply. You can use the area model to find 3 × 74 by writing 74 in expanded form and using the **Distributive Property** to find **partial products**. After you find all the partial products, you can add them together to find the actual product of 3 × 74.

Complete each exercise.

1. Write 74 in expanded form.

   3 × 74 = 3 (_____ + _____)

2. Use the Distributive Property.

   3 × 74 = (_____ × _____) + (_____ × _____)

The area models below show the steps to find the solution to 3 × 74.

STEP 1 74 =

70	+	4
3	3 × 70 = 210		3

Multiply the tens.

(3 × 70) = _____

STEP 2 74 =

70	+	4
3		3 × 4 = 12	3

Multiply the ones.

(3 × 4) = _____

STEP 3 74 =

70	+	4
3	3 × 70 = 210	3 × 4 = 12	3

Add the
partial products.

```
  210
+  12
_____
```

3. What is the actual product of 3 × 74? _____

VOCABULARY
Algebraic Notation Method

▶ Use the Algebraic Notation Method to Multiply

Another numerical multiplication method that can be represented by an area model is the **Algebraic Notation Method**. This method also decomposes the two-digit factor into tens and ones and then uses the Distributive Property.

Use the Algebraic Notation Method to solve each problem. Complete the steps.

4. 8 · 62

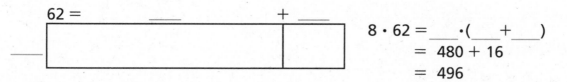

62 = _____ + _____

$8 \cdot 62 = \_\_\_ \cdot (\_\_\_ + \_\_\_)$
$\quad = 480 + 16$
$\quad = 496$

5. 2 · 97

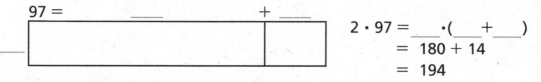

97 = _____ + _____

$2 \cdot 97 = \_\_\_ \cdot (\_\_\_ + \_\_\_)$
$\quad = 180 + 14$
$\quad = 194$

Draw an area model and use the Algebraic Notation Method to solve the problem.

6. There are 9 members on the school's golf team. Each golfer hit a bucket of 68 golf balls at the driving range. How many golf balls did the entire team hit?

_____

7. What is the first step in the Algebraic Notation Method?

_____

Algebraic Notation Method

Name _____   Date _____

CA CC Content Standards **4.NBT.5**
Mathematical Practices **MP.2, MP.6, MP.7, MP.8**

▶ Numerical Multiplication Methods

You have used the area model to help you multiply. In this lesson, you will compare the numerical multiplication methods that are related to this area model.

Place Value Sections Method

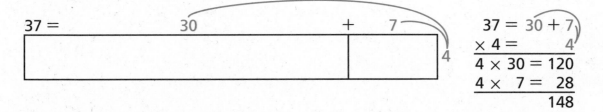

$37 =$ 30 $+$ 7

4 | $4 \times 30 = 120$ | $4 \times 7 = 28$ | 4

$$\begin{array}{r} 120 \\ +\ 28 \\ \hline 148 \end{array}$$

Expanded Notation Method

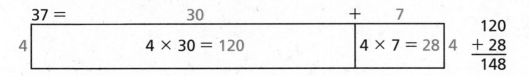

$37 =$ 30 $+$ 7

4

$$\begin{array}{r} 37 = 30 + 7 \\ \times\ 4 = \qquad 4 \\ \hline 4 \times 30 = 120 \\ 4 \times\ 7 = \ \ 28 \\ \hline 148 \end{array}$$

Algebraic Notation Method

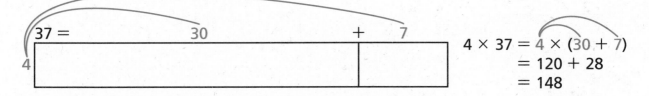

$37 =$ 30 $+$ 7

4

$4 \times 37 = 4 \times (30 + 7)$
$\qquad\quad = 120 + 28$
$\qquad\quad = 148$

▶ Connect the Multiplication Methods

Refer to the examples above.

1. What two values are added together to give the answer in all three methods?

    _____

2. What is different about the three methods?

    _____

Name _____ Date _____

▶ Practice Different Methods

Fill in the blanks in the following solutions.

3. 4 × 86

Expanded Notation

$$86 = \underline{\quad} + 6$$
$$\underline{\times \ 4 =} \qquad \underline{\quad}$$
$$4 \ \times \underline{\quad} = \underline{\quad}$$
$$\underline{\underline{\quad} \times 6 = 24}$$
$$\underline{\quad}$$

Algebraic Notation

$$4 \cdot 86 = \underline{\quad} \cdot (80 + 6)$$
$$= 320 + \underline{\quad}$$
$$= \underline{\quad}$$

4. 4 × 68

Expanded Notation

$$\underline{\quad} = 60 + 8$$
$$\underline{\times \ 4 =} \qquad \underline{\quad}$$
$$4 \ \times \underline{\quad} = \underline{\quad}$$
$$\underline{\underline{\quad} \times 8 = 32}$$
$$\underline{\quad}$$

Algebraic Notation

$$4 \cdot 68 = 4 \cdot (\underline{\quad} + \underline{\quad})$$
$$= 240 + \underline{\quad}$$
$$= \underline{\quad}$$

Solve using a numerical method. Draw the related area model.

5. 5 × 64 = _____

6. 6 × 72 = _____

7. 7 × 92 = _____

8. 8 × 53 = _____

9. 5 × 46 = _____

10. 6 × 27 = _____

Compare Methods of One-Digit by Two-Digit Multiplication

Name _____ Date _____

CA CC Content Standards **4.NBT.5**
Mathematical Practices **MP.2, MP.6, MP.7**

► Compare Multiplication Methods

Compare these methods for solving 9 × 28.

Method A	Method B	Method C	Method D
$28 = 20 + 8$	$28 = 20 + 8$	28	28
$\times\ 9 =\qquad 9$	$\times\ 9 =\qquad 9$	$\times\ \ 9$	$\times\ \ 9$
$9 \times 20 = 180$	180	180	72
$9 \times 8 =\ 72$	72	72	180
252	252	252	252

1. How are all the methods similar? List at least two similarities.

_____

_____

_____

2. How are the methods different? List at least three differences.

_____

_____

_____

Discuss how the recording methods below show the partial products in different ways.

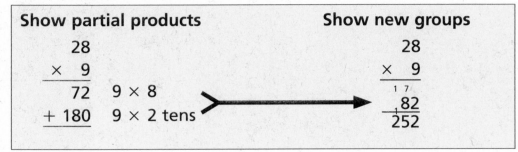

Show partial products	Show new groups

▶ Discuss the Shortcut Method

The steps for the Shortcut Method are shown below.

Shortcut Method with New Groups Above		
Method E:	**Step 1**	**Step 2**
	$\overset{7}{2}8$	$\overset{7}{2}8$
	$\times\ 9$	$\times\ 9$
	2	252

Shortcut Method with New Groups Below		
Method F:	**Step 1**	**Step 2**
	28	28
	$\times\ 9$	$\times\ 9$
	$^{7}2$	252

3. Where are the products 180 and 72 from Methods A–D?

_____

_____

_____

▶ Practice Multiplication

Solve using any method. Sketch a rectangle if necessary.

4. 63
   × 5

5. 39
   × 8

6. 98
   × 2

7. 86
   × 4

8. 25
   × 7

9. 47
   × 9

10. 76
    × 3

11. 54
    × 6

Name

Date

CA CC Content Standards **4.NBT.2, 4.NBT.5, 4.MD.2**
Mathematical Practices **MP.1, MP.2, MP.3, MP.6, MP.7**

▶ Use Rectangles to Multiply Hundreds

You can use a model to show multiplication with hundreds.
Study this model to see how we can multiply 7 × 300.

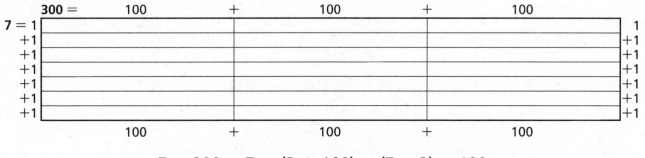

$$7 \times 300 = 7 \times (3 \times 100) = (7 \times 3) \times 100$$

$$= 21 \times 100$$

$$= 2,100$$

1. How many hundreds are represented in each column of the model?

_____

2. How does knowing that 7 × 3 = 21 help you find 7 × 300?

_____

_____

3. What property of multiplication is used in the equation, 7 × (3 × 100) = (7 × 3) × 100?

_____

4. Sketch a model of 6 × 400. Be ready to explain your model.

▶ Compare the Three Methods

You can use the **Place Value Sections Method** to multiply a one-digit number by a three-digit number.

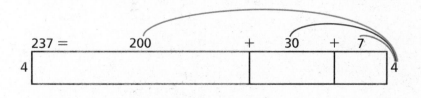

237 =	200	+	30	+ 7	
4	4 × 200 = 800		4 × 30 = 120	4 × 7 = 28	4

$$
\begin{array}{r}
800 \\
120 \\
+28 \\
\hline
948
\end{array}
$$

5. What are the two steps used to find the product of 4 × 237 using the Place Value Sections Method.

_____

The **Expanded Notation Method** uses the same steps as the Place Value Sections Method.

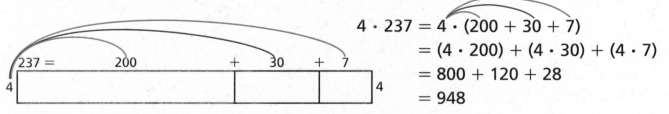

237 =	200	+	30	+ 7	
4					4

$$
\begin{array}{r}
237 = 200 + 30 + 7 \\
\times\ 4 = 4 \\
\hline
4 \times 200 = 800 \\
4 \times 30 = 120 \\
4 \times 7 = 28 \\
\hline
948
\end{array}
$$

6. What is the last step in the Expanded Notation Method and the Place Value Sections Method?

_____

The **Algebraic Notation Method** uses expanded form just like the other two methods. Even though the steps look different, they are the same as in the other methods.

237 =	200	+	30	+ 7	
4					4

$$
\begin{aligned}
4 \cdot 237 &= 4 \cdot (200 + 30 + 7) \\
&= (4 \cdot 200) + (4 \cdot 30) + (4 \cdot 7) \\
&= 800 + 120 + 28 \\
&= 948
\end{aligned}
$$

7. What is the first step in all three methods?

_____

Name _____ Date _____

▶ Practice Multiplication

Solve using any method. Show your work.
Draw an area model if necessary.

8. $7 \times 321 =$ _____

9. $5 \times 218 =$ _____

10. $612 \times 2 =$ _____

11. $154 \times 6 =$ _____

12. $236 \times 4 =$ _____

13. $3 \times 273 =$ _____

14. $482 \times 9 =$ _____

15. $8 \times 615 =$ _____

▶ Multiplication With Dollar Amounts

You can use your skills for multiplying a one-digit number by a three-digit number to multiply one-digit dollar amounts by three-digit numbers and one-digit numbers by three-digit dollar amounts.

Find the exact cost. Give your answer in dollars.   *Show your work.*

16. A car tire costs $158. If Danica needs to buy new tires, how much will 4 tires cost?

_____

17. The fourth grade is going on a field trip to the planetarium. A ticket costs $6. How much will it cost if 127 people go on the field trip?

_____

18. A round-trip airplane ticket costs $224. If a group of 5 people buy tickets, how much will their tickets cost?

_____

19. A book costs a bookstore $7 to order. If the store orders 325 copies of the book, how much does the store pay for the books?

_____

20. During the summer, Joe makes $115 each week mowing lawns. How much will Joe make in 9 weeks?

_____

21. A ticket to a show costs $8. There are 540 seats in the theater. If all the seats in the theater are occupied, how much money does the theater make for that show?

_____

2-11

Class Activity

Name

Date

CA CC Content Standards **4.OA.3, 4.NBT.5**
Mathematical Practices **MP.1, MP.2, MP.3, MP.5, MP.6**

▶ Discuss Problems With Too Much Information

A word problem may sometimes include more information than you need. Read the following problem and then answer each question.

Mrs. Sanchez is putting a border around her garden. Her garden is a rectangle with dimensions 12 feet by 18 feet. The border material costs $3.00 per foot. How many feet of border material is needed?

1. Identify any extra numerical information. Why isn't this information needed?

_____

_____

2. Solve the problem. _____

Solve each problem. Cross out information that is not needed.

Show your work.

3. Judy bought a CD for $10. It has 13 songs. Each song is 3 minutes long. How long will it take to listen to the whole CD?

_____

4. Jerry has 64 coins in his coin collection and 22 stamps in his stamp collection. His sister has 59 stamps in her collection. How many stamps do they have altogether?

_____

5. Adrian has been playing the piano for 3 years. He practices 20 minutes a day. He is preparing for a recital that is 9 days away. How many minutes of practice will he complete before the recital?

_____

▶ Discuss Problems With Too Little Information

When solving problems in real life, you need to determine what information is needed to solve the problem. Read the following problem and then answer each question.

The campers and staff of a day camp are going to an amusement park on a bus. Each bus holds 26 people. How many buses will be needed?

6. Do you have enough information to solve this problem? What additional information do you need?

_____

_____

Determine if the problem can be solved. If it cannot be solved, tell what information is missing. If it can be solved, solve it.

7. Richard is saving $5 a week to buy a bike. When will he have enough money?

_____

8. Natalie wants to find out how much her cat weighs. She picks him up and steps on the scale. Together, they weigh 94 pounds. How much does the cat weigh?

_____

9. Phyllis wants to make 8 potholders. She needs 36 loops for each potholder. How many loops does she need?

_____

10. For one of the problems that could not be solved, rewrite it so it can be solved and then solve it.

_____

_____

► Discuss Problems With Hidden Questions

Mrs. Norton bought 2 packages of white cheese with 8 slices in each pack. She bought 3 packages of yellow cheese with 16 slices in each pack. How many more slices of yellow cheese than white cheese did she buy?

11. What do you need to find?

_____

_____

12. What are the hidden questions?

_____

_____

13. Answer the hidden questions to solve the problem.

How many slices of white cheese? $2 \times 8 =$ _____

How many slices of yellow cheese? $3 \times 16 =$ _____

How many more slices of yellow cheese? $48 - 16 =$ _____

Read the problem. Then answer the questions.   *Show your work.*

Maurice has 6 boxes of markers. June has 5 boxes of markers. Each box contains 8 markers. How many markers do Maurice and June have altogether?

14. Write the hidden questions.

_____

_____

15. Solve the problem.

_____

_____

Name _____ Date _____

► Mixed Problem Solving

Solve each problem and show your work.   *Show your work.*

16. Mr. Collins counts 54 cartons and 5 boxes of paper clips.
Each carton contains 8 boxes. A box of paper clips
costs $2. How many boxes of paper clips does he have?

_____

17. Ms. Washington has 5 cartons of black printer ink.
She has 4 cartons of color printer ink. Each carton
contains 48 cartridges of ink. How many ink cartridges
are there in all?

_____

► What's the Error?

Dear Math Students,

My school is collecting cans for the annual
food drive. There are 608 students in the
entire school. A can of soup costs about
$1. Each student will bring in 3 cans for
the food drive. I wrote this multiplication
to find the number of cans the school will
collect in all.

I am not sure if my answer is correct.
Can you help me?

Your friend,
Puzzled Penguin

$$\begin{array}{r} \overset{2}{6}08 \\ \times\ \ 3 \\ \hline 1,864 \end{array}$$

18. Write a response to Puzzled Penguin.

_____

_____

► **Compare Models**

A coin-collecting book holds 24 coins on a page. There are 37 pages in the book. How many coins can the book hold? The models below all show the solution to 24×37.

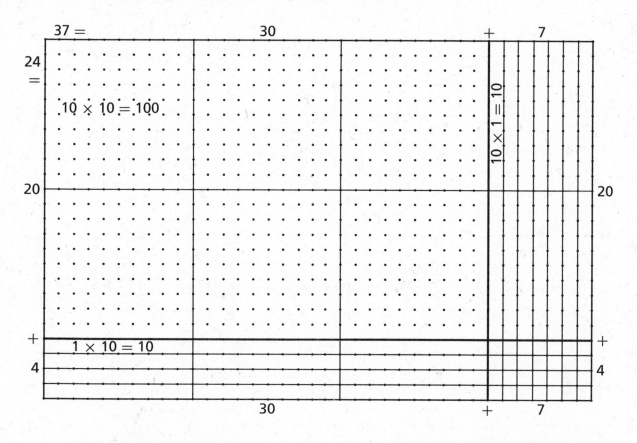

Area Model Sketch

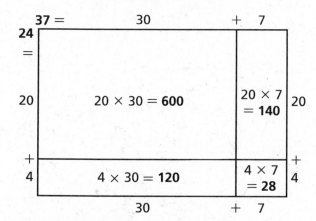

Place Value Sections Method

$20 \times 30 = \mathbf{600}$
$20 \times 7 = \mathbf{140}$
$4 \times 30 = \mathbf{120}$
$\underline{4 \times 7 = \mathbf{28}}$

1. Describe how each model shows 6 hundreds, 14 tens, 12 tens, and 28 ones.

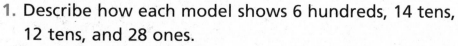

▶ Investigate Products in the Sketch

Complete each equation.

2. $20 \times 30 = 2 \times 10 \times 3 \times 10$
   $= 2 \times 3 \times \underline{10 \times 10}$
   $= 6 \times \underline{}$
   $= \underline{}$

3. $20 \times 7 = 2 \times 10 \times 7 \times 1$
   $= 2 \times 7 \times \underline{10 \times 1}$
   $= 14 \times \underline{}$
   $= \underline{}$

4. $4 \times 30 = 4 \times 1 \times 3 \times 10$
   $= 4 \times 3 \times \underline{1 \times 10}$
   $= 12 \times \underline{}$
   $= \underline{}$

5. $4 \times 7 = 4 \times 1 \times 7 \times 1$
   $= 4 \times 7 \times \underline{1 \times 1}$
   $= 28 \times \underline{}$
   $= \underline{}$

6. Explain how the underlined parts in Exercises 2–5 are shown in the dot drawing.

_____

_____

_____

_____

7. Find 24×37 by adding the products in Exercises 2–5.

_____

▶ Practice and Discuss Modeling

Use your MathBoard to sketch an area drawing for each exercise. Then find the product.

8. 36×58 _____

9. 28×42 _____

10. 63×27 _____

11. 26×57 _____

12. 86×35 _____

13. 38×65 _____

Name _____ **Date** _____

CA CC Content Standards **4.NBT.5**
Mathematical Practices **MP.1, MP.2, MP.6, MP.7**

► Compare Multiplication Methods

Each area model is the same. Study how these three methods of recording 43 × 67 are related to the area models.

Place Value Sections Method

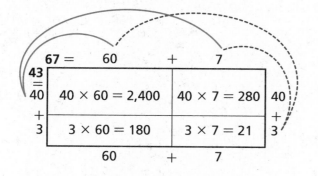

$$40 \times 60 = 2{,}400$$
$$40 \times 7 = 280$$
$$3 \times 60 = 180$$
$$\underline{3 \times 7 = + 21}$$
$$2{,}881$$

Expanded Notation Method

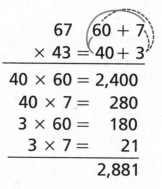

$$
\begin{array}{r}
67 \quad 60 + 7 \\
\times\ 43 = 40 + 3 \\
\hline
40 \times 60 = 2{,}400 \\
40 \times 7 = 280 \\
3 \times 60 = 180 \\
\underline{3 \times 7 = 21} \\
2{,}881
\end{array}
$$

Algebraic Notation Method

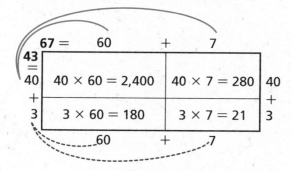

$$43 \cdot 67 = (40 + 3) \cdot (60 + 7)$$
$$= 2{,}400 + 280 + 180 + 21$$
$$= 2{,}881$$

1. What is alike about all the three methods?

_____

_____

▶ Other Ways to Record Multiplication

Discuss how the recording methods below show the partial products in different ways.

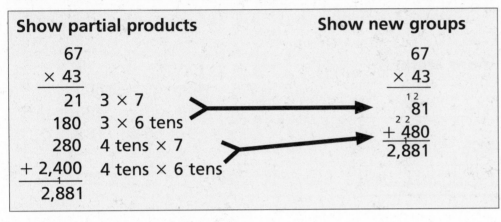

Show partial products		Show new groups
67		67
× 43		× 43
21	3 × 7	¹²81
180	3 × 6 tens	²²+ 480
280	4 tens × 7	2,881
+ 2,400	4 tens × 6 tens	
2,881		

▶ The Shortcut Method

The steps for the Shortcut Method are shown below.

New Groups Above

Step 1	Step 2	Step 3	Step 4	Step 5
²67	²67	²²67	²²67	²²67
× 43	× 43	× 43	× 43	× 43
1	201	201	201	201
		8	268	+ 268
				2,881

New Groups Below

Step 1	Step 2	Step 3	Step 4	Step 5
67	67	67	67	67
× 43	× 43	× 43	× 43	× 43
²1	²201	²²201	²²201	²²201
		8	268	+ 268
				2,881

Discuss how the area drawing below relates to the Shortcut Method.

67

40	40 × 67 = 2,680
+	
3	3 × 67 = 201

Different Methods for Two-Digit Multiplication

Name _____ **Date** _____

CA CC Content Standards **4.NBT.5**
Mathematical Practices **MP.3, MP.6**

► Estimate Products

Two-digit products can be estimated by rounding each number to the nearest ten.

Estimate and then solve.

1. 28×74

_____

2. 84×27

_____

3. 93×57

_____

4. 87×54

_____

5. 38×62

_____

6. 65×39

_____

7. 26×43

_____

8. 59×96

_____

9. 53×74

_____

10. Write a multiplication word problem. Estimate the product and then solve.

_____

_____

_____

_____

_____

11. Would using an estimate be problematic in the situation you wrote for Exercise 10? Explain why or why not.

_____

_____

_____

► **What's the Error?**

Dear Math Students,

My friends and I are helping build flower boxes for a community garden. We are going to build 42 flower boxes. The building plans say each box needs 13 nails. I rounded to estimate how many nails we'll need. Since 40 × 10 = 400, I bought a box of 400 nails.

My friends say we won't have enough nails. Did I make a mistake? Can you help me estimate how many nails we need?

Your friend,
Puzzled Penguin

12. Write a response to Puzzle Penguin.

_____

_____

_____

Estimate and then solve. Explain whether the estimate is problematic in each situation.

13. Sally's family is taking an 18-day vacation and needs to have someone take care of their cat. A veterinarian charges $14 per day to care for the cat. How much money do they need to save to care for the cat?

_____

_____

14. An artist uses 47 tiles to make a mosaic. The artist needs to make 21 mosaics for a fair. How many tiles does the artist need to buy?

_____

_____

CA CC Content Standards **4.OA.3, 4.NBT.5**
Mathematical Practices **MP.1, MP.2**

▶ Practice Multiplication Methods

1. Multiply 38×59.

Shortened Expanded Notation Method	**Shortcut Method**

$$\begin{array}{r} 38 \\ \times\ 59 \\ \hline \end{array}$$ $\qquad\qquad$ $$\begin{array}{r} 38 \\ \times\ 59 \\ \hline \end{array}$$

Solve using any method and show your work.
Check your work with estimation.

2. 43×22

_____

3. 25×15

_____

4. 31×62

_____

5. 54×72

_____

6. 81×33

_____

7. 49×62

_____

▶ Practice Multiplication

With practice, you will be able to solve a multiplication problem using fewer written steps.

Solve.   *Show your work.*

8. Between his ninth and tenth birthdays, Jimmy read 1 book each week. There are 52 weeks in a year. If each book had about 95 pages, about how many pages did he read during the year?

   _____

9. Sam's father built a stone wall in their back yard. The wall was 14 stones high and 79 stones long. How many stones did he use to build the wall?

   _____

10. Balloon Bonanza sells party balloons in packages of 25 balloons. There are 48 packages in the store. How many balloons are in 48 packages?

    _____

11. Brian is buying T-shirts for the marching band. He knows that at parades the band forms 24 rows. Each row has 13 students. If T-shirts come in boxes of 100, how many boxes of T-shirts should Brian buy?

    _____

▶ Use Rectangles to Multiply Thousands

You can use a model to multiply greater numbers.
Notice that each of the smaller rectangles in this model
represents one thousand. Each of the columns represents
seven one-thousands or 7,000.

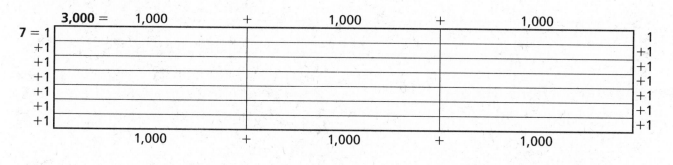

$$7 \times 3,000 = 7 \times (3 \times 1,000) = (7 \times 3) \times 1,000$$
$$= 21 \times 1,000$$
$$= 21,000$$

1. While multiplying by thousands, how many zeros can
   you expect in the product?

   _____

2. How does thinking of 3,000 as $3 \times 1,000$ help you to
   multiply $7 \times 3,000$?

   _____

   _____

   _____

   _____

3. Draw a model for $4 \times 8,000$. Then find the product.

Name _____   Date _____

▶ Compare Multiplication Methods

You can use the multiplication methods you have learned to multiply a one-digit number times a four-digit number.

Find 8 × 3,248.

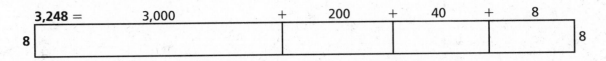

3,248 =	3,000	+	200	+	40	+	8	
8								8

Place Value Sections Method

$8 \times 3,000 = 24,000$
$8 \times 200 = 1,600$
$8 \times 40 = 320$
$8 \times 8 = 64$
$25,984$

Expanded Notation Method

$3,248 = 3,000 + 200 + 40 + 8$
$\times \quad 8 = \qquad\qquad 8$
$8 \times 3,000 = 24,000$
$8 \times 200 = 1,600$
$8 \times 40 = 320$
$8 \times 8 = 64$
$25,984$

Algebraic Notation Method

$8 \times 3,248 = 8 \times (3,000 + 200 + 40 + 8)$
$= (8 \times 3,000) + (8 \times 200) + (8 \times 40) + (8 \times 8)$
$= 24,000 + 1,600 + 320 + 64$
$= 25,984$

Make a rectangle drawing for each problem on your MathBoard. Then solve the problem using the method of your choice.

4. $3 \times 8,153 =$ _____

5. $4 \times 2,961 =$ _____

6. $6 \times 5,287 =$ _____

7. $7 \times 1,733 =$ _____

Name

Date

CA CC Content Standards **4.NBT.3, 4.NBT.5**
Mathematical Practices **MP.2, MP.3, MP.6, MP.7**

► Compare Methods of Multiplication

**Look at the drawing and the five numerical solutions
for $4 \times 2,237$.**

2,237 =	2,000	+	200	+	30	+	7

4   4

Method A	Method B	Method C	Method D	Method E	Method F
$2,237 = 2,000 + 200 + 30 + 7$	$2,237 = 2,000 + 200 + 30 + 7$	$2,237$	$2,237$	$\overset{1\,2}{2,237}$	$2,237$
$\times\ \ 4 =$	$\times\ \ 4 =$	$\times\ \ 4$	$\times\ \ 4$	$\times\ \ 4$	$\times\ \ 4$
$\underline{}$	$\underline{}$	$\overline{}$	$\overline{}$	$\overline{}$	$\underline{}$
$4 \times 2,000 = 8,000$	$8,000$	$8,000$	28	$8,948$	$\overset{1\,2}{}$
$4 \times 200 =\ \ \ 800$	800	800	120		$8,948$
$4 \times 30 =\ \ \ 120$	120	120	800		
$4 \times 7 =\ \ \ \ \ 28$	28	28	$8,000$		
$8,948$	$8,948$	$8,948$	$8,948$		

1. How are the solutions similar? List at least two ways.

_____

_____

_____

2. How are the solutions different? List at least three
comparisons between methods.

_____

_____

_____

_____

_____

3. How do Methods A–D relate to the drawing? List at least
two ways.

_____

_____

_____

Name _____   Date _____

▶ Analyze the Shortcut Method

Look at this breakdown of solution steps for Method E and Method F.

Method E			
Step 1	Step 2	Step 3	Step 4
$\overset{2}{2{,}237}$	$\overset{1\,2}{2{,}237}$	$\overset{1\,2}{2{,}237}$	$\overset{1\,2}{2{,}237}$
× 4	× 4	× 4	× 4
8	48	948	8,948

Method F			
Step 1	Step 2	Step 3	Step 4
2,237	2,237	2,237	2,237
× 4	× 4	× 4	× 4
8	48	948	8,948

4. Describe what happens in Step 1.

_____

_____

_____

5. Describe what happens in Step 2.

_____

_____

_____

_____

6. Describe what happens in Step 3.

_____

_____

_____

7. Describe what happens in Step 4.

_____

_____

_____

Use the Shortcut Method

▶ Round and Estimate With Thousands and Hundreds

You can use what you know about rounding and multiplication with thousands to estimate the product of $4 \times 3{,}692$.

8. Find the product if you round up: $4 \times 4{,}000 =$ _____

9. Find the product if you round down: $4 \times 3{,}000 =$ _____

10. Which one of the two estimates will be closer to the actual solution? Why?

_____

11. Calculate the actual solution. _____

12. Explain why neither estimate is very close to the actual solution.

_____

_____

13. What would be the estimate if you added 4×600 to $4 \times 3{,}000$; $(4 \times 3{,}000) + (4 \times 600)$? _____

14. What would be the estimate if you added 4×700 to $4 \times 3{,}000$; $(4 \times 3{,}000) + (4 \times 700)$? _____

15. Estimate $4 \times 7{,}821$ by rounding 7,821 to the nearest thousand.

_____

16. Find the actual product. _____

17. Find a better estimate for $4 \times 7{,}821$. Show your work.

_____

_____

Round, estimate, and fix the estimate as needed.

18. $6 \times 3{,}095$

19. $7 \times 2{,}784$

_____   _____

_____   _____

Name _____   Date _____

▶ Estimate Products

You can use estimation to decide if an answer is reasonable.

Solve and then estimate to check if your answer is reasonable. Show your estimate.

20. 5 × 3,487 = _____

_____

_____

21. 7 × 8,894 = _____

_____

_____

22. 4 × 7,812 = _____

_____

_____

23. 3 × 4,109 = _____

_____

_____

▶ What's the Error?

Dear Math Students,

My school collected 2,468 empty cartons of milk during the day today. If the school collects about the same number of cartons each day for 5 days, I estimated that the school will collect 17,500 empty cartons of milk. I wrote this estimate.

$$(5 \times 3,000) + (5 \times 500) = 17,500$$

I am not sure if this is a reasonable estimate. Can you help me?

Your Friend,
Puzzled Penguin

24. Write a response to Puzzled Penguin.

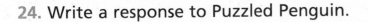

_____

_____

_____

Use the Shortcut Method

CA CC Content Standards 4.OA.3, 4.NBT.5, 4.MD.2
Mathematical Practices MP.1, MP.6

▶ Practice Mixed Multiplication

Solve using any method and show your work. Check your work with estimation.

1. 35×9

_____

2. 56×17

_____

3. 228×2

_____

4.   23
   $\times\ 7$

5.   77
   $\times\ 9$

6.   59
   $\times\ 3$

7.   92
   $\times\ 84$

8.   49
   $\times\ 12$

9.   61
   $\times\ 36$

10.   459
   $\times\ 4$

11.   588
   $\times\ 6$

12.   216
   $\times\ 7$

13.   3,473
   $\times\ \ \ \ 5$

14.   1,156
   $\times\ \ \ \ 8$

15.   2,937
   $\times\ \ \ \ 3$

© Houghton Mifflin Harcourt Publishing Company

▶ Practice with Word Problems

Solve using any method and show your work.
Check your work with estimation.

Show your work.

16. The lines on a doubles tennis court are painted to be 78 feet long and 36 feet wide. The lines on a singles tennis court are painted to be 78 feet long and 27 feet wide. What is the difference between the areas of a doubles tennis court and a singles tennis court?

_____

17. A movie theater has 287 crates of popcorn. Each crate holds 8 pounds of popcorn. There are 13 people who work at the theater. How many pounds of popcorn are there altogether?

_____

18. Jenny goes to a 55-minute-long dance class 3 days each week. There are 9 weeks until the class recital. How many minutes of dance class are there until the recital?

_____

19. Alex is shopping for school clothes. He buys 4 shirts for $12 each. He also buys 3 pairs of shorts for $17 each. How much does Alex spend on school clothes in all?

_____

20. Casey draws a rectangular array that is 1,167 units long and 7 units wide. What is the area of Casey's array?

_____

Practice Multiplying

Name _____ **Date** _____

CA CC Content Standards **4.OA.3, 4.NBT.5**
Mathematical Practices **MP.1, MP.2**

► Math and Games

This is a game called *Big City Building*. The goal of the game is to design and build a successful city within a budget. To win the game, the city must have all of the features of a real-life city such as apartments, schools, parks, and shops, so its residents will be happy.

1. Each city in *Big City Building* requires a fire station, a police station, and a post office. These each cost $2,657 in taxes per year to maintain. How much does it cost to maintain the fire station, the police station, and the post office building for one year?

_____

2. In *Big City Building*, the roads are standard two-lane roads. The total width of the road is 9 meters. If each block is 82 meters long, what is the area of the road of one city block in square meters?

_____

▶ Big City Building

The table shows the cost of different features on the *Big City Building* game. Below is Scott's design, so far, for his city in *Big City Building*.

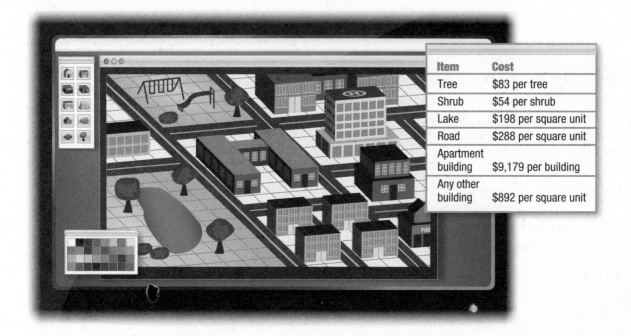

Item	Cost
Tree	$83 per tree
Shrub	$54 per shrub
Lake	$198 per square unit
Road	$288 per square unit
Apartment building	$9,179 per building
Any other building	$892 per square unit

Currently, Scott has $156,324 in *Big City Building* money to create his city.

3. Scott buys 42 trees to put in the park. The trees cost $83 each. How much money does Scott pay for the trees?

_____

4. Each apartment building contains 59 apartment units. Scott has 4 apartment buildings in his city. How many apartment units does Scott's city have?

_____

5. If Scott's city is 27 units long and 19 units wide, what is the area of Scott's city in square units?

_____

Focus on Mathematical Practices

1. Use the numbers on the tiles to complete the steps to find 20 × 40 by factoring the tens.

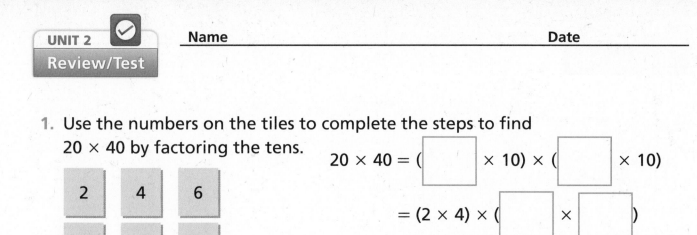

2	4	6
8	10	20
600	800

$20 \times 40 = (\boxed{} \times 10) \times (\boxed{} \times 10)$

$= (2 \times 4) \times (\boxed{} \times \boxed{})$

$= \boxed{} \times 100$

$= \boxed{}$

2. Select the expression that is equivalent to 36 × 25. Mark all that apply.

Ⓐ 30 × 6 + 20 × 5

Ⓑ (30 × 20) + (30 × 5) + (6 × 20) + (6 × 5)

Ⓒ (5 × 6) + (5 × 3 tens) + (2 tens × 6) + (2 tens × 3 tens)

Ⓓ 30 × (20 + 5) + 6 × (20 + 5)

Ⓔ 30 + 15 + 12 + 6

3. There are 24 pencils in a box. If there are 90 boxes, how many pencils are there?

_____ pencils

4. A clown bought 18 bags of round balloons with 20 balloons in each bag. He bought 26 bags of long balloons with 35 balloons in each bag. How many more long balloons are there than round balloons? Show your work.

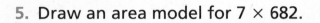
5. Draw an area model for 7 × 682.

Explain how you used the model to find the product.

6. For numbers 6a–6e, choose Yes or No to tell whether the equation is true.

6a. 8 × 4 = 32   ○ Yes   ○ No

6b. 8 × 400 = 32,000   ○ Yes   ○ No

6c. 80 × 40 = 3,200   ○ Yes   ○ No

6d. 8 × 4,000 = 32,000   ○ Yes   ○ No

6e. 800 × 40 = 320,000   ○ Yes   ○ No

7. Find the product of 4 × 52.

8. Use the numbers on the tiles to complete the area model for 29 × 48.

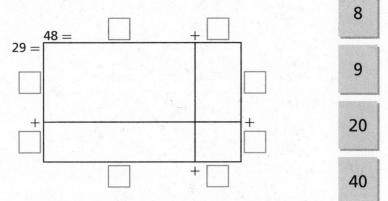

8	
9	
20	
40	

Show how to use the area model and expanded notation to find 29 × 48.

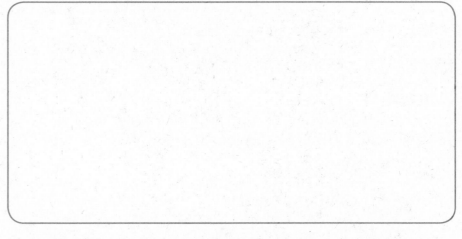

9. Estimate 15 × 34 by rounding each number to the nearest ten.

10. For numbers 10a–10d, choose True or False to describe the statement.

10a. 8 × 93 is greater than 8 × 90. ○ True ○ False

10b. An estimate of 8 × 93 is 2,700. ○ True ○ False

10c. 8 × 93 = (8 × 9) + (8 × 3) ○ True ○ False

10d. 8 × 93 is less than 800. ○ True ○ False

11. Find 4 × 7,342.

Use estimation to explain why your answer is reasonable.

12. For numbers 12a–12d, choose Yes or No to tell whether the equation is true.

12a. 5 × 60 = 30	○ Yes	○ No
12b. 500 × 6 = 30,000	○ Yes	○ No
12c. 50 × 600 = 30,000	○ Yes	○ No
12d. 5 × 60,000 = 300,000	○ Yes	○ No

13. The best estimate for 78 × 50 is that it must be greater than ___?___ but less than ___?___.

Select one number from each column to make the sentence true.

Greater than	Less than
○ 3,200	○ 3,200
○ 3,500	○ 3,500
○ 4,000	○ 4,000
○ 4,200	○ 4,200

14. Choose the number from the box to complete the statement.

The product of 39 and 22 is closest to

300
400
800
8,000

.

15. A bus tour of New York City costs $48 per person. A group of 7 people go on the tour. What is the cost for the group? Explain how you found your answer.

16. There is a book sale at the library. The price for each book is $4. If 239 books are sold, how much money will be made at the sale?

Ⓐ $235

Ⓑ $243

Ⓒ $826

Ⓓ $956

17. Volunteers are needed at the animal shelter. If 245 boys and 304 girls each volunteer to work 3 hours, how many volunteer hours is this?

Part A
Identify any extra information given in the problem.
Explain your reasoning.

Part B
Solve the problem. Show your work.

18. Select an expression that is equivalent to 7×800.
Mark all that apply.

Ⓐ $8 + (100 \times 7) + 10$ Ⓒ $(7 \times 80) \times 10$

Ⓑ $(8 \times 7) \times (100 \times 1)$ Ⓓ $(8 + 7) \times (100 + 1)$

19. Joe makes belts. He has 9 buckles. He uses 12 rivets on each of 4 belts and 15 rivets on each of 2 belts. He has 22 rivets left over. How many rivets are on the belts?

Part A
Identify any extra information given in the problem.

Part B
Solve the problem. Show your work.

20. Draw an area model for $7 \times 5,432$. Then write an equation to match your model.

Equation: _____ × _____ = _____

21. Use the numbers on the tiles to complete the steps to find the solution to 4×65.

$4 \times 65 =$ _____ $\times (60 +$ _____$)$

    $= (4 \times$ _____$) + (4 \times$ _____$)$

    $=$ _____ $+ 20$

    $=$ _____

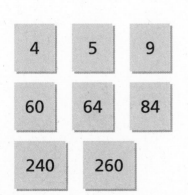

4	5	9
60	64	84
240	260	

Family Letter

Content Overview

Dear Family,

Your child is familiar with multiplication from earlier units. Unit 3 of *Math Expressions* extends the concepts used in multiplication to teach your child division. The main goals of this unit are to:

- Learn methods for dividing whole numbers up to four digits.

- Use estimates to check the reasonableness of answers.

- Solve problems involving division and remainders.

Your child will learn and practice techniques such as the Place Value Sections, Expanded Notation, and Digit-by-Digit methods to gain speed and accuracy in division. At first, your child will learn to use patterns and multiplication to divide. Later, your child will learn to use the methods with divisors from 2 to 9. Then your child will learn to divide when there is a zero in the quotient or dividend and to watch out for potential problems involving these situations.

Examples of Division Methods:

Place Value Sections Method	Expanded Notation Method	Digit-by-Digit Method

$$60 + 6 = 66$$

$$5 \overline{\begin{array}{c|c} 330 & 30 \\ \hline -300 & 30 \\ \hline 30 & 0 \end{array}}$$

$$\begin{array}{r} 6 \\ 60 \end{array} \Bigr] 66$$
$$5\overline{)330}$$
$$-300$$
$$\overline{30}$$
$$-30$$
$$\overline{0}$$

$$\begin{array}{r} 66 \\ 5\overline{)330} \\ -30 \\ \hline 30 \\ -30 \\ \hline 0 \end{array}$$

Your child may use whatever method he or she chooses as long as he or she can explain it. Some children like to use different methods.

Your child will also learn to interpret remainders in the context of the problem being solved; for example, when the remainder alone is the answer to a word problem.

Finally, your child will apply this knowledge to solve mixed problems with one or more steps and using all four operations.

If you have questions or problems, please contact me.

Sincerely,
Your child's teacher

 CA CC

Unit 3 addresses the following standard from the *Common Core State Standards for Mathematics with California Additions*: **4.NBT.6** and all Mathematical Practices.

Estimada familia:

En unidades anteriores su niño se ha familiarizado con la multiplicación. La Unidad 3 de *Math Expressions* amplía los conceptos usados en la multiplicación para que su niño aprenda la división. Los objetivos principales de esta unidad son:

- aprender métodos para dividir números enteros de hasta cuatro dígitos.

- usar la estimación para comprobar si las respuestas son razonables.

- resolver problemas que requieran división y residuos.

Su niño aprenderá y practicará técnicas tales como las de Secciones de valor posicional, Notación extendida y Dígito por dígito, para adquirir rapidez y precisión en la división. Al principio, su niño aprenderá a usar patrones y la multiplicación para dividir. Más adelante, usará los métodos con divisores de 2 a 9. Luego, aprenderá a dividir cuando haya un cero en el cociente o en el dividendo, y a detectar problemas que pueden surgir en esas situaciones.

Ejemplos de métodos de división:

Secciones de valor posicional	Notación extendida	Dígito por dígito

$$60 + 6 = 66$$

$$
\begin{array}{c|c|c}
5 & 330 & 30 \\
 & -300 & 30 \\
 & 30 & 0
\end{array}
$$

$$
\begin{array}{r}
6 \\
60 \rbrack 66 \\
5\overline{)330} \\
-300 \\
\hline
30 \\
-30 \\
\hline
0
\end{array}
$$

$$
\begin{array}{r}
66 \\
5\overline{)330} \\
-30 \\
\hline
30 \\
-30 \\
\hline
0
\end{array}
$$

Su niño puede usar el método que elija siempre y cuando pueda explicarlo. A algunos niños les gusta usar métodos diferentes.

Su niño también aprenderá a interpretar los residuos en el contexto del problema que se esté resolviendo; por ejemplo, cuando solamente el residuo es la respuesta a un problema.

Por último, su niño aplicará este conocimiento para resolver problemas mixtos de uno o más pasos, usando las cuatro operaciones.

Si tiene alguna pregunta o comentario, por favor comuníquese conmigo.

Atentamente,
El maestro de su niño

© Houghton Mifflin Harcourt Publishing Company

CA CC

En la Unidad 3 se aplican los siguientes estándares auxiliares, contenidos en los *Estándares estatales comunes de matemáticas con adiciones para California*: **4.NBT.6** y todos los de prácticas matemáticas.

VOCABULARY
divisor
quotient
dividend

► **Division Vocabulary and Models**

Although multiplication and division are inverse operations, each operation has its own language.

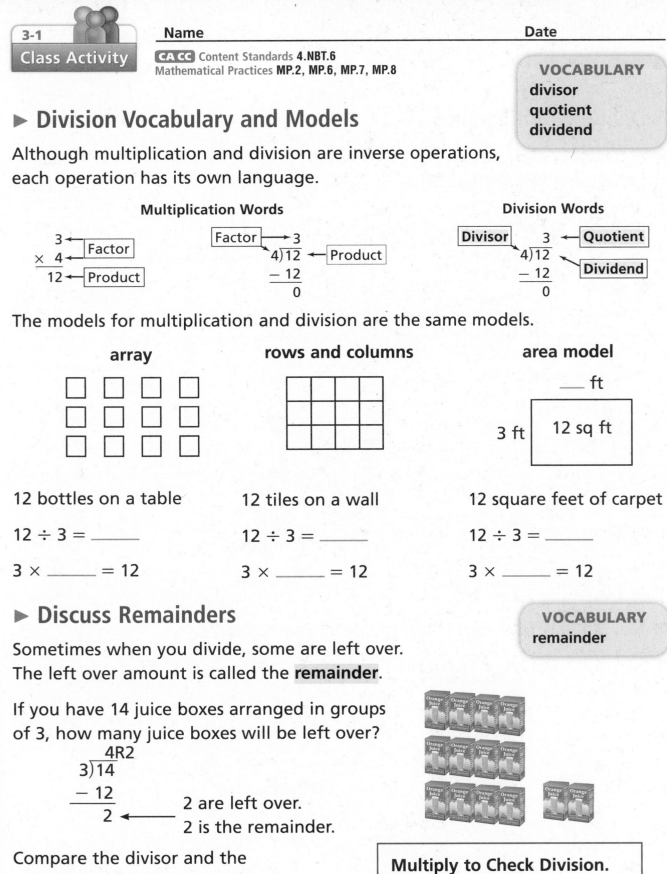

Multiplication Words

$3 \leftarrow$ Factor
$\times\ 4 \leftarrow$ Factor
$\overline{12} \leftarrow$ Product

Factor $\rightarrow 3$
$4\overline{)12} \leftarrow$ Product
$\underline{-12}$
0

Division Words

Divisor $\quad 3 \leftarrow$ Quotient
$4\overline{)12} \leftarrow$ Dividend
$\underline{-12}$
0

The models for multiplication and division are the same models.

array

12 bottles on a table

$12 \div 3 =$ _____

$3 \times$ _____ $= 12$

rows and columns

12 tiles on a wall

$12 \div 3 =$ _____

$3 \times$ _____ $= 12$

area model

___ ft

3 ft | 12 sq ft

12 square feet of carpet

$12 \div 3 =$ _____

$3 \times$ _____ $= 12$

► **Discuss Remainders**

VOCABULARY
remainder

Sometimes when you divide, some are left over. The left over amount is called the **remainder**.

If you have 14 juice boxes arranged in groups of 3, how many juice boxes will be left over?

```
    4R2
3)14
  -12
    2  ← 2 are left over.
       2 is the remainder.
```

Compare the divisor and the remainder. The remainder must be less than the divisor.

$2 < 3$, so the remainder is correct.

**Multiply to Check Division.
Add the remainder.**

$4 \times 3 = 12$
$12 + 2 = 14$

3-1
Class Activity

Name _____   Date _____

▶ Divide with Remainders

The remainder must be less than the divisor.
If it is not, increase the quotient.

$$
\begin{array}{r} 3 \\ 5\overline{)23} \\ -15 \\ \hline 8 \text{ no} \\ 8 > 5 \end{array}
\qquad \longrightarrow \qquad
\begin{array}{r} 4 \text{ R3} \\ 5\overline{)23} \\ -20 \\ \hline 3 \text{ yes} \\ 3 < 5 \end{array}
$$

$$
\begin{array}{r} 8 \\ 9\overline{)87} \\ -72 \\ \hline 15 \text{ no} \\ 15 > 9 \end{array}
\qquad \longrightarrow \qquad
\begin{array}{r} 9 \text{ R6} \\ 9\overline{)87} \\ -81 \\ \hline 6 \text{ yes} \\ 6 < 9 \end{array}
$$

Divide with remainders.

1. $2\overline{)19}$ 2. $7\overline{)50}$ 3. $9\overline{)48}$

4. $5\overline{)48}$ 5. $6\overline{)19}$ 6. $3\overline{)25}$

Divide. Multiply to check the last problem in each row.

7. $6\overline{)27}$ 8. $4\overline{)30}$ 9. $\begin{array}{r} 5 \text{ R4} \\ 7\overline{)39} \\ -35 \\ \hline 4 \end{array}$ $7 \cdot 5 + 4 =$
                                                                                                 $35 + 4 = 39$

10. $8\overline{)43}$ 11. $5\overline{)26}$ 12. $9\overline{)41}$

13. $5\overline{)32}$ 14. $4\overline{)21}$ 15. $3\overline{)22}$

► Multiply and Divide with Zeros

When you multiply or divide with zeros, you can see a pattern.

$4 \times 1 = 4$	$4 \div 4 = 1$	$7 \times 5 = 35$	$35 \div 7 = 5$
$4 \times 10 = 40$	$40 \div 4 = 10$	$7 \times 50 = 350$	$350 \div 7 = 50$
$4 \times 100 = 400$	$400 \div 4 = 100$	$7 \times 500 = 3,500$	$3,500 \div 7 = 500$
$4 \times 1,000 = 4,000$	$4,000 \div 4 = 1,000$	$7 \times 5,000 = 35,000$	$35,000 \div 7 = 5,000$

16. What pattern do you notice when you multiply with zeros?

_____

_____

17. What pattern do you notice when you divide with zeros?

_____

_____

Find the unknown factor. Multiply to check the division.

18. $4\overline{)320}$ $\qquad$ $4 \cdot$ _____ $= 320$ $\qquad$ **19.** $6\overline{)420}$ $\qquad$ $6 \cdot$ _____ $= 420$

20. $7\overline{)49}$ $\qquad$ $7 \cdot$ _____ $= 49$ $\qquad$ **21.** $3\overline{)1,800}$ $\qquad$ $3 \cdot$ _____ $= 1,800$

22. $5\overline{)4,500}$ $\qquad$ $5 \cdot$ _____ $= 4,500$ $\qquad$ **23.** $9\overline{)3,600}$ $\qquad$ $9 \cdot$ _____ $= 3,600$

24. $6\overline{)3,000}$ $\qquad$ $6 \cdot$ _____ $= 3,000$ $\qquad$ **25.** $5\overline{)4,000}$ $\qquad$ $5 \cdot$ _____ $= 4,000$

Name _____ **Date** _____

► Divide With Zeros and Remainders

Divide. Multiply to check your answer.

26.
$$
\begin{array}{r}
300 \text{ R}6 \\
7\overline{)2{,}106} \\
-2{,}100 \\
\hline
6
\end{array}
$$

27. $8\overline{)643}$

28. $9\overline{)275}$

29. $2\overline{)1{,}601}$

30. $3\overline{)1{,}802}$

31. $4\overline{)2{,}803}$

32. $5\overline{)4{,}503}$

33. $6\overline{)4{,}205}$

Divide With Remainders

▶ Multiplying and Dividing

Complete the steps.

1. Sam divides 738 by 6. He uses the Place Value
   Sections Method and the Expanded Notation Method.

   a. Sam thinks: I'll draw the Place Value Sections that I know from
      multiplication. To divide, I need to find how many hundreds,
      tens, and ones to find the unknown factor.

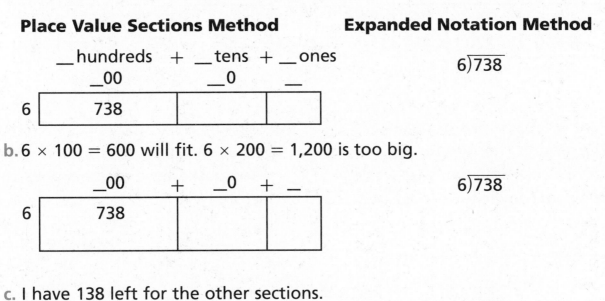

Place Value Sections Method   **Expanded Notation Method**

__ hundreds + __ tens + __ ones   6)738

b. 6 × 100 = 600 will fit. 6 × 200 = 1,200 is too big.

c. I have 138 left for the other sections.
   6 × 20 = 120 will fit. 6 × 30 = 180 is too big.

d. 6 × 3 = 18

Name _____   Date _____

▶ Practice the Place Value Sections Method

Solve. Use Place Value Sections Method for division.

The sidewalk crew knows that the new sidewalk at the mall will be 3,915 square feet. It will be 9 feet wide. How long will it be? _____

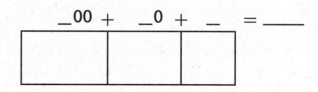

$$\underline{400} + \underline{30} + \underline{5} = 435$$

	400	30	5
9 ft	3,915 −3,600	315 −270	45 −45
	315	45	0

2. The sidewalk at the theater will be 2,748 square feet. It will be 6 feet wide. How long will it be?

_____

$$\underline{}00 + \underline{}0 + \underline{} = \underline{}$$

3. Pens are packaged in boxes of 8. The store is charged for a total of 4,576 pens. How many boxes of pens did they receive? _____

$$\underline{}00 + \underline{}0 + \underline{} = \underline{}$$

4. A factory has 2,160 erasers. They package them in groups of 5. How many packages of erasers does the factory have? _____

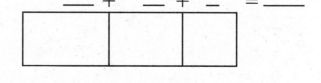

$$\underline{} + \underline{} + \underline{} = \underline{}$$

5. A party planner has 834 small flowers to make party favors. She will put 3 flowers in each party favor. How many party favors can she make? _____

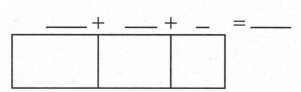

$$\underline{} + \underline{} + \underline{} = \underline{}$$

6. An artist has 956 tiles to use in a design. He plans to arrange the tiles in group of 4 tiles. How many groups of 4 tiles can he make?

_____

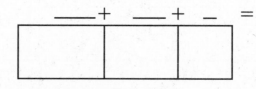

$$\underline{} + \underline{} + \underline{} = \underline{}$$

► Problem Solving with 3-Digit Quotients

Solve using the Expanded Notation Method for division.

7. A toy company has 740 games to donate to different schools. Each school will receive 4 games. How many schools will receive games?

8. A landscape architect designs a rectangular garden that is 1,232 square feet. It is 8 feet wide. How long is the garden? _____

9. The convention center is expecting 1,434 people for an event. Since each table can seat 6 people, how many tables will the convention center need to set up? _____

10. An adult lion weighs an average of 375 pounds. A lion cub weighs an average of 3 pounds at birth. How many times more does the adult lion weigh than the lion cub weighs at birth? _____

Name _____ **Date** _____

► Practice with the Expanded Notation Method

Solve using the Expanded Notation Method for division.

11. 3)552

12. 7)851

13. 2)978

14. 4)979

15. 3)1,098

16. 5)2,945

17. 7)1,652

18. 8)4,520

19. 6)3,938

Relate 3-Digit Multiplication to Division

Name _____ Date _____

CA CC Content Standards **4.NBT.6**
Mathematical Practices **MP.2, MP.7, MP.8**

▶ 2-Digit and 4-Digit Quotients

Solve. Use the Place Value Sections and the Expanded Notation Methods for division.

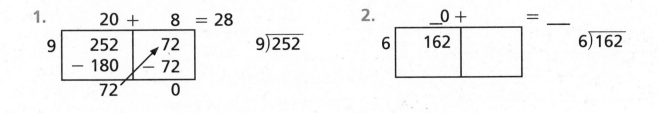

1.
$$20 + 8 = 28$$

20 +	8 = 28
252	72
− 180	− 72
72	0

9 ⟌ 252

2.
$$\_0 + \quad = \_$$

| 162 | |

6 ⟌ 162

3.
$$\_,000 + \_00 + \_0 + \_ = \_\_\_\_$$

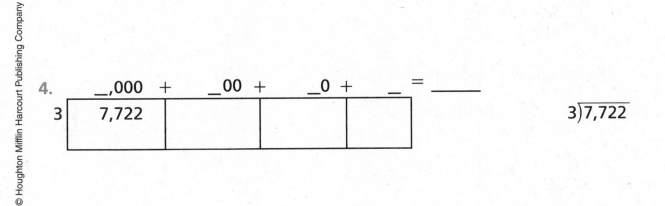

8 | 8,984 | | | |

8 ⟌ 8,984

4.
$$\_,000 + \_00 + \_0 + \_ = \_\_\_\_$$

3 | 7,722 | | | |

3 ⟌ 7,722

▶ Finding Group Size

5. An orchard has 516 apples ready for delivery. There are the same number of apples in each of 4 crates. How many apples are in each crate? _____

$516 \div 4 = ?$

4 groups

4)516

Divide 5 hundreds, 1 ten, 6 ones equally among 4 groups.

Complete the steps.

Step 1

4 groups

1 hundred
1 hundred
1 hundred
1 hundred

5 hundreds ÷ 4

Each group gets 1 hundred.

1 hundred is left.

$$\begin{array}{r} 1 \\ 4\overline{)516} \\ -4 \\ \hline 1 \end{array}$$

Regroup 1 hundred.

10 tens + 1 ten =

11 _____

$$\begin{array}{r} 1 \\ 4\overline{)516} \\ -4 \\ \hline 11 \end{array}$$

Step 2

4 groups

1 hundred + 2 tens
1 hundred + 2 tens
1 hundred + 2 tens
1 hundred + 2 tens

11 tens ÷ 4

Each group gets 2 tens.

3 _____ are left.

$$\begin{array}{r} 12 \\ 4\overline{)516} \\ -4 \\ \hline 11 \\ -8 \\ \hline 3 \end{array}$$

Regroup 3 tens.

30 ones + 6 ones =

_____ ones

$$\begin{array}{r} 12 \\ 4\overline{)516} \\ -4 \\ \hline 11 \\ -8 \\ \hline 36 \end{array}$$

Step 3

4 groups

1 hundred + 2 tens + 9
1 hundred + 2 tens + 9
1 hundred + 2 tens + 9
1 hundred + 2 tens + 9

36 ones ÷ 4

Each group gets 9 ones.

There are _____ ones left.

$$\begin{array}{r} 129 \\ 4\overline{)516} \\ -4 \\ \hline 11 \\ -8 \\ \hline 36 \\ -36 \\ \hline 0 \end{array}$$

There are _____

apples in each crate.

Discuss 2-Digit and 4-Digit Quotients

Name _____ Date _____

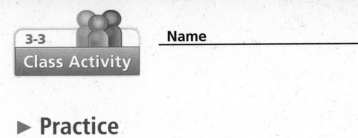

▶ Practice

Divide.

6. 4)868

7. 6)5,142

8. 3)4,395

9. 4)332

10. 7)1,617

11. 7)939

12. 2)4,276

13. 6)2,576

14. 7)441

15. 9)3,735

16. 7)406

17. 3)9,954

► Division Word Problems

Solve.

Show your work.

18. What is the length of a rectangle with an area of 756 square centimeters and a width of 4 centimeters?

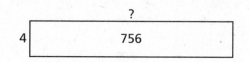

```
     ?
  ┌─────────────┐
4 │    756      │
  └─────────────┘
```

_____

19. At a county fair, there are 7 booths that sell raffle tickets. In one day, 4,592 tickets were sold. Each booth sold the same number of tickets. How many tickets did each booth sell?

_____

20. One part of a city football stadium has 5,688 seats. The seats are arranged in 9 sections. Each section has the same number of seats. How many seats are in each section?

_____

21. An art museum has a total of 475 paintings hanging in 5 different viewing rooms. If each room has the same number of paintings, how many paintings are in each room?

_____

22. A parking garage can hold a total of 762 cars. The same number of cars can park on each floor. There are 6 floors. How many cars can park on each floor?

_____

▶ The Digit-by-Digit Method

1. Suppose Judith wants to divide 948 by 4. She knows how to use the Place Value Sections Method and the Expanded Notation Method, but she doesn't want to write all the zeros.

Place Value Sections Method

$$200 + \quad 30 + \quad 7 = 237$$

	948	148	28
4	− 800	− 120	− 28
	148	28	0

Expanded Notation Method

$$\begin{array}{r} 7 \\ 30 \\ 200 \end{array} \bigg] 237$$

$$\begin{array}{r} 4\overline{)948} \\ -800 \\ \hline 148 \\ -120 \\ \hline 28 \\ -28 \\ \hline 0 \end{array}$$

Judith thinks: I'll look at the place values in decreasing order. I'll imagine zeros in the other places, but I don't need to think about them until I'm ready to divide in that place.

Step 1: Look at the greatest place value first. Divide the hundreds. Then subtract.

9 hundreds ÷ 4 = 2 hundreds

$$\begin{array}{r} 2 \\ 4\overline{)948} \\ -8 \\ \hline 1 \end{array}$$

Step 2: Bring down the 4. Divide the tens. Then subtract.

14 tens ÷ 4 = 3 tens

$$\begin{array}{r} 23 \\ 4\overline{)948} \\ -8\downarrow \\ \hline 14 \\ -12 \\ \hline 2 \end{array}$$

Step 3: Bring down the 8. Divide the ones. Then subtract.

28 ones ÷ 4 = 7 ones

$$\begin{array}{r} 237 \\ 4\overline{)948} \\ -8\downarrow \\ \hline 14 \\ -12\downarrow \\ \hline 28 \\ -28 \\ \hline 0 \end{array}$$

Name   Date

▶ What's the Error?

Dear Math Students,

Here is a division problem I tried to solve.

$$
\begin{array}{r}
5{,}796 \\
3\overline{)1{,}738} \\
-15 \\
\hline
23 \\
-21 \\
\hline
28 \\
-27 \\
\hline
18 \\
-18 \\
\hline
0
\end{array}
$$

Is my answer correct? If not, please help me understand why it is wrong.

Thank you,
Puzzled Penguin

2. Write a response to Puzzled Penguin.

_____

_____

_____

Solve. Use the Digit-by-Digit Method.

3. $4\overline{)3{,}036}$ 4. $7\overline{)5{,}292}$ 5. $6\overline{)853}$

Name Date

▶ Practice

Divide.

6. $5\overline{)965}$

7. $8\overline{)128}$

8. $8\overline{)928}$

9. $3\overline{)716}$

10. $4\overline{)4{,}596}$

11. $4\overline{)982}$

12. $3\overline{)6{,}342}$

13. $8\overline{)578}$

14. $5\overline{)1{,}155}$

15. $6\overline{)3{,}336}$

16. $7\overline{)672}$

17. $3\overline{)4{,}152}$

▶ Solve Division Problems

**Write an equation to represent the problem.
Then, solve.**

Show your work.

18. What is the length of a rectangle with an area of 528 square centimeters and a width of 6 centimeters?

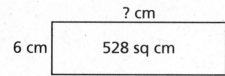

? cm

6 cm | 528 sq cm

_____

19. A cookbook features 414 recipes. There are 3 recipes on each page. How many pages are in the cookbook?

_____

20. A bus travels its route around a city once a day for 5 days. At the end of the 5th day, the bus had traveled 435 miles. How many miles did the bus travel each day?

_____

21. Ms. Tyler places a container of marbles at each table of 6 students. The students are told to share the marbles equally with the students at their table. If there are 714 marbles in the container, how many marbles should each student get?

_____

22. Sam's Used Bookstore is organizing their books on display shelves. They have 976 books and want 8 books displayed on each shelf. How many shelves will the books fill?

_____

▶ Compare Methods

Ellie, José, and Wanda each use their favorite method to
solve 1,194 ÷ 5. Discuss the methods.

Ellie's Place Value Sections Method	José's Expanded Notation Method	Wanda's Digit-by-Digit Method

Ellie's Place Value Sections Method

$$200 + 30 + 8 = 238 \text{ R4}$$

5	1,194	194	44
	−1,000	−150	−40
	194	44	4

José's Expanded Notation Method

$$\begin{array}{r} 8 \\ 30 \\ 200 \end{array} \Big] 238 \text{ R4}$$

$$5)\overline{1,194}$$
$$-\ 1,000$$
$$194$$
$$-\ 150$$
$$44$$
$$-\ 40$$
$$4$$

Wanda's Digit-by-Digit Method

$$238 \text{ R4}$$
$$5)\overline{1,194}$$
$$-\ 1\ 0$$
$$19$$
$$-\ 15$$
$$44$$
$$-\ 40$$
$$4$$

Use any method to solve.

1. $3,248 \div 5 =$ _____

2. $5,847 \div 6 =$ _____

Solve. Use any method.

3. $5)\overline{8,435}$ 4. $3)\overline{2,604}$ 5. $4)\overline{6,738}$ 6. $5)\overline{9,714}$

▶ Division Practice

Use any method to solve.

7. $6\overline{)2,238}$ 8. $5\overline{)2,431}$ 9. $7\overline{)2,198}$ 10. $8\overline{)2,512}$

11. $4\overline{)5,027}$ 12. $5\overline{)5,624}$ 13. $9\overline{)3,631}$ 14. $6\overline{)6,305}$

▶ What's the Error?

Dear Math Students,

This is a problem from my math homework. My teacher says my answer is not correct, but I can't figure out what I did wrong. Can you help me find and fix my mistake?

Your Friend,
Puzzled Penguin

$$\begin{array}{r} 7,069 \text{ R2} \\ 5\overline{)3,847} \\ -35 \\ \hline 34 \\ -30 \\ \hline 47 \\ -45 \\ \hline 2 \end{array}$$

15. Write a response to Puzzled Penguin.

_____

_____

_____

_____

Relate Three Methods

► Practice Division

Use any method to solve.

1. $8\overline{)960}$ 2. $4\overline{)632}$ 3. $7\overline{)809}$ 4. $5\overline{)736}$

5. $4\overline{)3,068}$ 6. $3\overline{)6,206}$ 7. $2\overline{)6,476}$ 8. $6\overline{)8,825}$

► Solve Division Word Problems

Solve.

9. A helper in the school store suggests selling notebooks in packages of 4. How many packages of 4 can be made from 192 notebooks?

_____

10. Another helper suggests selling notebooks in packages of 6. How many packages of 6 can be made from 192 notebooks?

_____

11. The store will sell packages of notebooks for $3.00 each.

   a. Which would be a better deal for students, packages of 4 or packages of 6?

   _____

   _____

   b. Which package size would make more money for the store?

   _____

   _____

▶ Solve Division Word Problems (continued)

Another helper in the school store suggests making packages of 7 or 8 notebooks.

Show your work.

12. How many packages of 7 notebooks can be made from 896 notebooks?

_____

13. How many packages of 8 notebooks can be made from 896 notebooks?

_____

14. The store will sell packages of notebooks for $6.00 each.

   a. Would you rather buy a package with 7 notebooks or a package with 8 notebooks? Explain.

_____

_____

   b. Would packages of 7 notebooks or packages of 8 notebooks make more money for the store? Explain.

_____

_____

15. The students at Walnut Street School collected 2,790 cans for a recycling center. Each student brought in 5 cans. How many students attend the school?

_____

16. A cube can be made from 6 square cards that are each the same size. How many cubes can be made out of 7,254 cards?

_____

17. There are 5,896 beads in a barrel at a factory. These beads will be sold in packets of 4. How many full packets can be made from the beads in the barrel?

_____

Divide by Any Method

Name _____ **Date** _____

CA CC **Content Standards 4.NBT.6**
Mathematical Practices **MP.1, MP.2, MP.3, MP.6**

▶ What's the Error?

Dear Math Students,

The Puzzled Penguin started to solve this division problem and realized there was a problem. Some friends suggested different ways to fix it.

Your friend,
Puzzled Penguin

$$\begin{array}{r} 7 \\ 4\overline{)3,476} \\ -28 \\ \hline 6 \end{array}$$

Jacob suggested that Puzzled Penguin erase the 7 and write 8 in its place. Puzzled Penguin would also need to erase the calculations and do them over. $$\begin{array}{r} 8 \\ 4\overline{)3,476} \\ -32 \\ \hline 2 \end{array}$$	Fred told Puzzled Penguin to cross out the 7 and write 8 above it. The next step would be to subtract one more 4. $$\begin{array}{r} 8 \\ \not{7} \\ 4\overline{)3,476} \\ -28 \\ \hline 6 \\ -4 \\ \hline \end{array}$$
Amad showed Puzzled Penguin how to use the Expanded Notation Method and just keep going. $$\begin{array}{r} 100 \\ 700 \\ 4\overline{)3,476} \\ -2,800 \\ \hline 676 \\ -400 \\ \hline 276 \end{array}$$	Kris showed Puzzled Penguin how, with the Place Value Sections Method, another section can be added. $$\begin{array}{c|c|c} & 700 + & 100 \\ \hline 4 & 3,476 & 676 \\ & -2,800 & -400 \\ \hline & 676 & 276 \end{array}$$

1. What was Puzzled Penguin's problem?

_____

2. Discuss the solutions above. Which friend was right?

_____

▶ Zeros in Quotients

Solve.

3. $6\overline{)1,842}$ 4. $8\overline{)5,125}$ 5. $4\overline{)4,152}$ 6. $5\overline{)9,522}$

7. $3\overline{)7,531}$ 8. $2\overline{)4,018}$ 9. $4\overline{)8,200}$ 10. $7\overline{)9,102}$

11. Cameron has a collection of 436 miniature cars that he displays on 4 shelves in a bookcase. If the cars are divided equally among the shelves, how many cars are on each shelf?

Show your work.

_____

12. The Tropical Tour Company has 2,380 brochures to distribute equally among its 7 resort hotels. How many brochures will each hotel receive?

_____

13. A factory packs 8,440 bottles of water in boxes each day. If each box contains 8 bottles, how many full boxes of water can the factory pack in one day?

_____

       Just-Under Quotient Digits

Name _____ Date _____

CA CC Content Standards **4.OA.3, 4.NBT.3, 4.NBT.6**
Mathematical Practices **MP.1, MP.2, MP.6**

▶ Check Quotients With Rounding and Estimation

Rounding and estimating can be used to check answers. Review your rounding skills, and then apply what you know to division problems.

Use rounding and estimating to decide whether each quotient makes sense.

1. $\quad$ 18 R2
    $3\overline{)56}$

2. $\quad$ 92 R3
    $5\overline{)463}$

3. $\quad$ 928
    $6\overline{)5,568}$

4. $\quad$ 129 R4
    $7\overline{)907}$

▶ Practice Dividing and Estimating

Solve, using any method. Then check your answer by rounding and estimating.

5. $3\overline{)29}$

6. $6\overline{)34}$

7. $7\overline{)59}$

8. $3\overline{)72}$

9. $6\overline{)83}$

10. $7\overline{)88}$

11. $7\overline{)628}$

12. $8\overline{)683}$

13. $9\overline{)717}$

14. $7\overline{)805}$

15. $8\overline{)869}$

16. $9\overline{)914}$

17. $6\overline{)1,723}$

18. $2\overline{)2,986}$

19. $7\overline{)8,574}$

20. $6\overline{)4,652}$

21. $2\overline{)5,235}$

22. $7\overline{)7,310}$

► Estimate or Exact Answer

Some problems require an exact answer. Others require
an estimate only.

Exact Answer If a problem asks for an exact answer, then you will have to do the calculation.	**Estimate** If a problem asks for a close answer and uses *about, approximately, almost,* or *nearly,* then you can estimate.
Example: The school cafeteria prepares 3,210 lunches each week. The same numbers of lunches are prepared 5 days each week. How many lunches are prepared each day?	**Example:** Milo has to read a 229-page book. He has 8 days to finish it. About how many pages should he read each day?
Discuss why you think this problem requires an exact answer.	Discuss why an estimate, and not an exact answer, is appropriate.

**Decide whether you need an exact answer or an estimate.
Then find the answer.**

23. Sam bought a board that was
72 inches long to make
bookshelves. He wants to cut the
board into three equal pieces and
use each one for a shelf. How long
will each shelf be?

_____

24. Carl's mother baked 62 mini
muffins for his class. There are
18 people in Carl's class, including
the teacher. About how many mini
muffins should each person get?

_____

25. Each 24-inch shelf can hold about
10 books. Approximately how
many inches wide is each book?

_____

26. Malcom wants to buy 3 concert
tickets. Each ticket costs $45.
How much money will he need?

_____

▶ Different Kinds of Remainders

Remainders in division have different meanings, depending upon the type of problem you solve.

$$\begin{array}{r} 2\ \text{R1} \\ 4\overline{)9} \\ -8 \\ \hline 1 \end{array}$$

The same numeric solution shown at the right works for the following five problems. Discuss why the remainder means something different in each problem.

A. **The remainder is not part of the question.** Thomas has one 9-foot pine board. He needs to make 4-foot shelves for his books. How many shelves can he cut?

B. **The remainder causes the answer to be rounded up.** Nine students are going on a field trip. Parents have offered to drive. If each parent can drive 4 students, how many parents need to drive?

C. **The remainder is a fractional part of the answer.** One Monday Kim brought 9 apples to school. She shared them equally among herself and 3 friends. How many apples did each person get?

D. **The remainder is a decimal part of the answer.** Raul bought 4 toy cars for $9.00. Each car costs the same amount. How much did each car cost?

E. **The remainder is the only part needed to answer the question.** Nine students have signed up to run a relay race. If each relay team can have 4 runners, how many students cannot run in the race?

▶ Discuss Real World Division Problems

Solve. Then discuss the meaning of the remainder.

1. Maddie tried to divide 160 stickers equally among herself and 5 friends. There were some stickers left over, so she kept them. How many stickers did Maddie get?

_____

_____

_____

_____

2. Kendra bought a bag of 200 cheese crackers for her class. If each student gets 7 crackers, how many students are there? How many crackers are left over?

_____

_____

_____

_____

3. Jerry bought shelves to hold the 132 DVDs in his collection. Each shelf can fit 8 DVDs. How many full shelves will Jerry have?

_____

_____

_____

4. Racheed had 87 pennies. He divided them equally among his 4 sisters. How many pennies did Racheed have left after he gave his sisters their shares?

_____

_____

_____

5. Mara wants to buy some new pencil boxes for her pencil collection. She has 47 pencils. If each pencil box holds 9 pencils, how many pencil boxes does Mara need to buy?

_____

_____

_____

6. Henry's coin bank holds only nickels. Henry takes $4.42 to the bank to exchange for nickels only. How many nickels will he get from the bank?

_____

_____

_____

Make Sense of Remainders

▶ Mixed One-Step Word Problems

The fourth- and fifth-grade classes at Jackson Elementary
School held a Just-for-Fun Winter Carnival. All of the students
in the school were invited.

**Discuss what operation you need to use to solve each
problem. Then solve the problem.**

1. Two students from each fourth- and fifth-grade class were on the planning committee. If Jackson School has 14 fourth- and fifth-grade classes in all, how many students planned the carnival?

   _____

   _____

2. To advertise the carnival, students decorated 4 hallway bulletin boards. They started with 2,025 pieces of colored paper. When they finished, they had 9 pieces left. How many pieces of paper did they use?

   _____

   _____

3. The parents ordered pizzas to serve at the carnival. Each pizza was cut into 8 slices. How many pizzas had to be ordered so that 1,319 people could each have one slice?

   _____

   _____

4. There were 825 students signed up to run in timed races. If exactly 6 students ran in each race, how many races were there?

   _____

   _____

5. At the raffle booth, 364 fourth-graders each bought one ticket to win a new school supply set. Only 8 fifth-graders each bought a ticket. How many students bought raffle tickets altogether?

   _____

   _____

6. Altogether, 1,263 students were enrolled in the first through fifth grades at Jackson School. On the day of the carnival, 9 students were absent. How many students could have participated in the carnival activities?

   _____

   _____

Name _____   **Date** _____

▶ Mixed Multistep Word Problems

Solve these problems about Pine Street School's Olympic Games.

7. At the start of the games, 193 fourth-graders signed up to play in three events. Eighty-seven played in the first event. The rest of the students were evenly divided between the second and third events. How many students played in the third event?

_____

_____

8. Three teams stacked paper cups into pyramids. Each team had 176 cups to use. Team 1 used exactly half of their cups. Team 2 used four times as many cups as Team 3. Team 3 used 32 cups. Which team stacked the most cups?

_____

_____

9. The Parents' Club provided 357 celery sticks, 676 carrot sticks, and 488 apple slices. If each student was given 3 snack pieces, how many students got a snack?

_____

_____

10. Seventy-five first-graders and 84 second-graders skipped around the gym. After a while, only 8 students were still skipping. How many students had stopped skipping?

_____

_____

11. A team from each school had 250 foam balls and a bucket. The Jackson team dunked 6 fewer balls than the Pine Street team. The Pine Street team dunked all but 8 of their balls. How many balls did the two teams dunk in all?

_____

_____

12. When the day was over, everybody had earned at least 1 medal, and 32 students each got 2 medals. In all, 194 each of gold, silver, and bronze medals were given out. How many students played in the games?

_____

_____

► **Math and Amusement Parks**

There are many things to do at an Amusement Park: ride the rides, play some games, try new foods. Many people like to ride roller coasters while at the Amusement Park.

The tallest roller coaster in the world is 456 feet tall and is located in Jackson, New Jersey. In fact, the top three tallest roller coasters in the world are in the United States.

The fourth and fifth grade classes went on a field trip to the Amusement Park.

1. There are 58 fourth grade students who are in line to ride the Loop-the-Loop roller coaster. Each roller coaster car holds 4 people. How many roller coaster cars are needed so they all can ride the roller coaster once?

Show your work.

_____

2. There are 41 fifth grade students who are in line to ride the Mile Long wooden roller coaster. Each roller coaster car holds 6 people. How many students will be in a roller coaster car that is not full?

_____

Name _____   **Date** _____

▶ More Amusement Park Fun

After riding the roller coasters, the fourth and fifth grade classes spend the rest of the day getting lunch, going shopping, and riding the rest of the rides at the Amusement Park.

Solve.   *Show your work.*

3. There are 27 students in Evan's group. Each student decides to get a kids meal for lunch at the food stand. If each kids meal is $7, how much did the students spend in lunch altogether?

   _____

4. Thirty-one students are in line to ride the Ferris wheel. Four students are needed to fill each Ferris wheel car. How many Ferris wheel cars will be full?

   _____

5. In the souvenir shop, a worker opens a box of posters. The posters in the box are bundled in groups of 8. There are a total of 2,864 posters in a box. How many bundles of posters are in the box?

   _____

Focus on Mathematical Practices

1. For 1a–1d, choose True or False to indicate if the statement is correct.

   1a. $245 \div 6 = 40 \, R5$ ○ True ○ False

   1b. $803 \div 2 = 400$ ○ True ○ False

   1c. $492 \div 7 = 69 \, R7$ ○ True ○ False

   1d. $355 \div 5 = 71$ ○ True ○ False

2. A train has a total of 216 seats in 3 cars. Each train car has the same number of seats. How many seats are in each train car?

   _____ seats

3. Kayla puts together gift boxes of fruit to sell at her fruit stand. She places exactly 6 pieces of fruit in each box. She only sells full boxes of fruit.

   Part A

   Kayla has 256 apples. How many boxes of fruit can she fill? Explain how you found your answer.

   Part B

   Kayla has enough peaches to fill 31 gift boxes. How many apples and peaches did Kayla put in gift boxes to sell at her fruit stand? Show your work.

4. Margaret is dividing 829 by 4.

Part A

Explain why Margaret needs to write a zero in the tens place of the quotient.

Part B

How would the digit in the tens place of the quotient change if Margaret were dividing 829 by 2?

5. A storage shelf where Carmen works can hold about 165 pounds. The storage shelf can hold 8 boxes of car parts. About how many pounds does each box weigh? Does this problem require an exact answer or an estimate? Then find the answer.

6. What is 945 ÷ 5?

  Ⓐ 189   Ⓒ 199

  Ⓑ 190   Ⓓ 209

Name _____ **Date** _____

7. Divide 4,124 by 2.

```
┌─────────┐
│         │
│         │
└─────────┘
```

8. Joshua carried 52 loads of sand to make a play area. Each load weighed 21 pounds. How many pounds of sand does Joshua use to make the play area? Use the numbers and symbols on the keypad to write the expression needed to solve this problem. Then solve the problem.

7	8	9
4	5	6
1	2	3
0	÷	×

expression: _____

_____ pounds

9. There are 118 boys and 121 girls signed up for a volleyball league. The coaches first make teams of 9 players and then assign any remaining players to make some of the teams have 10 players.

Part A
How many teams of 10 players will there be? Explain.

Part B
How many teams of 9 players will there be? Explain.

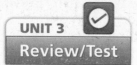
10. A florist has 2,388 flowers to make into small bouquets. She wants 6 flowers in each bouquet. How many bouquets can she make? Complete the Place Value Sections to solve.

___00   +   ___0   +   ___   = _____ bouquets

11. Divide 7,433 by 7. Show your work.

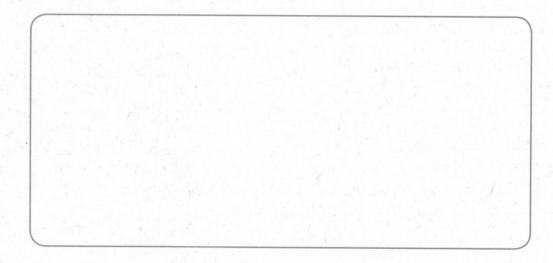

12. For numbers 12a–12d, choose Yes or No to tell if the quotient is reasonable.

            39 R3
12a. 6)297   ○ Yes   ○ No

            814
12b. 4)3,256   ○ Yes   ○ No

            228 R5
12c. 8)4,229   ○ Yes   ○ No

            1,007 R1
12d. 8)5,136   ○ Yes   ○ No

13. Hailey finds 24 seashells on Friday and another 38 seashells on Saturday. She shares as many of the seashells as she can equally among herself and 3 friends. She keeps the leftover seashells for herself. How many seashells does Hailey get? Show your work.

14. Ethan has 203 geodes to put into display cases. Each case holds 8 geodes. How many cases does Ethan need to hold all the geodes? Explain how you know.

15. Select one number from each column to make the equation true.

$$5,155 \div 3 = \blacksquare \text{ R } \blacksquare$$

Quotient	Remainder
○ 1,715	○ 1
○ 1,717	○ 2
○ 1,718	○ 3
○ 1,720	○ 4

16. Julie divided 2,526 by 6 and found a quotient of 421.
For 16a–16c, choose True or False to tell if the
statement is correct.

16a. 2,400 ÷ 6 = 400, so 421 makes sense. ○ True   ○ False

16b. 2,526 ÷ 6 = 421 R5   ○ True   ○ False

16c. 421 × 6 = 2,526, so 421 makes sense. ○ True   ○ False

17. Which expression has a quotient of 400? Circle all that apply.

| 1,600 ÷ 4 | 2,000 ÷ 5 | 400 ÷ 4 | 3,600 ÷ 9 |

18. Kyle wrote his first step in dividing 3,325 ÷ 5 using the Expanded
Notation Method.

$$
\begin{array}{r}
500 \\
5\overline{)3{,}325} \\
-2{,}500 \\
\hline
825
\end{array}
$$

Part A

Write a number sentence that will calculate a reasonable estimate
for the quotient of 3,325 ÷ 5.

Part B

Explain how Kyle's division work would be different if he had used
your estimate instead of 500 as his first step? Then find the exact
quotient of 3,325 ÷ 5.

© Houghton Mifflin Harcourt Publishing Company

Family Letter

Content Overview

Dear Family,

In Unit 4 of Math Expressions, your child will apply the skills he or she has learned about operations with whole numbers while solving real world problems involving addition, subtraction, multiplication, and division.

Your child will simplify and evaluate expressions. Parentheses will be introduced to show which operation should be done first. The symbols "=" and "≠" will be used to show whether numbers and expressions are equal.

Other topics of study in this unit include situation and solution equations for addition and subtraction, as well as multiplication and division. Your child will use situation equations to represent real world problems and solution equations to solve the problems. This method of representing a problem is particularly helpful when the problems contain greater numbers and students cannot solve mentally.

Your child will also solve multiplication and addition comparison problems and compare these types of problems identifying what is the same or different.

Addition Comparison	Multiplication Comparison
Angela is 14 years old. She is 4 years older than Damarcus. How old is Damarcus?	Shawn colored 5 pages in a coloring book. Anja colored 4 times as many pages as Shawn colored. How many pages did Anja color?

Students learn that in the addition problem they are adding 4, while in the multiplication problem, they are multiplying by 4.

Your child will apply this knowledge to solve word problems using all four operations and involving one or more steps.

Finally, your child will find factor pairs for whole numbers and generate and analyze numerical and geometric patterns.

If you have any questions or comments, please call or write to me.

Sincerely,
Your child's teacher

 CA CC

Unit 4 addresses the following standards from the *Common Core State Standards for Mathematics with California Additions:* **4.OA.1, 4.OA.2, 4.OA.3, 4.OA.4, 4.OA.5, 4.NBT.4, 4.NBT.5, 4.NBT.6, 4.MD.2,** and all Mathematical Practices.

Properties and Algebraic Notation **135**

Un vistazo general al contenido

Estimada familia:

En la Unidad 4 de Math Expressions, su hijo aplicará las destrezas relacionadas con operaciones de números enteros que ha adquirido, resolviendo problemas cotidianos que involucran suma, resta, multiplicación y división.

Su hijo simplificará y evaluará expresiones. Se introducirán los paréntesis como una forma de mostrar cuál operación deberá completarse primero. Los signos "=" y "≠" se usarán para mostrar si los números o las expresiones son iguales o no.

Otros temas de estudio en esta unidad incluyen ecuaciones de situación y de solución para la suma y resta, así como para la multiplicación y división. Su hijo usará ecuaciones de situación para representar problemas de la vida cotidiana y ecuaciones de solución para resolver esos problemas. Este método para representar problemas es particularmente útil cuando los problemas involucran números grandes y los estudiantes no pueden resolverlos mentalmente.

Su hijo también resolverá problemas de comparación de multiplicación y suma, y comparará este tipo de problemas para identificar las semejanzas y diferencias.

Comparación de suma	Comparación de multiplicación
Ángela tiene 14 años. Ella es 4 años mayor que Damarcus. ¿Cuántos años tiene Damarcus?	Shawn coloreó 5 páginas de un libro. Ana coloreó 4 veces ese número de páginas. ¿Cuántas páginas coloreó Ana?

Los estudiantes aprenderán que en el problema de suma están sumando 4, mientras que en el problema de multiplicación, están multiplicando por 4.

Su hijo aplicará estos conocimientos para resolver problemas de uno o más pasos usando las cuatro operaciones.

Finalmente, su hijo hallará pares de factores para números enteros y generará y analizará patrones numéricos y geométricos.

Si tiene alguna pregunta por favor comuníquese conmigo.

Atentamente,
El maestro de su niño

CA CC

En la Unidad 4 se aplican los siguientes estándares auxiliares, contenidos en los *Estándares estatales comunes de matemáticas con adiciones para California*: **4.OA.1, 4.OA.2, 4.OA.3, 4.OA.4, 4.OA.5, 4.NBT.4, 4.NBT.5, 4.NBT.6, 4.MD.2** y todos los de prácticas matemáticas.

Properties and Algebraic Notation

Name _____ **Date** _____

CA CC Content Standards **4.NBT.4, 4.NBT.5, 4.NBT.6**
Mathematical Practices **MP.2, MP.7, MP.8**

VOCABULARY
expression
equation
simplify
term

▶ Properties and Algebraic Notation

An **expression** is one or more numbers, variables, or numbers and variables with one or more operations.	An **equation** is a statement that two expressions are equal. It has an equal sign.
Examples: 4 $6x$ $6x - 5$ $7 + 4$	Examples: $40 + 25 = 65$ $(16 \div 4) - 3 = 1$

We **simplify** an expression or equation by performing operations to combine like **terms**.

Use the Identity Property to simplify each expression.

1. $n + 5n =$ _____

2. $17t + t =$ _____

3. $x + 245x =$ _____

4. $9e - e =$ _____

5. $8c + c + c =$ _____

6. $(5z - z) - z =$ _____

Solve.

7. $30 \div (35 \div 7) =$ _____

8. $(72 \div 9) \div 4 =$ _____

9. $80 \div (32 \div 8) =$ _____

10. $13 - (9 - 1) =$ _____

11. $(600 - 400) - 10 =$ _____

12. $100 - (26 - 6) =$ _____

Use properties to find the value of ▢ or a.

13. $49 + 17 = ▢ + 49$

▢ = _____

14. $(a \cdot 2) \cdot 3 = 4 \cdot (2 \cdot 3)$

$a =$ _____

15. $▢ \cdot 6 = 6 \cdot 8$

▢ = _____

16. $6 \cdot (40 + a) = (6 \cdot 40) + (6 \cdot 5)$

$a =$ _____

17. $(▢ \cdot 5) + (▢ \cdot 9) = 7 \cdot (5 + 9)$

▢ = _____

18. $29 + 8 = ▢ + 29$ ⟶ Is ▢ $= 4 + 2$ or $4 \cdot 2$? _____

19. $a \cdot 14 = 14 \cdot 15$ ⟶ Is $a = 5 \cdot 3$ or $5 + 3$? _____

20. $60 + 10 = ▢ + 60$ ⟶ Is ▢ $= 2 + 5$ or $2 \cdot 5$? _____

VOCABULARY
evaluate

▶ Parentheses in Equations

Solve.

21. $9 \cdot n = 144$

$n = $ _____

22. $s + 170 = 200$

$s = $ _____

23. $105 \div h = 7$

$h = $ _____

24. $(10 - 4) \cdot 7 = \boxed{} \cdot 7$

$\boxed{} = $ _____

25. $4 \cdot (9 - 3) = g$

$g = $ _____

26. $(10 - 6) \div 2 = b$

$b = $ _____

27. $9 \cdot (6 + 2) = \boxed{} \cdot 8$

$\boxed{} = $ _____

28. $\boxed{} \cdot 6 = 96$

$\boxed{} = $ _____

29. $(15 \div 3) \cdot (4 + 1) = v$

$v = $ _____

30. $(12 - 5) - (12 \div 6) = $ _____

31. $(23 + 4) \div (8 - 5) = $ _____

32. $(24 \div 3) \cdot (12 - 7) = $ _____

33. $(22 + 8) \div (17 - 11) = $ _____

▶ Substitute a Value

To **evaluate** an expression or equation:

1) Substitute the value of each letter.

2) Then simplify the expression by performing the operations.

Evaluate each expression.

34. $a = 4$

$19 - (a + 6)$

_____

35. $a = 10$

$(80 \div a) - 5$

_____

36. $b = 3$

$(8 \div 4) \cdot (7 - b)$

_____

37. $b = 7$

$21 \div (b - 4)$

_____

38. $b = 11$

$(b + 9) \div (7 - 2)$

_____

39. $c = 8$

$(20 - 10) + (7 + c)$

_____

40. $x = 9$

$16 \cdot (13 - x)$

_____

41. $d = 3$

$(24 \div 3) \cdot (d + 7)$

_____

42. $d = 0$

$(63 \div 7) \cdot d$

_____

Properties and Algebraic Notation

Name _____ Date _____

CA CC Content Standards **4.NBT.4**
Mathematical Practices **MP.1, MP.2, MP.3, MP.4, MP.6, MP.7**

VOCABULARY
sum
difference

▶ Discuss the = and ≠ Signs

An equation is made up of two equal quantities or expressions. An equal sign (=) is used to show that the two sides of the equation are equal.

$5 = 3 + 2$ $3 + 2 = 5$ $5 = 5$ $3 + 2 = 2 + 3$ $7 - 2 = 1 + 1 + 3$

The "is not equal to" sign (≠) shows that two quantities are not equal.

$4 \neq 3 + 2$ $5 \neq 3 - 1$ $5 \neq 4$ $3 - 2 \neq 1 + 3$ $3 + 2 \neq 1 + 1 + 2$

An equation can have one or more numbers or letters on each side of the equal sign. A **sum** or **difference** can be written on either side of the equal sign.

1. Use the = sign to write four equations. Vary how many numbers you have on each side of your equations.

_____   _____

_____   _____

2. Use the ≠ sign to write four "is not equal to" statements. Vary how many numbers you have on each side of your statements.

_____   _____

_____   _____

Write = or ≠ to make each statement true.

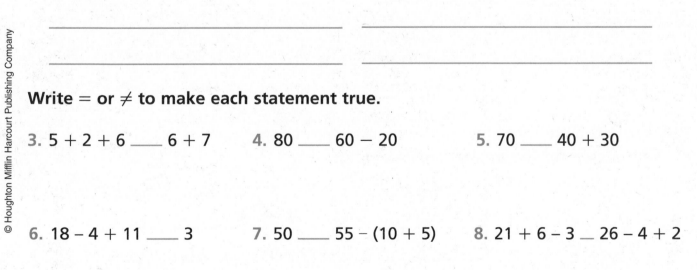

3. $5 + 2 + 6$ ____ $6 + 7$ 4. 80 ____ $60 - 20$ 5. 70 ____ $40 + 30$

6. $18 - 4 + 11$ ____ 3 7. 50 ____ $55 - (10 + 5)$ 8. $21 + 6 - 3$ ____ $26 - 4 + 2$

▶ Discuss Inverse Operations

When you add, you put two groups together. When you subtract, you find an unknown addend or take away one group from another. Addition and subtraction are inverse operations. They undo each other.

Addends are numbers that are added to make a sum. You can find two addends for a sum by breaking apart the number.

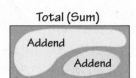

A break-apart drawing can help you find all eight related addition and subtraction equations for two addends.

Total (Sum)
81

72   9
Addend   Addend

$81 = 72 + 9$ $72 + 9 = 81$

$81 = 9 + 72$ $9 + 72 = 81$

$72 = 81 - 9$ $81 - 9 = 72$

$9 = 81 - 72$ $81 - 72 = 9$

9. Which equations show the Commutative Property?

_____

10. What is the total in each equation? Where is the total in a subtraction equation?

_____

Solve each equation.

11. $50 = 30 + p$

$p = $ _____

12. $q + 20 = 60$

$q = $ _____

13. $90 - v = 50$

$v = $ _____

14. Write the eight related addition and subtraction equations for the break-apart drawing.

56

48   8

_____   _____

_____   _____

_____   _____

_____   _____

Situation and Solution Equations for Addition and Subtraction

VOCABULARY
situation equation
solution equation

▶ Write Equations to Solve Problems

A situation equation shows the structure of the information in a problem. A solution equation shows the operation that can be used to solve a problem.

Show your work.

Write an equation to solve the problem. Draw a model if you need to.

15. In a collection of 2,152 coins, 628 coins are pennies. How many coins are not pennies?

_____

_____

16. Susanna took $3,050 out of her bank account. Now she has $11,605 left in the account. How much money was in Susanna's account to start?

_____

_____

17. In the month of May, Movieland rented 563 action movies and 452 comedy movies. How many action and comedy movies in all did Movieland rent in May?

_____

_____

▶ Practice Solving Problems

Write an equation to solve the problem. Draw a model if you need to.

18. The workers at a factory made 3,250 pink balloons in the morning. There were 5,975 pink balloons at the factory at the end of the day. How many pink balloons did the factory workers make in the afternoon?

_____

_____

▶ **Practice Solving Problems (continued)**   *Show your work.*

19. Terrence is planning a 760-mile trip. He travels 323 miles the first two days. How many miles does Terrence have left to travel on this trip?

    _____

    _____

20. There were some people at the football stadium early last Sunday, and then 5,427 more people arrived. Then there were 79,852 people at the stadium. How many people arrived early?

    _____

    _____

▶ **What's the Error?**

Dear Math Students,

The problem shown below was part of my homework assignment.

Mrs. Nason has a collection of 1,845 stamps. She bought some more stamps. Now she has 2,270 stamps. How many stamps did Mrs. Nason buy?

To solve the problem, I wrote this equation: $s - 1{,}845 = 2{,}270$. I solved the equation and wrote $s = 4{,}115$.

My teacher says that my answer is not correct. Can you help me understand what I did wrong and explain how to find the correct answer?

Your Friend,
Puzzled Penguin

21. Write a response to Puzzled Penguin.

    _____

    _____

Name _____ **Date** _____

CA CC Content Standards **4.NBT.5, 4.NBT.6**
Mathematical Practices **MP.1, MP.2, MP.4**

▶ Discuss Inverse Operations

Multiplication and division are inverse operations. They undo each other.

A **factor pair** for a number is a pair of whole numbers whose product is that number. For example, a factor pair for 15 is 3 and 5. A rectangle model is a diagram that shows a factor pair and the product.

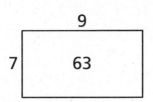

1. Which numbers in the rectangle model above are the factors? Where are the factors located?

_____

2. Which number is the product? Where is the product located?

_____

A rectangle model can you help you find all eight related multiplication and division equations for two factors. You can write these equations for the rectangle model above.

$$63 = 7 \times 9 \qquad\qquad 7 \times 9 = 63$$
$$63 = 9 \times 7 \qquad\qquad 9 \times 7 = 63$$
$$7 = 63 \div 9 \qquad\qquad 63 \div 9 = 7$$
$$9 = 63 \div 7 \qquad\qquad 63 \div 7 = 9$$

3. Write the eight related multiplication and division equations for the rectangle model below.

► Write Equations to Solve Problems

Read the problem and answer the questions.

4. Brenda planted 234 trees on her farm. The farm has 9 rows of trees. How many trees are in each row?

	n
9	234

   a. The number of trees on the farm is known. Write the number.

   b. The number of rows of trees is known. Write the number.

   c. The number of trees in each row is unknown. Use the letter *n* to represent the number of trees in each row. Write a situation equation to solve the problem.

   d. Write a solution equation.

   e. Solve your equation.

Write an equation to solve the problem. Draw a model if you need to.

Show your work.

5. Evan is starting a cycling program. He will ride 315 miles each month for the next 6 months. How many miles does he plan to ride in all?

6. Suki has 152 stickers to place in a sticker album. How many pages will Suki fill with stickers if each page in the album holds 8 stickers?

7. Al bought a wall pattern with 27 rows of 28 squares. How many squares are in the wall pattern?

Situation and Solution Equations for Multiplication and Division

VOCABULARY
compare
comparison bars

▶ Discuss Comparison Problems

To prepare for a family gathering, Sara and Ryan made soup. Sara made 2 quarts. Ryan made 6 quarts.

You can **compare** amounts, using multiplication and division.

Let r equal the number of quarts Ryan made.
Let s equal the number of quarts Sara made.

Ryan made 3 times as many quarts as Sara.

$$r = 3 \cdot s, r = 3s, \text{ or } s = r \div 3$$

Ryan (r)	2	2	2	6
Sarah (s)	2	2	2	

Solve.

Natasha made 12 quarts of soup. Manuel made 3 quarts.

1. Draw **comparison bars** to show the amount of soup each person made.

2. _____ made 4 times as many quarts as _____.

3. Write a multiplication equation that compares the amounts. _____

4. Write a division equation that compares the amounts.

   _____

5. Multiplication is the putting together of equal groups. How can this idea be used to explain why a *times as many* comparing situation is multiplication?

   _____

   _____

▶ Share Solutions

**Write an equation to solve each problem.
Draw a model if you need to.**

Show your work.

6. There are 24 students in the science club. There are 2 times as many students in the drama club. How many students are in the drama club?

   a. Draw comparison bars to compare the numbers of students in each club.

   b. Write an equation to solve the problem.

   _____

7. There are 180 pennies in Miguel's coin collection and that is 5 times as many as the number of quarters in his coin collection. How many quarters does Miguel have?

   _____

8. Fred has 72 football cards and Scott has 6 football cards. How many times as many football cards does Fred have as Scott has?

   _____

9. Audrey has 1,263 centimeters of fabric, and that is 3 times as much fabric as she needs to make some curtains. How many centimeters of fabric does Audrey need to make the curtains?

   _____

> VOCABULARY
> comparison situations

► Discuss Comparison Situations

In Lesson 4-4, you learned about multiplication and division **comparison situations**. You can also compare by using addition and subtraction. You can find *how much more* or *how much less* one amount is than another.

The amount more or less is called the difference. In some problems, the difference is not given. You have to find it. In other problems, the lesser or the greater amount is not given.

Mai has 9 apples and 12 plums.

- How many more plums than apples does Mai have?

- How many fewer apples than plums does Mai have?

Plums	12

Apples	9	d

Comparison bars can help us show which is more. We show the difference in an oval.

Draw comparison bars for each problem. Write and solve an equation. Discuss other equations you could use.

1. A nursery has 70 rose bushes and 50 tea-tree bushes. How many fewer tea-tree bushes than rose bushes are at the nursery?

2. Dan wants to plant 30 trees. He has dug 21 holes. How many more holes does Dan need to dig?

Name _____   Date _____

▶ Share Solutions

**Draw comparison bars for each problem.
Write and solve an equation.**

Show your models here.

3. Kyle and Mackenzie are playing a computer game. Kyle scored 7,628 points. Mackenzie scored 2,085 fewer points than Kyle. How many points did Mackenzie score?

_____

4. The school fair fundraiser made $632 more from baked goods than from games. The school fair made $935 from games. How much money did the school fair make from baked goods?

_____

5. A college football stadium in Michigan seats 109,901 people. A college football stadium in Louisiana seats 92,542 people. How many fewer people does the stadium in Louisiana seat than the stadium in Michigan?

_____

6. The soccer team drilled for 150 minutes last week. The team drilled for 30 minutes more than it scrimmaged. For how long did the team scrimmage?

_____

Discuss Comparison Problems

Name _____   Date _____

▶ Solve Comparison Problems

Show your models here.

For each problem, draw a model and write *addition* or *multiplication* to identify the type of comparison. Then write and solve an equation to solve the problem.

7. Nick and Liz both collect marbles. Liz has 4 times as many marbles as Nick. If Nick has 240 marbles, how many marbles does Liz have?

    Type of comparison: _____

    Equation and answer: _____

8. Samantha has 145 fewer songs on her portable media player than Luke has on his portable media player. If Samantha has 583 songs, how many songs does Luke have?

    Type of comparison: _____

    Equation and answer: _____

9. A large bookstore sold 19,813 books on Saturday and 22,964 books on Sunday. How many fewer books did the bookstore sell on Saturday than on Sunday?

    Type of comparison: _____

    Equation and answer: _____

10. Last weekend, Mr. Morgan rode his bike 3 miles. This weekend, he rode his bike 21 miles. How many times as many miles did Mr. Morgan ride his bike this weekend as last weekend?

    Type of comparison: _____

    Equation and answer: _____

    _____

► Practice

**Write and solve an equation to solve each problem.
Draw comparison bars when needed.**

Show your work.

11. On the last day of school, 100 more students wore shorts than wore jeans. If 130 students wore jeans, how many students wore shorts?

    _____

12. Matthew completed a puzzle with 90 pieces. Wendy completed a puzzle with 5 times as many pieces. How many pieces are in Wendy's puzzle?

    _____

13. There were 19,748 adults at a baseball game. There were 5,136 fewer children at the baseball game than there were adults. How many children were at the baseball game?

    _____

► What's the Error?

Dear Math Students,

I was asked to find the number of stamps that Amanda has if her friend Jesse has 81 stamps and that is 9 times as many stamps as Amanda has.

To solve the problem, I wrote this equation: $81 \times 9 = s$. I solved the equation and wrote $s = 729$. My teacher says that my answer is not correct. Can you help me understand what I did wrong?

Your friend,
Puzzled Penguin

14. Write a response to Puzzled Penguin.

    _____

    _____

Discuss Comparison Problems

Name _____ **Date** _____

CA CC Content Standards **4.OA.1, 4.OA.2**
Mathematical Practices **MP.1, MP.2**

VOCABULARY
pictograph

▶ Use a Pictograph

A **pictograph** is a graph that uses pictures or symbols to represent data. This pictograph shows how many books 5 students checked out of a library in one year.

Books Checked Out of Library

Student	
Najee	📖 📖
Tariq	📖 📖 📖 📖 📖 📖
Celine	📖 📖 📖 📖 📖 📖 📖
Jamarcus	📖 📖 📖
Brooke	📖 📖 📖 📖

📖 = 5 books

Use the pictograph to solve.

1. Write an addition equation and a subtraction equation that compare the number of books Tariq checked out (*t*) to the number of books Jamarcus checked out (*j*).

   _____

2. Write a multiplication equation and a division equation that compare the number of books Najee checked out (*n*) to the number of books Celine checked out (*c*).

   _____

3. Celine checked out twice as many books as which student?

   _____

4. Which student checked out 30 fewer books than Celine?

   _____

5. The number of books Dawson checked out is not shown. If Jamarcus checked out 10 more books than Dawson, how many books did Dawson check out?

   _____

▶ Use a Bar Graph

The bar graph below shows the number of home runs hit by five members of a baseball team.

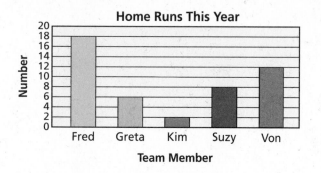

Home Runs This Year

Use the bar graph to solve.

6. Write an addition equation and a subtraction equation that compare the number of home runs Suzy hit (*s*) to the number of home runs Kim hit (*k*).

   _____

7. Write a multiplication equation and a division equation that compare the number of home runs Greta hit (*g*) to the number of runs Fred hit (*f*).

   _____

8. How many more home runs did Von hit than Greta?

   _____

9. Which player hit 10 fewer home runs than Von?

   _____

10. This year, Fred hit 2 times as many home runs as he hit last year. How many home runs did Fred hit last year?

    _____

11. **Math Journal** Write a sentence about the graph that contains the words *times as many*.

▶ Discuss the Steps of the Problem

Sometimes you will need to work through more than one step to solve a problem. The steps can be shown in one or more equations.

Solve.

1. At Parkes Elementary School, there are 6 fourth-grade classes with 17 students in each class. On Friday, 23 fourth-graders brought lunch from home and the rest of the students bought lunch in the cafeteria. How many fourth-graders bought lunch in the cafeteria on Friday?

_____

2. Solve the problem again by finishing Tommy's and Lucy's methods. Then discuss how the two methods are alike and how they are different.

Tommy's Method	Lucy's Method
Write an equation for each step.	**Write an equation for the whole problem.**
Find the total number of students who are in fourth grade.	Let n = the number of students who bought lunch.
$6 \times 17 =$ _____	Students in each fourth grade class. Students who brought lunch from home.
Subtract the number of students who brought lunch from home.	
$102 - 23 =$ _____	$6 \quad \times \quad \text{_____} \quad - \quad \text{_____} \quad = n$
	_____ $= n$

3. Use an equation to solve. Discuss the steps you used.

Susan buys 16 packages of hot dogs for a barbecue. Each package contains 12 hot dogs. Hot-dog buns are sold in packages of 8. How many packages of hot-dog buns does Susan need to buy so she has one bun for each hot dog?

_____

▶ **Share Solutions**

Use an equation to solve.

Show your work.

4. Admission to the theme park is $32 for each adult. A group of 5 adults and 1 child pays $182 to enter the theme park. How much is a child's ticket to the theme park?

_____

5. Kenny collects CDs and DVDs. He has a total of 208 CDs. He also has 8 shelves with 24 DVDs on each shelf. How many more CDs does Kenny have than DVDs?

_____

6. Carla plants 14 tomato plants. Her gardening book says that each plant should grow 12 tomatoes. She plans to divide the tomatoes equally among herself and 7 friends. How many tomatoes would each person get?

_____

7. Alex and his family go on a roadtrip. On the first day, they drive 228 miles. On the second day, they drive 279 miles. Their destination is 1,043 miles away. How many miles do they have left to drive to reach their destination?

_____

8. A public library has more than 50,000 books. There are 249 science books and 321 technology books. Mary sorts the science and technology books on shelves with 6 books on each shelf. How many shelves will Mary fill with science and technology books?

_____

▶ Discuss the Steps

1. Mr. Stills makes bags of school supplies for the 9 students in his class. He has 108 pencils and 72 erasers. He puts the same number of pencils and the same number of erasers into each bag. How many more pencils than erasers are in each bag of school supplies?

   Solve the problem by finishing Nicole's and David's methods. Discuss what is alike and what is different about the methods.

Nicole's Method

Write an equation for each step.

Divide to find the number of pencils that Mr. Stills puts in each bag of school supplies. $108 \div 9 =$ _____

Divide to find the number of erasers that Mr. Stills puts in each bag of school supplies. $72 \div 9 =$ _____

Subtract the number of erasers in each bag from the number of pencils in each bag. $12 - 8 =$ _____

There are _____ more pencils than erasers in each bag of school supplies.

David's Method

Write an equation for the whole problem.

Let $p =$ how many more pencils than erasers are in each bag of school supplies

The number of pencils in   The number of erasers in each
each bag of school supplies.   bag of school supplies.

_____ $\div$ 9 $-$ _____ $\div$ 9 $= p$

12 $-$ 8 $= p$

_____ $= p$

There are _____ more pencils than erasers in each bag of school supplies.

► Discuss the Steps (continued)

2. John is selling bags of popcorn for a school fundraiser. So far, John has sold 45 bags of popcorn for $5 each. His goal is to earn $300 for the school fundraiser. How many more bags of popcorn must John sell to reach his goal?

   Solve the problem by writing an equation for each step. Then solve the problem by writing one equation for the whole problem.

Write an equation for each step.

Multiply to find how much money John has earned so far selling popcorn.

_____ × $5 = $ _____

Subtract to find how much money John has left to earn to reach his goal.

$300 − $ _____ = $ _____

Divide to find the number of bags of popcorn John must sell to reach his goal.

$75 ÷ $5 = _____

John must sell _____ more bags of popcorn to reach his goal.

Write an equation for the whole problem.

Let b = the number of bags of popcorn John must sell to reach his goal.

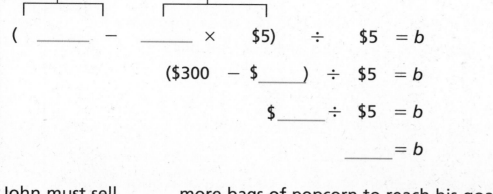

John's fundraiser goal amount.   Amount of money John has raised so far.

(_____ − _____ × $5) ÷ $5 = b

($300 − $ _____) ÷ $5 = b

$ _____ ÷ $5 = b

_____ = b

John must sell _____ more bags of popcorn to reach his goal.

Solve Multistep Problems

► **Multistep Word Problems**

Use an equation to solve.

Show your work.

3. Sara bought some bags of beads. Each bag had 9 beads and cost $2. Sara used the beads to make 18 necklaces, each with 25 beads. How much money did Sara pay for the beads for all of the necklaces that she made?

_____

4. There are 5 fourth-grade classes going on a field trip. Two of the classes have 16 students each and 3 of the classes have 17 students each. They are travelling in vans that hold 9 students each. How many vans must they have to transport all the students?

_____

5. A movie theater has 13 screens. On weekends, each screen shows a movie 7 times in one day. On weekdays, each screen shows a movie 5 times in one day. How many more showings are there on Saturdays than on Tuesdays?

_____

6. Justin goes to the store and buys 3 T-shirts for $14 each. He also buys 2 pairs of jeans for $23 each. He gives the cashier $100. How much change does Justin receive?

_____

7. Terrence has 24 model cars arranged in equal rows of 6 model cars. Natalie has 18 model cars arranged in equal rows of 3 model cars. How many rows of model cars in all do they have?

Name _____ Date _____

▶ What's the Error?

Dear Math Students,

My friend and I are planning a hike. We will hike from point *A* to point *B*, which is a distance of 28 miles. Then we will hike from Point *B* to Point *C*, which is a distance of 34 miles. We will walk 7 miles each day for 8 days. We are trying to figure out how many miles we need to walk on the ninth day to reach Point *C*.

I wrote and solved this equation.

$28 + 34 - 7 \times 8 = t$

$62 - 7 \times 8 = t$

$55 \times 8 = t$

$440 = t$

This answer doesn't make sense. Did I do something wrong? What do you think?

Your friend,
Puzzled Penguin

8. Write a response to Puzzled Penguin.

_____

_____

_____

_____

_____

_____

Solve Multistep Problems

▶ Discuss Multistep Word Problems

Use equations to solve.

Show your work.

1. Eli reads 6 pages in a book each night. Shelby reads 8 pages each night. How many pages altogether will Eli and Shelby read in one week?

   _____

2. Min Soo is ordering 5 pizzas for a party. Each pizza will be cut into 8 slices. Three pizzas will have multiple toppings, and the others will be plain cheese. How many slices of plain cheese pizza is Min Soo ordering for the party?

   _____

3. Jasmine and Mori each received the same number of party favor bags at a friend's party. Each bag contained 8 favors. If Jasmine and Mori received a total of 48 favors, how many party favor bags did they each receive?

   _____

4. In art class, Ernesto made some fruit bowls for his mother and brother. Nine apples can be placed in each bowl. Ernesto's brother placed 18 apples in the bowls he was given, and Ernesto's mother placed 36 apples in the bowls she was given. How many fruit bowls did Ernesto make?

   _____

5. On Tuesday, a bicycle shop employee replaced all of the tires on 6 bicycles. On Wednesday, all of the tires on 5 tricycles were replaced. What is the total number of tires that were replaced on those days?

   _____

▶ Solve Multistep Word Problems

Use equations to solve.   *Show your work.*

6. Mrs. Luong bought 9 trees for $40 each. She paid for her purchase with four $100 bills. How much change did she receive?

_____

7. Chan Hee is carrying a box that weighs 37 pounds. In the box are five containers of equal weight, and a book that weighs 2 pounds. What is the weight of each container?

_____

8. A pet shop is home to 6 cats, 10 birds, 3 dogs, and 18 tropical fish. Altogether, how many legs do those pets have?

_____

9. Dan has 7 fish in his aquarium. Marilyn has 4 times as many fish in her aquarium. How many fish do Dan and Marilyn have altogether?

_____

10. Write a problem that is solved using more than one step. Then show how to solve the problem.

_____

_____

_____

_____

_____

_____

Name _____

Date _____

CA CC Content Standards 4.OA.4, 4.OA.5
Mathematical Practices MP.3, MP.5, MP.6, MP.7, MP.8

▶ Find Factor Pairs

A factor pair for a number is two whole numbers whose product is that number. For example, 2 and 5 is a factor pair for 10.

1. Draw arrays to show all the factor pairs for 12 on the grid below. The array for 1 and 12 is shown.

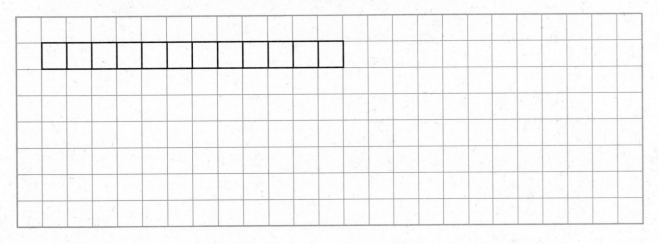

2. List all the factor pairs for 12. _____

Use the table to find all the factors pairs for each number.

3. 32

1	32
2	

4. 44

1	44

5. 100

1	100

List all the factor pairs for each number.

6. 29

7. 63

_____   _____

Name _Mia_   Date _____

▶ Identify Prime and Composite Numbers

A number greater than 1 that has 1 and itself as its only factor pair is a **prime number**. Some prime numbers are 2, 5, 11, and 23.

A number greater than 1 that has more than one factor pair is a **composite number**. Some composite numbers are 4, 12, 25, and 100.

The number 1 is neither prime nor composite.

8. Use counters to model the arrays for all factor pairs for 24. The array for 2 and 12 is shown below.

9. Is 24 a *prime number* or a *composite number*? Explain your answer.

_____

_____

Write whether each number is *prime* or *composite*.

10. 99   11. 72   12. 31

_____   _____   _____

13. 45   14. 19   15. 88

_____   _____   _____

16. 67   17. 100   18. 53

_____   _____   _____

19. Is 2 the only even prime number? Explain.

_____

_____

Factors and Prime Numbers

VOCABULARY
multiple

▶ Factors and Multiples

A **multiple** of a number is a product of that number and a counting number.

20. What are the first five multiples of 4? Explain your method.

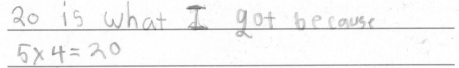

20 is what I got because
5×4=20

21. Write the first ten multiples of 8.

_____

22. Is 54 a multiple of 6? Explain how you know.

_____

_____

23. Is 6 a factor of 40? Explain how you know.

_____

24. What are the first five multiples of 9? Explain your method.

_____

_____

25. What are the factors of 63?

_____

26. Is 63 a multiple of each factor that you listed for Exercise 25? Explain how you know.

_____

_____

_____

▶ Practice With Factors and Multiples

Tell whether 7 is a factor of each number. Write *yes* or *no*.

27. 7

28. 84

29. 93

30. 49

_____   _____   _____   _____

Tell whether each number is a multiple of 9. Write *yes* or *no*.

31. 27

32. 30

33. 81

34. 99

_____   _____   _____   _____

Use a pattern to find the unknown multiples.

35. $3 \times 11 = 33$

$4 \times 11 = 44$

$5 \times 11 =$ _____

$6 \times 11 =$ _____

$7 \times 11 =$ _____

36. $5 \times 6 = 30$

$6 \times 6 =$ _____

$7 \times 6 =$ _____

$8 \times 6 =$ _____

$9 \times 6 =$ _____

Use the rule to complete the pattern.

37. Rule: skip count by 6

6, _____, _____, 24, _____, 36, _____, 48, _____, 60

38. Rule: skip count by 5

5, 10, _____, 20, 25, _____, 35, 40, _____, _____, 55, _____

39. Rule: skip count by 7

7, 14, 21, _____, _____, _____, _____, _____, _____, _____

40. Rule: skip count by 12

12, 24, _____, _____, _____, _____, _____, _____, _____

Name _____ **Date** _____

CA CC Content Standards **4.OA.5**
Mathematical Practices **MP.6, MP.7, MP.8**

> **VOCABULARY**
> pattern

▶ Numerical Patterns

A **pattern** is a sequence that can be described by a rule.

Use the rule to find the next three terms in the pattern.

1. 22, 24, 26, 28, 30, …
Rule: add 2

_____

2. 5, 10, 20, 40, …
Rule: multiply by 2

_____

3. 1, 3, 9, 27, …
Rule: multiply by 3

_____

4. 2, 9, 16, 23, 30, …
Rule: add 7

_____

Use the rule to find the first ten terms in the pattern.

5. First term: 9   Rule: add 5

_____

6. First term: 10   Rule: add 60

_____

▶ Real World Applications

Solve.

7. Amy lives in the twentieth house on Elm Street. The first house on Elm Street is numbered 3. The second is 6. The third is 9. The fourth is 12. If this pattern continues, what is Amy's house number likely to be?

_____

House	1st	2nd	3rd	4th	20th
Number	3	6	9	12	

8. Theo runs 5 miles every morning. He tracks his progress on a chart to log how many miles he has run in all. How many miles will Theo write on the 100th day?

_____

Day	1	2	3	4	5	100
Miles	5	10	15	20	25	

© Houghton Mifflin Harcourt Publishing Company

► **Extend Patterns**

9. What are the repeating terms of the pattern?

_____

10. What will be the tenth term in the pattern? _____

11. What will be the fifteenth term in the pattern? _____

► **Growing Patterns**

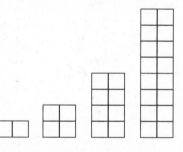

12. How does each figure in the pattern change from one term to the next?

_____

_____

13. Describe the number of squares in the next term in the pattern?

_____

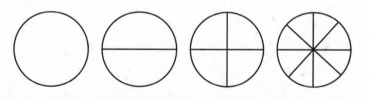

14. How does each figure in the pattern change from one term to the next?

_____

15. How many equal parts will be in the seventh term?

_____

Name _____ **Date** _____

CA CC Content Standards **4.OA.1, 4.OA.2, 4.OA.3, 4.OA.5, 4.NBT.4, 4.NBT.5, 4.NBT.6, 4.MD.2**
Mathematical Practices **MP.1, MP.2, MP.4, MP.8**

▶ Math and Pottery

Pottery are objects that are first shaped of wet clay and then hardened by baking. Four steps are needed to make a pottery product: preparing the clay mixture, shaping the clay, decorating and glazing the product, and baking the product. Pottery includes products such as works of art, dinnerware, vases, and other household items. Some of the places you can find pottery include art studios, crafts shows, pottery stores, and most households.

Write an equation to solve.

Show your work.

1. A small pottery store has 9 boxes full of pottery items. The boxes weigh 765 pounds in all. How much does each box weigh?

   _____

2. Julio and Myra had a pottery stand at the annual craft fair. They sold some of their pottery at the original price of $13 each and made $780. Later in the day, they decreased the price of each item by $4 and sold 20 more items. How much money did they make in all that day?

   _____

Write an equation to solve.

Show your work.

3. Last month, Mr. Smith bought 65 small cans of paint for his pottery shop. This month he bought 3 times as many small cans of paint. How many small cans of paint did he buy this month?

_____

4. The employees at a pottery warehouse are packing boxes of vases to be delivered by truck. They packed 824 small vases in boxes that each hold 8 vases. They also packed 296 large vases in boxes that each hold 4 vases. How many boxes did the workers pack in all?

_____

5. Last year, there were 3,875 different pottery items for sale at a large crafts show. This year, there were 1,260 fewer pottery items for sale at the crafts show. How many pottery items were for sale at the crafts show this year?

_____

Solve.

6. Isabella saw a pottery design that she liked at a crafts store. She wants to copy the design and paint it on a pot she is making. Part of the design is shown below.

a. What shape should Isabella paint next to continue the design's pattern?

_____

b. What will be the fourteenth term in Isabella's design?

_____

1. The number of ash trees on a tree farm is 5 times the number of pine trees. Choose one expression from each column to create an equation that compares the number of ash trees (*a*) and pine trees (*p*).

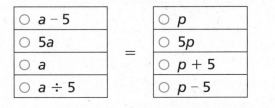

○ $a - 5$	○ p
○ $5a$	○ $5p$
○ a	○ $p + 5$
○ $a \div 5$	○ $p - 5$

$=$

2. Katie canned 182 quarts of tomatoes last week. She canned 259 quarts of tomatoes this week. How many quarts of tomatoes (*q*) did Katie can over these two weeks? Write an equation. Then solve.

Equation: _____

$q =$ _____ quarts

3. Eliot sends 217 text messages each week. Write equations to find how many text messages he sends in 4 weeks and in 7 weeks.

Equations: _____

_____

Use the equations to complete the table.

Weeks	Total Text Messages
1	217
4	
7	

4. Solve for *n*.

$(16 + 12) \div (11 - 7) = n$ $n =$ ☐

5. There are 1,342 players in the baseball league. That is 2 times the number of players in the football league. How many players are in the football league? Write an equation. Then solve.

6. A school ordered 688 T-shirts in 3 sizes: small, medium, and large. There are 296 small and 268 medium T-shirts. How many large T-shirts were ordered? Select numbers from the list to complete the equation. Then solve.

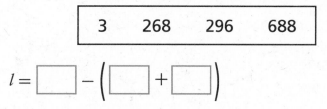

| 3 | 268 | 296 | 688 |

$$l = \boxed{} - \left(\boxed{} + \boxed{} \right)$$

$l =$ _____ large T-shirts

7. Select the factor pair for 45. Mark all that apply.

Ⓐ 4, 11   Ⓒ 6, 7   Ⓔ 1, 45

Ⓑ 3, 15   Ⓓ 4, 12   Ⓕ 5, 9

8. Is a multiple of the prime number 3 also a prime number? Circle your answer.

                                    Yes   No

Explain your reasoning.

9. For numbers 9a–9e, choose Yes or No to tell whether the number is prime.

9a. 49 ○ Yes ○ No

9b. 53 ○ Yes ○ No

9c. 63 ○ Yes ○ No

9d. 37 ○ Yes ○ No

9e. 51 ○ Yes ○ No

10. Classify each number from the list as being a multiple of 2, 3, or 5. Write each number in the correct box. A number can be written in more than one box.

| 18 | 30 | 20 | 24 | 55 | 39 |

Multiple of 2	Multiple of 3	Multiple of 5

11. Use the rule to find the next 3 terms in the pattern.

Rule: multiply by 2

4, 8, 16, 32, ☐ , ☐ , ☐ , ...

12. Draw the next term of the pattern.

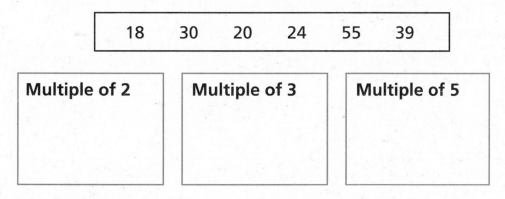

13. A team of workers is building a 942-foot trail. They plan to complete 6 feet per hour. How many hours will it take to build the trail?

Choose the equation that can be used to solve this problem. Mark all that apply.

(A) $942 \times 6 = h$ (D) $6 \times h = 942$

(B) $942 \div 6 = h$ (E) $6 = 942 \times h$

(C) $942 \div h = 6$ (F) $942 = 6 \div h$

14. Roger first ships a large number of packages. Then he ships 3,820 more packages. Roger ships 22,540 packages in all. How many packages did he ship first? Identify the type of comparison as addition or multiplication. Then write and solve an equation to solve the problem.

Type of comparison: _____

Equation: _____

Answer: _____ packages

15. For numbers 15a–15d, select True or False for the calculation.

15a. $72 \div (6 + 2) = 9$ ○ True   ○ False

15b. $(2 + 7) + (6 - 2) = 36$ ○ True   ○ False

15c. $(12 + 8) \div 4 = 10 \div (5 - 3)$ ○ True   ○ False

15d. $(35 - 8) \div (2 + 1) = 32$ ○ True   ○ False

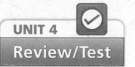
16. Charlotte made this pictograph to show the number of dogs attending a dog training class this week.

Dogs in Training Class

Monday	🐾 🐾 🐾
Wednesday	🐾 🐾
Friday	🐾 🐾 🐾 🐾 🐾 🐾 🐾
Saturday	🐾 🐾 🐾 🐾 🐾 🐾 🐾 🐾

🐾 = 3 dogs

Part A

How many fewer dogs were in training class on Monday than on Friday? Write and solve an equation.

Equation: _____

Answer: _____ fewer dogs

Part B

Choose the number that makes the sentence true.

Charlotte forgot to include Thursday on her graph. There were two times as many dogs at Thursday's class than at Monday's class.

There were
| 2 |
| 6 |
| 15 |
| 18 |
dogs in the training class on Thursday.

Part C

Explain how you determined the number of dogs at Thursday's class.

17. The Ruiz family bought 2 adult tickets and 4 child tickets to the fair. The adult tickets cost $8 each. The child tickets cost $3 each.

Part A

Complete the equation Zach and Alannah wrote to find the total cost of the tickets bought by the Ruiz family.

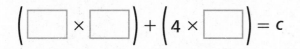

$$\left(\boxed{} \times \boxed{} \right) + \left(4 \times \boxed{} \right) = c$$

Part B

Zach's answer is $72, and Alannah's answer is $28. Who has the wrong answer? Explain what error he or she made.

18. A store has 4 bins of planet posters with 23 posters in each bin. It has 3 bins of planet calendars with 26 calendars in each bin. Yesterday, 72 calendars were sold. How many planet posters and calendars are left in all? Explain how you found your answer, and how you know if your answer is reasonable.

Reference Tables

Table of Measures

Metric	Customary

Length/Area

Metric	Customary
1,000 millimeters (mm) = 1 meter (m)	1 foot (ft) = 12 inches (in.)
100 centimeters (cm) = 1 meter	1 yard (yd) = 36 inches
10 decimeters (dm) = 1 meter	1 yard = 3 feet
1 dekameter (dam) = 10 meters	1 mile (mi) = 5,280 feet
1 hectometer (hm) = 100 meters	1 mile = 1,760 yards
1 kilometer (km) = 1,000 meters	

Liquid Volume

Metric	Customary
1,000 milliliters (mL) = 1 liter (L)	6 teaspoons (tsp) = 1 fluid ounce (fl oz)
100 centiliters (cL) = 1 liter	2 tablespoons (tbsp) = 1 fluid ounce
10 deciliters (dL) = 1 liter	1 cup (c) = 8 fluid ounces
1 dekaliter (daL) = 10 liters	1 pint (pt) = 2 cups
1 hectoliter (hL) = 100 liters	1 quart (qt) = 2 pints
1 kiloliter (kL) = 1,000 liters	1 gallon (gal) = 4 quarts

Mass / Weight

Mass	Weight
1,000 milligrams (mg) = 1 gram (g)	1 pound (lb) = 16 ounces
100 centigrams (cg) = 1 gram	1 ton (T) = 2,000 pounds
10 decigrams (dg) = 1 gram	
1 dekagram (dag) = 10 grams	
1 hectogram (hg) = 100 grams	
1 kilogram (kg) = 1,000 grams	
1 metric ton = 1,000 kilograms	

Reference Tables (continued)

Table of Units of Time

Time

1 minute (min) = 60 seconds (sec)	1 year = 365 days
1 hour (hr) = 60 minutes	1 leap year = 366 days
1 day = 24 hours	1 decade = 10 years
1 week (wk) = 7 days	1 century = 100 years
1 month, about 30 days	1 millennium = 1,000 years
1 year (yr) = 12 months (mo) or about 52 weeks	

Table of Formulas

Perimeter

Polygon

P = sum of the lengths of the sides

Rectangle

$P = 2(l + w)$ or $P = 2l + 2w$

Square

$P = 4s$

Area

Rectangle

$A = lw$ or $A = bh$

Square

$A = s \cdot s$

Properties of Operations

Associative Property of Addition

$(a + b) + c = a + (b + c)$ $\qquad$ $(2 + 5) + 3 = 2 + (5 + 3)$

Commutative Property of Addition

$a + b = b + a$ $\qquad$ $4 + 6 = 6 + 4$

Addition Identity Property of 0

$a + 0 = 0 + a = a$ $\qquad$ $3 + 0 = 0 + 3 = 3$

Associative Property of Multiplication

$(a \cdot b) \cdot c = a \cdot (b \cdot c)$ $\qquad$ $(3 \cdot 5) \cdot 7 = 3 \cdot (5 \cdot 7)$

Commutative Property of Multiplication

$a \cdot b = b \cdot a$ $\qquad$ $6 \cdot 3 = 3 \cdot 6$

Multiplicative Identity Property of 1

$a \cdot 1 = 1 \cdot a = a$ $\qquad$ $8 \cdot 1 = 1 \cdot 8 = 8$

Distributive Property of Multiplication over Addition

$a \cdot (b + c) = (a \cdot b) + (a \cdot c)$ $\qquad$ $2 \cdot (4 + 3) = (2 \cdot 4) + (2 \cdot 3)$

Problem Types

Addition and Subtraction Problem Types

	Result Unknown	Change Unknown	Start Unknown
Add to	A glass contained $\frac{3}{4}$ cup of orange juice. Then $\frac{1}{4}$ cup of pineapple juice was added. How much juice is in the glass now? *Situation and solution equation:* [1] $\frac{3}{4} + \frac{1}{4} = c$	A glass contained $\frac{3}{4}$ cup of orange juice. Then some pineapple juice was added. Now the glass contains 1 cup of juice. How much pineapple juice was added? *Situation equation:* $\frac{3}{4} + c = 1$ *Solution equation:* $c = 1 - \frac{3}{4}$	A glass contained some orange juice. Then $\frac{1}{4}$ cup of pineapple juice was added. Now the glass contains 1 cup of juice. How much orange juice was in the glass to start? *Situation equation* $c + \frac{1}{4} = 1$ *Solution equation:* $c = 1 - \frac{1}{4}$
Take from	Micah had a ribbon $\frac{5}{6}$ yard long. He cut off a piece $\frac{1}{6}$ yard long. What is the length of the ribbon that is left? *Situation and solution equation:* $\frac{5}{6} - \frac{1}{6} = r$	Micah had a ribbon $\frac{5}{6}$ yard long. He cut off a piece. Now the ribbon is $\frac{4}{6}$ yard long. What is the length of the ribbon he cut off? *Situation equation:* $\frac{5}{6} - r = \frac{4}{6}$ *Solution equation:* $r = \frac{5}{6} - \frac{4}{6}$	Micah had a ribbon. He cut off a piece $\frac{1}{6}$ yard long. Now the ribbon is $\frac{4}{6}$ yard long. What was the length of the ribbon he started with? *Situation equation:* $r - \frac{1}{6} = \frac{4}{6}$ *Solution equation:* $r = \frac{4}{6} + \frac{1}{6}$

[1] A situation equation represents the structure (action) in the problem situation. A solution equation shows the operation used to find the answer.

	Total Unknown	Addend Unknown	Both Addends Unknown
Put Together/ Take Apart	A baker combines $1\frac{2}{3}$ cups of white flour and $\frac{2}{3}$ cup of wheat flour. How much flour is this altogether? *Math drawing:*[1] f $1\frac{2}{3}$ $\frac{2}{3}$ *Situation and solution equation:* $1\frac{2}{3} + \frac{2}{3} = f$	Of the $2\frac{1}{3}$ cups of flour a baker uses, $1\frac{2}{3}$ cups are white flour. The rest is wheat flour. How much wheat flour does the baker use? *Math drawing:* $2\frac{1}{3}$ $1\frac{2}{3}$ f *Situation equation:* $2\frac{1}{3} = 1\frac{2}{3} + f$ *Solution equation:* $f = 2\frac{1}{3} - 1\frac{2}{3}$	A baker uses $2\frac{1}{3}$ cups of flour. Some is white flour and some is wheat flour. How much of each type of flour does the baker use? *Math drawing:* $2\frac{1}{3}$ f w *Situation equation:* $2\frac{1}{3} = f + w$

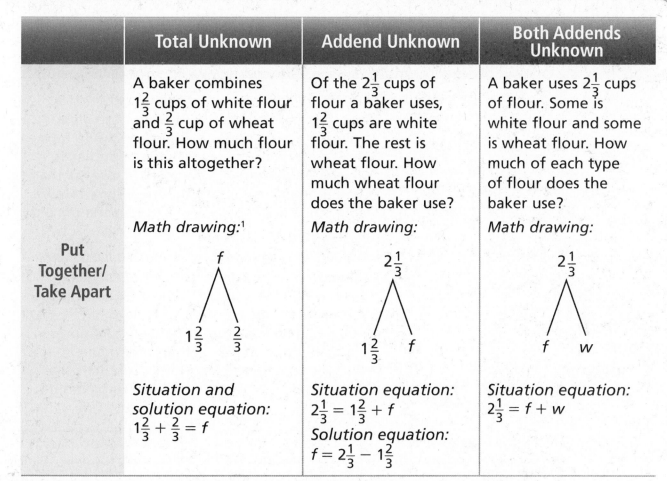

[1]These math drawings are called math mountains in Grades 1–3 and break apart drawings in Grades 4 and 5.

Problem Types continued

Addition and Subtraction Problem Types (continued)

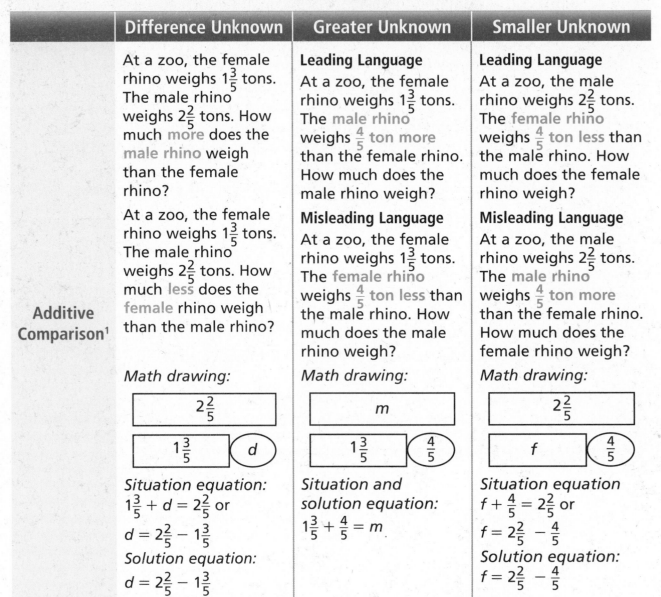

	Difference Unknown	Greater Unknown	Smaller Unknown
Additive Comparison[1]	At a zoo, the female rhino weighs $1\frac{3}{5}$ tons. The male rhino weighs $2\frac{2}{5}$ tons. How much more does the male rhino weigh than the female rhino?	**Leading Language** At a zoo, the female rhino weighs $1\frac{3}{5}$ tons. The male rhino weighs $\frac{4}{5}$ ton more than the female rhino. How much does the male rhino weigh?	**Leading Language** At a zoo, the male rhino weighs $2\frac{2}{5}$ tons. The female rhino weighs $\frac{4}{5}$ ton less than the male rhino. How much does the female rhino weigh?
	At a zoo, the female rhino weighs $1\frac{3}{5}$ tons. The male rhino weighs $2\frac{2}{5}$ tons. How much less does the female rhino weigh than the male rhino?	**Misleading Language** At a zoo, the female rhino weighs $1\frac{3}{5}$ tons. The female rhino weighs $\frac{4}{5}$ ton less than the male rhino. How much does the male rhino weigh?	**Misleading Language** At a zoo, the male rhino weighs $2\frac{2}{5}$ tons. The male rhino weighs $\frac{4}{5}$ ton more than the female rhino. How much does the female rhino weigh?
	Math drawing:	Math drawing:	Math drawing:
	Situation equation: $1\frac{3}{5} + d = 2\frac{2}{5}$ or $d = 2\frac{2}{5} - 1\frac{3}{5}$ Solution equation: $d = 2\frac{2}{5} - 1\frac{3}{5}$	Situation and solution equation: $1\frac{3}{5} + \frac{4}{5} = m$	Situation equation $f + \frac{4}{5} = 2\frac{2}{5}$ or $f = 2\frac{2}{5} - \frac{4}{5}$ Solution equation: $f = 2\frac{2}{5} - \frac{4}{5}$

[1]A comparison sentence can always be said in two ways. One way uses *more*, and the other uses *fewer* or *less*. Misleading language suggests the wrong operation. For example, it says *the female rhino weighs $\frac{4}{5}$ ton less than the male*, but you have to add $\frac{4}{5}$ ton to the female's weight to get the male's weight.

Multiplication and Division Problem Types

	Unknown Product	Group Size Unknown	Number of Groups Unknown
Equal Groups	A teacher bought 10 boxes of pencils. There are 20 pencils in each box. How many pencils did the teacher buy? *Situation and solution equation:* $p = 10 \cdot 20$	A teacher bought 10 boxes of pencils. She bought 200 pencils in all. How many pencils are in each box? *Situation equation:* $10 \cdot n = 200$ *Solution equation:* $n = 200 \div 10$	A teacher bought boxes of 20 pencils. She bought 200 pencils in all. How many boxes of pencils did she buy? *Situation equation* $b \cdot 20 = 200$ *Solution equation:* $b = 200 \div 20$

	Unknown Product	Unknown Factor	Unknown Factor
Arrays[1]	An auditorium has 60 rows with 30 seats in each row. How many seats are in the auditorium? *Math drawing:* 30 60 | s | *Situation and solution equation:* $s = 60 \cdot 30$	An auditorium has 60 rows with the same number of seats in each row. There are 1,800 seats in all. How many seats are in each row? *Math drawing:* n 60 | 1,800 | *Situation equation:* $60 \cdot n = 1{,}800$ *Solution equation:* $n = 1{,}800 \div 60$	The 1,800 seats in an auditorium are arranged in rows of 30. How many rows of seats are there? *Math drawing:* 30 r | 1,800 | *Situation equation* $r \cdot 30 = 1{,}800$ *Solution equation:* $r = 1{,}800 \div 30$

[1]We use rectangle models for both array and area problems in Grades 4 and 5 because the numbers in the problems are too large to represent with arrays.

Multiplication and Division Problem Types (continued)

	Unknown Product	Unknown Factor	Unknown Factor
Area	Sophie's backyard is 80 feet long and 40 feet wide. What is the area of Sophie's backyard? *Math drawing:* 80 40 A *Situation and solution equation:* $A = 80 \cdot 40$	Sophie's backyard has an area of 3,200 square feet. The length of the yard is 80 feet. What is the width of the yard? *Math drawing:* 80 w 3,200 *Situation equation:* $80 \cdot w = 3,200$ *Solution equation:* $w = 3,200 \div 80$	Sophie's backyard has an area of 3,200 square feet. The width of the yard is 40 feet. What is the length of the yard? *Math drawing:* l 40 3,200 *Situation equation* $l \cdot 40 = 3,200$ *Solution equation:* $l = 3,200 \div 40$
Multiplicative Comparison	**Whole Number Multiplier** Sam has 4 times as many marbles as Brady has. Brady has 70 marbles. How many marbles does Sam have? *Math drawing:* s	70	70	70	70 | b	70 | *Situation and solution equation:* $s = 4 \cdot 70$	**Whole Number Multiplier** Sam has 4 times as many marbles as Brady has. Sam has 280 marbles. How many marbles does Brady have? *Math drawing:* 280 s				| b	| *Situation equation:* $4 \cdot b = 280$ *Solution equation:* $b = 280 \div 4$	**Whole Number Multiplier** Sam has 280 marbles. Brady has 70 marbles. The number of marbles Sam has is how many times the number Brady has? *Math drawing:* 280 s	70	70	70	70 | b	70 | *Situation equation* $m \cdot 70 = 280$ *Solution equation:* $m = 280 \div 70$

Vocabulary Activities

▶ Word Review PAIRS

Work with a partner. Choose a word from a current unit or a review word from a previous unit. Use the word to complete one of the activities listed on the right. Then ask your partner if they have any edits to your work or questions about what you described. Repeat, having your partner choose a word.

Activities

▶ Give the meaning in words or gestures.

▶ Use the word in the sentence.

▶ Give another word that is related to the word in some way and explain the relationship.

▶ Crossword Puzzle PAIRS OR INDIVIDUALS

Create a crossword puzzle similar to the example below. Use vocabulary words from the unit. You can add other related words, too. Challenge your partner to solve the puzzle.

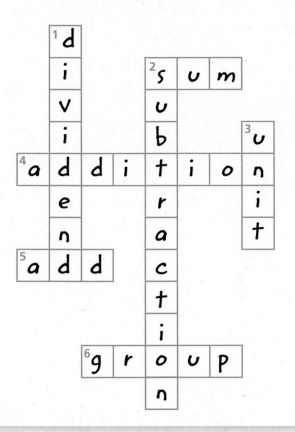

Across

2. The answer to an addition problem

4. _____ and subtraction are inverse operations.

5. To put amounts together

6. When you trade 10 ones for 1 ten, you _____.

Down

1. The number to be divided in a division problem

2. The operation that you can use to find out how much more one number is than another.

3. A fraction with a numerator of 1 is a _____ fraction.

Vocabulary Activities (continued)

▶ Word Wall   `PAIRS` OR `SMALL GROUPS`

With your teacher's permission, start a word wall in your classroom. As you work through each lesson, put the math vocabulary words on index cards and place them on the word wall. You can work with a partner or a small group choosing a word and giving the definition.

▶ Word Web   `INDIVIDUALS`

Make a word web for a word or words you do not understand in a unit. Fill in the web with words or phrases that are related to the vocabulary word.

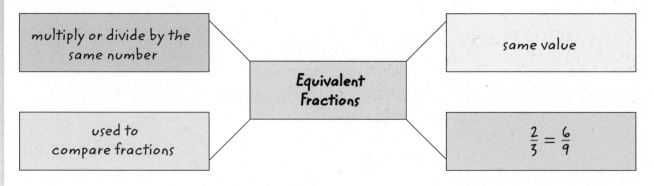

▶ Alphabet Challenge   `PAIRS` OR `INDIVIDUALS`

Take an alphabet challenge. Choose 3 letters from the alphabet. Think of three vocabulary words for each letter. Then write the definition or draw an example for each word.

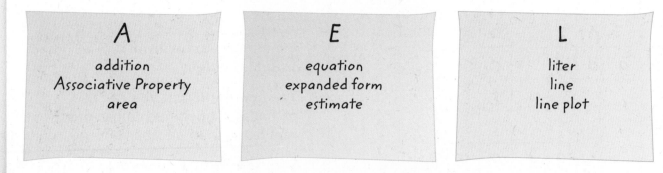

▶ Concentration PAIRS

Write the vocabulary words and related words from a unit on index cards. Write the definitions on a different set of index cards. Mix up both sets of cards. Then place the cards facedown on a table in an array, for example, 3 by 3 or 3 by 4. Take turns turning over two cards. If one card is a word and one card is a definition that matches the word, take the pair. Continue until each word has been matched with its definition.

area		
		The number of square units that cover a figure.

▶ Math Journal INDIVIDUALS

As you learn new words, write them in your Math Journal. Write the definition of the word and include a sketch or an example. As you learn new information about the word, add notes to your definition.

Angle: A figure formed by two rays with the same endpoint.

Degree: A unit for measuring angles.

Vocabulary Activities (continued)

▶ **What's the Word?** PAIRS

Work together to make a poster or bulletin board display of
the words in a unit. Write definitions on a set of index cards.
Mix up the cards. Work with a partner, choosing a definition
from the index cards. Have your partner point to the word
on the poster and name the matching math vocabulary word.
Switch roles and try the activity again.

array

place value

addend

inverse operations

expanded form

word form

standard form

digit

one of two or more numbers
added together to find a sum

Glossary

A

acute angle An angle smaller than a right angle.

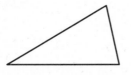

acute triangle A triangle with three acute angles.

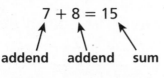

addend One of two or more numbers added together to find a sum.

Example: 7 + 8 = 15

addend   addend   sum

adjacent (sides) Two sides that meet at a point.

Example: Sides a and b are adjacent.

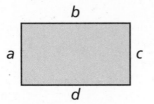

Algebraic Notation Method A strategy based on the Distributive Property in which a factor is decomposed to create simpler algebraic expressions, and the Distributive Property is applied.

Example: $9 \cdot 28 = 9 \cdot (20 + 8)$
$= (9 \cdot 20) + (9 \cdot 8)$
$= 180 + 72$
$= 252$

analog clock A clock with a face and hands.

angle A figure formed by two rays with the same endpoint.

area The number of square units that cover a figure.

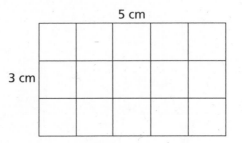

array An arrangement of objects, symbols, or numbers in rows and columns.

Associative Property of Addition Grouping the addends in different ways does not change the sum.

Example: $3 + (5 + 7) = 15$
$(3 + 5) + 7 = 15$

Glossary (continued)

Associative Property of Multiplication
Grouping the factors in different ways does not change the product.

Example: $3 \times (5 \times 7) = 105$
$(3 \times 5) \times 7 = 105$

B

bar graph A graph that uses bars to show data. The bars may be vertical or horizontal.

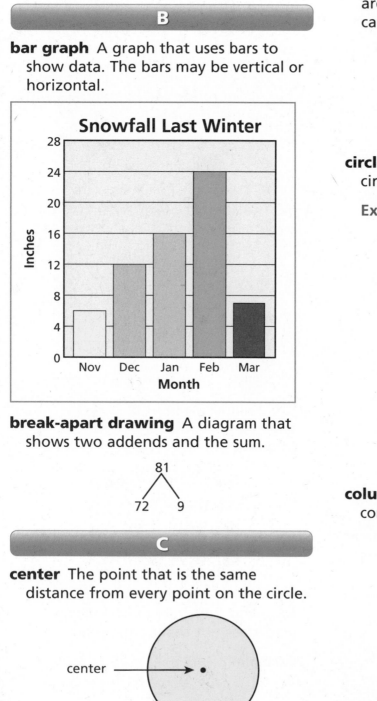

Snowfall Last Winter

break-apart drawing A diagram that shows two addends and the sum.

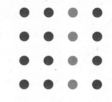

C

center The point that is the same distance from every point on the circle.

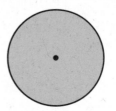

center

centimeter A unit of measure in the metric system that equals one hundredth of a meter. $100 \text{ cm} = 1 \text{ m}$

circle A plane figure that forms a closed path so that all the points on the path are the same distance from a point called the center.

circle graph A graph that uses parts of a circle to show data.

Example:

Favorite Fiction Books

Humor

Fantasy

Adventure

Mystery

column A part of a table or array that contains items arranged vertically.

● ● ● ●
● ● ● ●
● ● ● ●
● ● ● ●

common denominator A common multiple of two or more denominators.

Example: A common denominator of $\frac{1}{2}$ and $\frac{1}{3}$ is 6 because 6 is a multiple of 2 and 3.

Commutative Property of Addition Changing the order of addends does not change the sum.

Example: 3 + 8 = 11
8 + 3 = 11

Commutative Property of Multiplication Changing the order of factors does not change the product.

Example: 3 × 8 = 24
8 × 3 = 24

compare Describe quantities as greater than, less than, or equal to each other.

comparison bars Bars that represent the larger amount and smaller amount in a comparison situation.

For addition and subtraction:

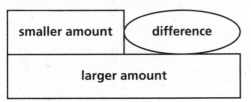

For multiplication and division:

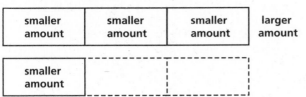

comparison situation A situation in which two amounts are compared by addition or by multiplication. An *addition comparison situation* compares by asking or telling how much more (how much less) one amount is than another. A *multiplication comparison situation* compares by asking or telling how many times as many one amount is as another. The multiplication comparison may also be made using fraction language. For example, you can say, "Sally has one fourth as much as Tom has," instead of saying "Tom has 4 times as much as Sally has."

composite number A number greater than 1 that has more than one factor pair. Examples of composite numbers are 10 and 18. The factor pairs of 10 are 1 and 10, 2 and 5. The factor pairs of 18 are 1 and 18, 2 and 9, 3 and 6.

cup A unit of liquid volume in the customary system that equals 8 fluid ounces.

D
---

data A collection of information.

decimal number A representation of a number using the numerals 0 to 9, in which each digit has a value 10 times the digit to its right. A dot or **decimal point** separates the whole-number part of the number on the left from the fractional part on the right.

Examples: 1.23 and 0.3

Glossary (continued)

decimal point A symbol used to separate dollars and cents in money amounts or to separate ones and tenths in decimal numbers.

Examples:

$8.59   1.2

decimal point

decimeter A unit of measure in the metric system that equals one tenth of a meter. 10 dm = 1 m

degree (°) A unit for measuring angles.

denominator The number below the bar in a fraction. It shows the total number of equal parts in the fraction.

Example:

$\frac{3}{4}$ ← denominator

diagonal A line segment that connects vertices of a polygon, but is not a side of the polygon.

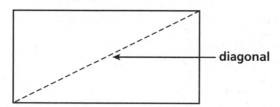

diagonal

difference The result of a subtraction.

Example: 54 − 37 = 17 ← difference

digit Any of the symbols 0, 1, 2, 3, 4, 5, 6, 7, 8, or 9.

digital clock A clock that shows us the hour and minutes with numbers.

Digit-by-Digit A method used to solve a division problem.

Put in only one digit at a time.

```
      5                54               546
7 ) 3,822        7 ) 3,822        7 ) 3,822
  − 3 5             − 3 5             − 3 5
    32               32                32
                   − 28              − 28
                     42                42
                                     − 42
```

Distributive Property You can multiply a sum by a number, or multiply each addend by the number and add the products; the result is the same.

Example:
$$3 \times (2 + 4) = (3 \times 2) + (3 \times 4)$$
$$3 \times 6 \quad = \quad 6 \quad + \quad 12$$
$$18 \quad = \quad 18$$

dividend The number that is divided in division.

Example: $9\overline{)63}$ 63 is the dividend.

divisible A number is divisible by another number if the quotient is a whole number with a remainder of 0.

divisor The number you divide by in division.

Example: $9\overline{)63}$ 9 is the divisor.

dot array An arrangement of dots in rows and columns.

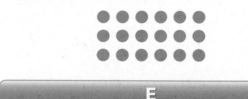

E

elapsed time The time that passes between the beginning and the end of an activity.

endpoint The point at either end of a line segment or the beginning point of a ray.

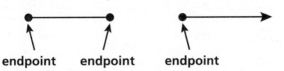

endpoint   endpoint   endpoint

equation A statement that two expressions are equal. It has an equal sign.

Examples: $32 + 35 = 67$
$67 = 32 + 34 + 1$
$(7 \times 8) + 1 = 57$

equilateral Having all sides of equal length.

Example: An equilateral triangle

equivalent fractions Two or more fractions that represent the same number.

Example: $\frac{2}{4}$ and $\frac{4}{8}$ are equivalent because they both represent one half.

estimate A number close to an exact amount or to find about how many or how much.

evaluate Substitute a value for a letter (or symbol) and then simplify the expression.

expanded form A way of writing a number that shows the value of each of its digits.

Example: Expanded form of 835:
$800 + 30 + 5$
8 hundreds + 3 tens + 5 ones

Expanded Notation A method used to solve multiplication and division problems.

Examples:

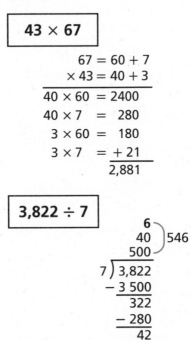

43×67

$$
\begin{array}{r}
67 = 60 + 7 \\
\times\,43 = 40 + 3 \\
\hline
40 \times 60 = 2400 \\
40 \times 7 \quad = \quad 280 \\
3 \times 60 \quad = \quad 180 \\
3 \times 7 \quad = +\;21 \\
\hline
2{,}881
\end{array}
$$

$3{,}822 \div 7$

$$
\begin{array}{r}
6 \\
40\;\big)\,546 \\
500 \\
7\,\big)\,3{,}822 \\
-\,3\,500 \\
\hline
322 \\
-\,280 \\
\hline
42 \\
-\,42 \\
\hline
0
\end{array}
$$

expression One or more numbers, variables, or numbers and variables with one or more operations.

Examples: 4
$6x$
$6x - 5$
$7 + 4$

F

factor One of two or more numbers multiplied to find a product.

Example:

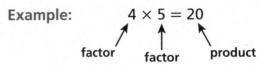

$4 \times 5 = 20$

factor   factor   product

Glossary (continued)

factor pair A factor pair for a number is a pair of whole numbers whose product is that number.

Example: 5 × 7 = 35

factor pair   product

fluid ounce A unit of liquid volume in the customary system.
8 fluid ounces = 1 cup

foot A U.S. customary unit of length equal to 12 inches.

formula An equation with letters or symbols that describes a rule.

The formula for the area of a rectangle is:

$A = l \times w$

where A is the area, l is the length, and w is the width.

fraction A number that is the sum of unit fractions, each an equal part of a set or part of a whole.

Examples: $\frac{3}{4} = \frac{1}{4} + \frac{1}{4} + \frac{1}{4}$

$\frac{5}{4} = \frac{1}{4} + \frac{1}{4} + \frac{1}{4} + \frac{1}{4} + \frac{1}{4}$

G

gallon A unit of liquid volume in the customary system that equals 4 quarts.

gram The basic unit of mass in the metric system.

greater than (>) A symbol used to compare two numbers. The greater number is given first below.

Example: 33 > 17
33 is greater than 17.

group To combine numbers to form new tens, hundreds, thousands, and so on.

H

hundredth A unit fraction representing one of one hundred parts, written as 0.01 or $\frac{1}{100}$.

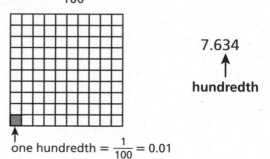

7.634

hundredth

one hundredth = $\frac{1}{100}$ = 0.01

I

Identity Property of Multiplication The product of 1 and any number equals that number.

Example: 10 × 1 = 10

inch A U.S. customary unit of length.

Example: |——————|
1 inch

inequality A statement that two expressions are not equal.

Examples: 2 < 5
4 + 5 > 12 − 8

inverse operations Opposite or reverse operations that undo each other. Addition and subtraction are inverse operations. Multiplication and division are inverse operations.

Examples: 4 + 6 = 10 so, 10 − 6 = 4
and 10 − 4 = 6.
3 × 9 = 27 so, 27 ÷ 9 = 3
and 27 ÷ 3 = 9.

isosceles triangle A triangle with at least two sides of equal length.

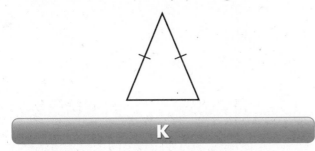

K
---

kilogram A unit of mass in the metric system that equals one thousand grams. 1 kg = 1,000 g

kiloliter A unit of liquid volume in the metric system that equals one thousand liters. 1 kL = 1,000 L

kilometer A unit of length in the metric system that equals 1,000 meters. 1 km = 1,000 m

---
L
---

least common denominator The least common multiple of two or more denominators.

Example: The least common denominator of $\frac{1}{2}$ and $\frac{1}{3}$ is 6 because 6 is the smallest multiple of 2 and 3.

length The measure of a line segment or one side of a figure.

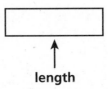

length

less than (<) A symbol used to compare two numbers. The smaller number is given first below.

Example: 54 < 78
54 is less than 78.

line A straight path that goes on forever in opposite directions.

Example: line *AB*

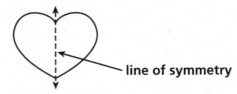

line of symmetry A line on which a figure can be folded so that the two halves match exactly.

line of symmetry

line plot A diagram that shows the frequency of data on a number line. Also called a dot plot.

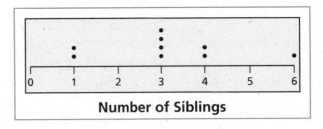

Number of Siblings

line segment Part of a line that has two endpoints.

line symmetry A figure has line symmetry if it can be folded along a line to create two halves that match exactly.

liquid volume A measure of the space a liquid occupies.

liter The basic unit of liquid volume in the metric system. 1 liter = 1,000 milliliters

Glossary (continued)

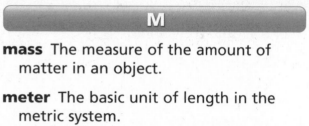

M

mass The measure of the amount of matter in an object.

meter The basic unit of length in the metric system.

metric system A base ten system of measurement.

mile A U.S. customary unit of length equal to 5,280 feet.

milligram A unit of mass in the metric system. 1,000 mg = 1g

milliliter A unit of liquid volume in the metric system. 1,000 mL = 1 L

millimeter A unit of length in the metric system. 1,000 mm = 1 m

mixed number A number that can be represented by a whole number and a fraction.

Example: $4\frac{1}{2} = 4 + \frac{1}{2}$

multiple A number that is the product of a given number and any whole number.

Examples:

$4 \times 1 = 4$, so 4 is a multiple of 4.
$4 \times 2 = 8$, so 8 is a multiple of 4.

N

number line A line that extends, without end, in each direction and shows numbers as a series of points. The location of each number is shown by its distance from 0.

numerator The number above the bar in a fraction. It shows the number of equal parts.

Example:

O

obtuse angle An angle greater than a right angle and less than a straight angle.

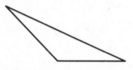

obtuse triangle A triangle with one obtuse angle.

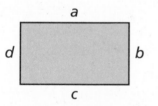

opposite sides Sides that are across from each other; they do not meet at a point.

Example: Sides *a* and *c* are opposite.

Order of Operations A set of rules that state the order in which operations should be done.

STEPS: -Compute inside parentheses first.

-Multiply and divide from left to right.

-Add and subtract from left to right.

ounce A unit of weight.
16 ounces = 1 pound
A unit of liquid volume (also called a fluid ounce).
8 ounces = 1 cup

P

parallel Lines in the same plane that never intersect are parallel. Line segments and rays that are part of parallel lines are also parallel.

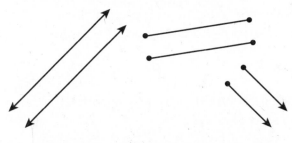

parallelogram A quadrilateral with both pairs of opposite sides parallel.

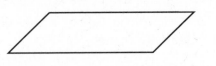

partial product The product of the ones, or tens, or hundreds, and so on in multidigit multiplication.

Example:

```
    24
  ×  9
  ────
    36   ←  partial product (9 × 4)
   180   ←  partial product (9 × 20)
  ────
   216
```

perimeter The distance around a figure.

perpendicular Lines, line segments, or rays are perpendicular if they form right angles.

Example: These two lines are perpendicular.

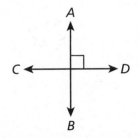

pictograph A graph that uses pictures or symbols to represent data.

Books Checked Out of Library	
Student	
Najee	📖 📖
Tariq	📖 📖 📖 📖 📖 📖
Celine	📖 📖 📖 📖 📖 📖 📖 📖
Jamarcus	📖 📖 📖
Brooke	📖 📖 📖 📖
	📖 = 5 books

pint A customary unit of liquid volume that equals 16 fluid ounces.

place value The value assigned to the place that a digit occupies in a number.

Example: 235

The 2 is in the hundreds place, so its value is 200.

Glossary (continued)

place value drawing A drawing that represents a number. Thousands are represented by vertical rectangles, hundreds are represented by squares, tens are represented by vertical lines, and ones by small circles.

Example:

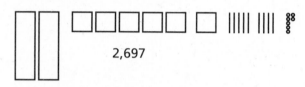

2,697

Place Value Sections A method using rectangle drawings to solve multiplication or division problems.

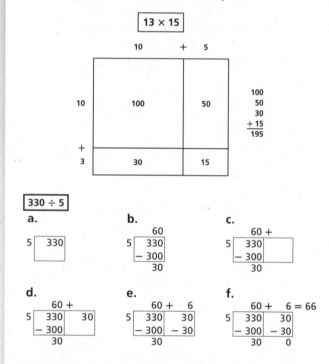

point A location in a plane. It is usually shown by a dot.

polygon A closed plane figure with sides made of straight line segments.

pound A unit of weight in the U.S. customary system.

prefix A letter or group of letters placed before a word to make a new word.

prime number A number greater than 1 that has 1 and itself as the only factor pair. Examples of prime numbers are 2, 7, and 13. The only factor pair of 7 is 1 and 7.

product The answer to a multiplication problem.

Example: $9 \times 7 = 63$

↑
product

protractor A semicircular tool for measuring and constructing angles.

Q

quadrilateral A polygon with four sides.

quart A customary unit of liquid volume that equals 32 ounces or 4 cups.

quotient The answer to a division problem.

Example: $9\overline{)63}$ 7 is the quotient.

R

ray Part of a line that has one endpoint and extends without end in one direction.

rectangle A parallelogram with four right angles.

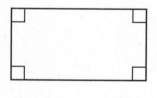

reflex angle An angle with a measure that is greater than 180° and less than 360°.

remainder The number left over after dividing two numbers that are not evenly divisible.

Example: $5\overline{)43}$ → 8 R3   The remainder is 3.

rhombus A parallelogram with sides of equal length.

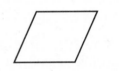

right angle One of four angles made by perpendicular line segments.

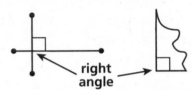

right angle

right triangle A triangle with one right angle.

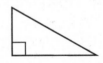

round To find the nearest ten, hundred, thousand, or some other place value. The usual rounding rule is to round up if the next digit to the right is 5 or more and round down if the next digit to the right is less than 5.

Examples: 463 rounded to the nearest ten is 460.
463 rounded to the nearest hundred is 500.

row A part of a table or array that contains items arranged horizontally.

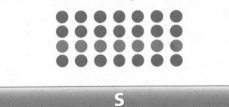

S

scalene A triangle with no equal sides is a scalene triangle.

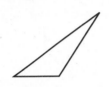

Shortcut Method A strategy for multiplying. It is the current common method in the United States.

Step 1	Step 2
$\overset{7}{2}8$	$\overset{7}{2}8$
$\times\ 9$	$\times\ 9$
2	252

simplest form A fraction is in simplest form if there is no whole number (other than 1) that divides evenly into the numerator and denominator.

Example: $\frac{3}{4}$ This fraction is in simplest form because no number divides evenly into 3 and 4.

simplify an expression Combine like terms and perform operations until all terms have been combined.

simplify a fraction To divide the numerator and the denominator of a fraction by the same number to make an equivalent fraction made from fewer but larger unit fractions.

Example: $\frac{5}{10} = \frac{5 \div 5}{10 \div 5} = \frac{1}{2}$

Glossary (continued)

situation equation An equation that shows the structure of the information in a problem.

Example: $35 + n = 40$

solution equation An equation that shows the operation that can be used to solve the problem.

Example: $n = 40 - 35$

square A rectangle with 4 sides of equal length and 4 right angles. It is also a rhombus.

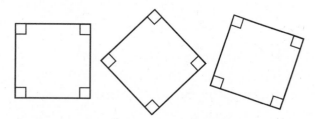

square array An array in which the number of rows equals the number of columns.

square centimeter A unit of area equal to the area of a square with one-centimeter sides.

square decimeter A unit of area equal to the area of a square with one-decimeter sides.

square foot A unit of area equal to the area of a square with one-foot sides.

square inch A unit of area equal to the area of a square with one-inch sides.

square kilometer A unit of area equal to the area of a square with one-kilometer sides.

square meter A unit of area equal to the area of a square with one-meter sides.

square mile A unit of area equal to the area of a square with one-mile sides.

square millimeter A unit of area equal to the area of a square with one-millimeter sides.

square unit A unit of area equal to the area of a square with one-unit sides.

square yard A unit of area equal to the area of a square with one-yard sides.

standard form The form of a number written using digits.

Example: 2,145

straight angle An angle that measures 180°.

sum The answer when adding two or more addends.

Example:

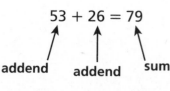

T

table Data arranged in rows and columns.

tenth A unit fraction representing one of ten equal parts of a whole, written as 0.1 or $\frac{1}{10}$.

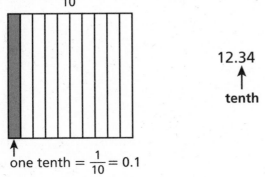

one tenth = $\frac{1}{10}$ = 0.1

12.34
↑
tenth

term in an expression A number, variable, product, or quotient in an expression. Each term is separated by an operation sign (+, −).

Example: $3n + 5$ has two terms, $3n$ and 5.

thousandth A unit fraction representing one of one thousand equal parts of a whole, written as 0.001 or $\frac{1}{1,000}$.

ton A unit of weight that equals 2,000 pounds.

tonne A metric unit of mass that equals 1,000 kilograms.

total Sum. The result of addition.

Example: 53 + 26 = 79

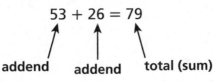

addend   addend   total (sum)

trapezoid A quadrilateral with exactly one pair of parallel sides.

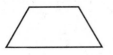

triangle A polygon with three sides.

unit A standard of measurement.

Examples: Centimeters, pounds, inches, and so on.

unit fraction A fraction whose numerator is 1. It shows one equal part of a whole.

Example: $\frac{1}{4}$

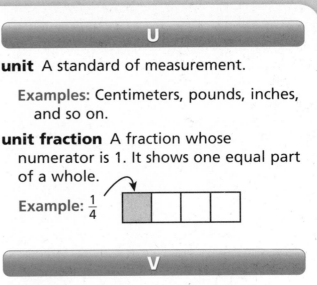

variable A letter or a symbol that represents a number in an algebraic expression.

vertex A point that is shared by two sides of an angle or two sides of a polygon.

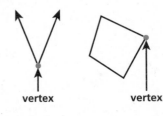

vertex   vertex

width The measure of one side of a figure.

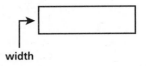

width

word form The form of a number written using words instead of digits.

Example: Six hundred thirty-nine

yard A U.S. customary unit of length equal to 3 feet.

© Houghton Mifflin Harcourt Publishing Company

California Common Core Standards for Mathematical Content

4.OA Operations and Algebraic Thinking

Use the four operations with whole numbers to solve problems.

4.OA.1	Interpret a multiplication equation as a comparison, e.g., interpret $35 = 5 \times 7$ as a statement that 35 is 5 times as many as 7 and 7 times as many as 5. Represent verbal statements of multiplicative comparisons as multiplication equations.	Unit 4 Lessons 4, 5, 6, 12
4.OA.2	Multiply or divide to solve word problems involving multiplicative comparison, e.g., by using drawings and equations with a symbol for the unknown number to represent the problem, distinguishing multiplicative comparison from additive comparison.	Unit 4 Lessons 4, 5, 6, 12
4.OA.3	Solve multistep word problems posed with whole numbers and having whole-number answers using the four operations, including problems in which remainders must be interpreted. Represent these problems using equations with a letter standing for the unknown quantity. Assess the reasonableness of answers using mental computation and estimation strategies including rounding.	Unit 1 Lessons 8, 11 Unit 2 Lessons 11, 15, 18, 19 Unit 3 Lessons 8, 9, 10 Unit 4 Lessons 7, 8, 9, 12

Gain familiarity with factors and multiples.

4.OA.4	Find all factor pairs for a whole number in the range 1–100. Recognize that a whole number is a multiple of each of its factors. Determine whether a given whole number in the range 1–100 is a multiple of a given one-digit number. Determine whether a given whole number in the range 1–100 is prime or composite.	Unit 4 Lessons 10, 12

Generate and analyze patterns.

4.OA.5	Generate a number or shape pattern that follows a given rule. Identify apparent features of the pattern that were not explicit in the rule itself.	Unit 4 Lessons 10, 11, 12 Unit 8 Lesson 12

4.NBT Number and Operations in Base Ten

Generalize place value understanding for multi-digit whole numbers.

4.NBT.1	Recognize that in a multi-digit whole number, a digit in one place represents ten times what it represents in the place to its right.	Unit 1 Lessons 1, 2, 4 Unit 2 Lessons 2, 3
4.NBT.2	Read and write multi-digit whole numbers using base-ten numerals, number names, and expanded form. Compare two multi-digit numbers based on meanings of the digits in each place, using $>$, $=$, and $<$ symbols to record the results of comparisons.	Unit 1 Lessons 2, 3, 4, 5 Unit 2 Lessons 4, 10, 12, 16, 19
4.NBT.3	Use place value understanding to round multi-digit whole numbers to any place.	Unit 1 Lessons 3, 5, 8, 14 Unit 2 Lessons 5, 17 Unit 3 Lesson 8

Use place value understanding and properties of operations to perform multi-digit arithmetic.

4.NBT.4	Fluently add and subtract multi-digit whole numbers using the standard algorithm.	Unit 1 Lessons 6, 7, 8, 9, 10, 11, 12, 13, 14 Unit 4 Lessons 1, 2, 12
4.NBT.5	Multiply a whole number of up to four digits by a one-digit whole number, and multiply two two-digit numbers, using strategies based on place value and the properties of operations. Illustrate and explain the calculation by using equations, rectangular arrays, and/or area models.	Unit 2 Lessons 1, 2, 3, 4, 5, 6, 7, 8, 9, 10, 11, 12, 13, 14, 15, 16, 17, 18, 19 Unit 4 Lessons 1, 3, 12
4.NBT.6	Find whole-number quotients and remainders with up to four-digit dividends and one-digit divisors, using strategies based on place value, the properties of operations, and/or the relationship between multiplication and division. Illustrate and explain the calculation by using equations, rectangular arrays, and/or area models.	Unit 3 Lessons 1, 2, 3, 4, 5, 6, 7, 8, 9, 10, 11 Unit 4 Lessons 1, 3, 12

4.NF Number and Operations—Fractions

Extend understanding of fraction equivalence and ordering.

4.NF.1	Explain why a fraction $\frac{a}{b}$ is equivalent to a fraction $\frac{(n \times a)}{(n \times b)}$ by using visual fraction models, with attention to how the number and size of the parts differ even though the two fractions themselves are the same size. Use this principle to recognize and generate equivalent fractions.	Unit 7 Lessons 4, 5, 6, 13
4.NF.2	Compare two fractions with different numerators and different denominators, e.g., by creating common denominators or numerators, or by comparing to a benchmark fraction such as $\frac{1}{2}$. Recognize that comparisons are valid only when the two fractions refer to the same whole. Record the results of comparisons with symbols >, =, or <, and justify the conclusions, e.g., by using a visual fraction model.	Unit 6 Lessons 2, 4, 10 Unit 7 Lessons 1, 2, 3, 6, 13

Build fractions from unit fractions by applying and extending previous understandings of operations on whole numbers.

4.NF.3	Understand a fraction $\frac{a}{b}$ with $a > 1$ as a sum of fractions $\frac{1}{b}$.	Unit 6 Lessons 1, 2, 3, 4, 5, 6, 10
4.NF.3a	Understand addition and subtraction of fractions as joining and separating parts referring to the same whole.	Unit 6 Lessons 2, 3, 4, 5, 6, 10
4.NF.3b	Decompose a fraction into a sum of fractions with the same denominator in more than one way, recording each decomposition by an equation. Justify decompositions, e.g., by using a visual fraction model.	Unit 6 Lessons 1, 2, 4, 5, 6, 9, 10

4.NF.3c	Add and subtract mixed numbers with like denominators, e.g., by replacing each mixed number with an equivalent fraction, and/or by using properties of operations and the relationship between addition and subtraction.	Unit 6 Lessons 5, 6, 9, 10
4.NF.3d	Solve word problems involving addition and subtraction of fractions referring to the same whole and having like denominators, e.g., by using visual fraction models and equations to represent the problem.	Unit 6 Lessons 3, 4, 6, 9, 10
4.NF.4	Apply and extend previous understandings of multiplication to multiply a fraction by a whole number.	Unit 6 Lessons 7, 8, 9, 10
4.NF.4a	Understand a fraction $\frac{a}{b}$ as a multiple of $\frac{1}{b}$.	Unit 6 Lessons 1, 7, 8, 9, 10
4.NF.4b	Understand a multiple of $\frac{a}{b}$ as a multiple of $\frac{1}{b}$, and use this understanding to multiply a fraction by a whole number.	Unit 6 Lessons 7, 8, 9, 10
4.NF.4c	Solve word problems involving multiplication of a fraction by a whole number, e.g., by using visual fraction models and equations to represent the problem.	Unit 6 Lessons 7, 8, 9, 10

Understand decimal notation for fractions, and compare decimal fractions.

4.NF.5	Express a fraction with denominator 10 as an equivalent fraction with denominator 100, and use this technique to add two fractions with respective denominators 10 and 100.	Unit 7 Lessons 6
4.NF.6	Use decimal notation for fractions with denominators 10 or 100.	Unit 7 Lessons 8, 9, 10, 11, 13
4.NF.7	Compare two decimals to hundredths by reasoning about their size. Recognize that comparisons are valid only when the two decimals refer to the same whole. Record the results of comparisons with the symbols >, =, or <, and justify the conclusions, e.g., by using a visual model.	Unit 7 Lessons 10, 12, 13

4.MD Measurement and Data

Solve problems involving measurement and conversion of measurements from a larger unit to a smaller unit.

4.MD.1	Know relative sizes of measurement units within one system of units including km, m, cm; kg, g; lb, oz.; l, ml; hr, min, sec. Within a single system of measurement, express measurements in a larger unit in terms of a smaller unit. Record measurement equivalents in a two-column table.	Unit 5 Lessons 1, 2, 3, 4, 5, 7, 8
4.MD.2	Use the four operations to solve word problems involving distances, intervals of time, liquid volumes, masses of objects, and money, including problems involving simple fractions or decimals, and problems that require expressing measurements given in a larger unit in terms of a smaller unit. Represent measurement quantities using diagrams such as number line diagrams that feature a measurement scale.	Unit 1 Lessons 6, 13 Unit 2 Lessons 4, 10, 18 Unit 4 Lessons 3, 12 Unit 5 Lessons 1, 2, 3, 4, 5, 7, 8 Unit 6 Lessons 3, 6, 8 Unit 7 Lessons 9, 10, 11, 12
4.MD.3	Apply the area and perimeter formulas for rectangles in real world and mathematical problems.	Unit 5 Lessons 6, 7, 8

Represent and interpret data.

4.MD.4	Make a line plot to display a data set of measurements in fractions of a unit ($\frac{1}{2}$, $\frac{1}{4}$, $\frac{1}{8}$). Solve problems involving addition and subtraction of fractions by using information presented in line plots.	Unit 5 Lesson 3 Unit 6 Lesson 6 Unit 7 Lessons 7, 13

Geometric measurement: understand concepts of angle and measure angles.

4.MD.5	Recognize angles as geometric shapes that are formed wherever two rays share a common endpoint, and understand concepts of angle measurement:	Unit 8 Lessons 1, 2, 3
4.MD.5a	An angle is measured with reference to a circle with its center at the common endpoint of the rays, by considering the fraction of the circular arc between the points where the two rays intersect the circle. An angle that turns through $\frac{1}{360}$ of a circle is called a "one-degree angle," and can be used to measure angles.	Unit 8 Lessons 2, 3
4.MD.5b	An angle that turns through n one-degree angles is said to have an angle measure of n degrees.	Unit 8 Lessons 2, 3
4.MD.6	Measure angles in whole-number degrees using a protractor. Sketch angles of specified measure.	Unit 8 Lessons 2, 3, 5
4.MD.7	Recognize angle measure as additive. When an angle is decomposed into non-overlapping parts, the angle measure of the whole is the sum of the angle measures of the parts. Solve addition and subtraction problems to find unknown angles on a diagram in real world and mathematical problems, e.g., by using an equation with a symbol for the unknown angle measure.	Unit 8 Lessons 3, 5, 6

4.G Geometry

Draw and identify lines and angles, and classify shapes by properties of their lines and angles.

4.G.1	Draw points, lines, line segments, rays, angles (right, acute, obtuse), and perpendicular and parallel lines. Identify these in two-dimensional figures.	Unit 8 Lessons 1, 2, 3, 4, 5, 7, 8, 9, 10, 12
4.G.2	Classify two-dimensional figures based on the presence or absence of parallel or perpendicular lines, or the presence or absence of angles of a specified size. Recognize right triangles as a category, and identify right triangles.	Unit 8 Lessons 4, 8, 9, 10, 12
4.G.3	Recognize a line of symmetry for a two-dimensional figure as a line across the figure such that the figure can be folded along the line into matching parts. Identify line-symmetric figures and draw lines of symmetry.	Unit 8 Lessons 11, 12

California Common Core Standards for Mathematical Practice

MP.1 Make sense of problems and persevere in solving them.

Mathematically proficient students start by explaining to themselves the meaning of a problem and looking for entry points to its solution. They analyze givens, constraints, relationships, and goals. They make conjectures about the form and meaning of the solution and plan a solution pathway rather than simply jumping into a solution attempt. They consider analogous problems, and try special cases and simpler forms of the original problem in order to gain insight into its solution. They monitor and evaluate their progress and change course if necessary. Older students might, depending on the context of the problem, transform algebraic expressions or change the viewing window on their graphing calculator to get the information they need. Mathematically proficient students can explain correspondences between equations, verbal descriptions, tables, and graphs or draw diagrams of important features and relationships, graph data, and search for regularity or trends. Younger students might rely on using concrete objects or pictures to help conceptualize and solve a problem. Mathematically proficient students check their answers to problems using a different method, and they continually ask themselves, "Does this make sense?" They can understand the approaches of others to solving complex problems and identify correspondences between different approaches.

Unit 1 Lessons 2, 5, 6, 7, 8, 10, 11, 12, 13, 14

Unit 2 Lessons 1, 3, 4, 5, 6, 7, 10, 11, 13, 14, 15, 16, 17, 18, 19

Unit 3 Lessons 2, 5, 6, 7, 8, 9, 10, 11

Unit 4 Lessons 2, 3, 4, 5, 6, 7, 8, 9, 12

Unit 5 Lessons 1, 2, 3, 4, 5, 6, 7, 8

Unit 6 Lessons 5, 6, 7, 9, 10

Unit 7 Lessons 1, 2, 3, 4, 5, 6, 7, 8, 9, 10, 11, 13

Unit 8 Lessons 5, 6, 7, 8, 12

MP.2 Reason abstractly and quantitatively.

Mathematically proficient students make sense of quantities and their relationships in problem situations. They bring two complementary abilities to bear on problems involving quantitative relationships: the ability to *decontextualize*—to abstract a given situation and represent it symbolically and manipulate the representing symbols as if they have a life of their own, without necessarily attending to their referents—and the ability to *contextualize*, to pause as needed during the manipulation process in order to probe into the referents for the symbols involved. Quantitative reasoning entails habits of creating a coherent representation of the problem at hand; considering the units involved; attending to the meaning of quantities, not just how to compute them; and knowing and flexibly using different properties of operations and objects.

Unit 1 Lessons 1, 3, 4, 5, 6, 8, 9, 14

Unit 2 Lessons 2, 4, 5, 6, 7, 8, 9, 10, 11, 13, 15, 16, 17, 19

Unit 3 Lessons 1, 3, 5, 7, 8, 11

Unit 4 Lessons 1, 2, 3, 4, 5, 6, 12

Unit 5 Lessons 2, 6, 7, 8

Unit 6 Lessons 1, 2, 3, 4, 7, 10

Unit 7 Lessons 1, 2, 9, 10, 13

Unit 8 Lessons 3, 5, 6, 12

MP.3 Construct viable arguments and critique the reasoning of others.

Mathematically proficient students understand and use stated assumptions, definitions, and previously established results in constructing arguments. They make conjectures and build a logical progression of statements to explore the truth of their conjectures. They are able to analyze situations by breaking them into cases, and can recognize and use counterexamples. They justify their conclusions, communicate them to others, and respond to the arguments of others. They reason inductively about data, making plausible arguments that take into account the context from which the data arose. Mathematically proficient students are also able to compare the effectiveness of two plausible arguments, distinguish correct logic or reasoning from that which is flawed, and—if there is a flaw in an argument—explain what it is. Elementary students can construct arguments using concrete referents such as objects, drawings, diagrams, and actions. Such arguments can make sense and be correct, even though they are not generalized or made formal until later grades. Later, students learn to determine domains to which an argument applies. Students at all grades can listen or read the arguments of others, decide whether they make sense, and ask useful questions to clarify or improve the arguments.

Unit 1 Lessons 1, 2, 3, 4, 5, 6, 7, 8, 9, 10, 11, 12, 13, 14
Unit 2 Lessons 1, 2, 3, 4, 5, 6, 7, 8, 9, 10, 11, 12, 13, 14, 15, 16, 17, 18, 19
Unit 3 Lessons 1, 2, 3, 4, 5, 6, 7, 8, 9, 10, 11
Unit 4 Lessons 1, 2, 3, 4, 5, 6, 7, 8, 9, 10, 11, 12
Unit 5 Lessons 1, 2, 3, 4, 5, 6, 7, 8
Unit 6 Lessons 1, 2, 3, 4, 5, 6, 7, 8, 9, 10
Unit 7 Lessons 1, 2, 3, 4, 5, 6, 7, 8, 9, 10, 11, 12, 13
Unit 8 Lessons 1, 2, 3, 4, 5, 6, 7, 8, 9, 10, 11, 12

MP.4 Model with mathematics.

Mathematically proficient students can apply the mathematics they know to solve problems arising in everyday life, society, and the workplace. In early grades, this might be as simple as writing an addition equation to describe a situation. In middle grades, a student might apply proportional reasoning to plan a school event or analyze a problem in the community. By high school, a student might use geometry to solve a design problem or use a function to describe how one quantity of interest depends on another. Mathematically proficient students who can apply what they know are comfortable making assumptions and approximations to simplify a complicated situation, realizing that these may need revision later. They are able to identify important quantities in a practical situation and map their relationships using such tools as diagrams, two-way tables, graphs, flowcharts and formulas. They can analyze those relationships mathematically to draw conclusions. They routinely interpret their mathematical results in the context of the situation and reflect on whether the results make sense, possibly improving the model if it has not served its purpose.

Unit 1 Lessons 3, 10, 12, 13, 14
Unit 2 Lessons 2, 6, 7, 19
Unit 3 Lessons 1, 2, 3, 10, 11
Unit 4 Lessons 2, 3, 4, 5, 8, 9, 12
Unit 5 Lessons 1, 4, 7, 8
Unit 6 Lessons 1, 3, 4, 5, 6, 7, 8, 10
Unit 7 Lessons 2, 3, 5, 7, 8, 13
Unit 8 Lessons 6, 12

MP.5 Use appropriate tools strategically.

Mathematically proficient students consider the available tools when solving a mathematical problem. These tools might include pencil and paper, concrete models, a ruler, a protractor, a calculator, a spreadsheet, a computer algebra system, a statistical package, or dynamic geometry software. Proficient students are sufficiently familiar with tools appropriate for their grade or course to make sound decisions about when each of these tools might be helpful, recognizing both the insight to be gained and their limitations. For example, mathematically proficient high school students analyze graphs of functions and solutions generated using a graphing calculator. They detect possible errors by strategically using estimation and other mathematical knowledge. When making mathematical models, they know that technology can enable them to visualize the results of varying assumptions, explore consequences, and compare predictions with data. Mathematically proficient students at various grade levels are able to identify relevant external mathematical resources, such as digital content located on a website, and use them to pose or solve problems. They are able to use technological tools to explore and deepen their understanding of concepts.

Unit 1 Lessons 1, 2, 3, 4, 6, 9, 14

Unit 2 Lessons 1, 4, 5, 6, 7, 8, 10, 11, 12, 16, 19

Unit 3 Lessons 3, 4, 10, 11

Unit 4 Lessons 2, 10, 12

Unit 5 Lessons 1, 4, 5, 6, 7, 8

Unit 6 Lessons 1, 2, 3, 4, 8, 9, 10

Unit 7 Lessons 1, 2, 4, 5, 9, 10, 11, 12, 13

Unit 8 Lessons 1, 2, 4, 5, 7, 8, 9, 10, 11, 12

MP.6 Attend to precision.

Mathematically proficient students try to communicate precisely to others. They try to use clear definitions in discussion with others and in their own reasoning. They state the meaning of the symbols they choose, including using the equal sign consistently and appropriately. They are careful about specifying units of measure, and labeling axes to clarify the correspondence with quantities in a problem. They calculate accurately and efficiently, express numerical answers with a degree of precision appropriate for the problem context. In the elementary grades, students give carefully formulated explanations to each other. By the time they reach high school they have learned to examine claims and make explicit use of definitions.

Unit 1 Lessons 1, 2, 3, 4, 5, 6, 7, 8, 9, 10, 11, 12, 13, 14

Unit 2 Lessons 1, 2, 3, 4, 5, 6, 7, 8, 9, 10, 11, 12, 13, 14, 15, 16, 17, 18, 19

Unit 3 Lessons 1, 2, 3, 4, 5, 6, 7, 8, 9, 10, 11

Unit 4 Lessons 1, 2, 3, 4, 5, 6, 7, 8, 9, 10, 11, 12

Unit 5 Lessons 1, 2, 3, 4, 5, 6, 7, 8

Unit 6 Lessons 1, 2, 3, 4, 5, 6, 7, 8, 9, 10

Unit 7 Lessons 1, 2, 3, 4, 5, 6, 7, 8, 9, 10, 11, 12, 13

Unit 8 Lessons 1, 2, 3, 4, 5, 6, 7, 8, 9, 10, 11, 12

MP.7 Look for and make use of structure.

Mathematically proficient students look closely to discern a pattern or structure. Young students, for example, might notice that three and seven more is the same amount as seven and three more, or they may sort a collection of shapes according to how many sides the shapes have. Later, students will see 7×8 equals the well remembered $7 \times 5 + 7 \times 3$, in preparation for learning about the distributive property. In the expression $x^2 + 9x + 14$, older students can see the 14 as 2×7 and the 9 as $2 + 7$. They recognize the significance of an existing line in a geometric figure and can use the strategy of drawing an auxiliary line for solving problems. They also can step back for an overview and shift perspective. They can see complicated things, such as some algebraic expressions, as single objects or as being composed of several objects. For example, they can see $5 - 3(x - y)^2$ as 5 minus a positive number times a square and use that to realize that its value cannot be more than 5 for any real numbers x and y.

Unit 1 Lessons 1, 2, 4, 9, 13, 14
Unit 2 Lessons 2, 3, 6, 8, 9, 10, 13, 16, 17, 19
Unit 3 Lessons 1, 3, 10, 11
Unit 4 Lessons 1, 2, 3, 5, 10, 11, 12
Unit 5 Lessons 1, 2, 4, 5, 8
Unit 6 Lessons 1, 4, 5, 10
Unit 7 Lessons 2, 6, 9, 10, 11, 12, 13
Unit 8 Lessons 1, 2, 4, 7, 8, 9, 10, 11, 12

MP.8 Look for and express regularity in repeated reasoning.

Mathematically proficient students notice if calculations are repeated, and look both for general methods and for shortcuts. Upper elementary students might notice when dividing 25 by 11 that they are repeating the same calculations over and over again, and conclude they have a repeating decimal. By paying attention to the calculation of slope as they repeatedly check whether points are on the line through (1, 2) with slope 3, middle school students might abstract the equation $(y - 2)/(x - 1) = 3$. Noticing the regularity in the way terms cancel when expanding $(x - 1)(x + 1)$, $(x - 1)$ $(x^2 + x + 1)$, and $(x - 1)(x^3 + x^2 + x + 1)$ might lead them to the general formula for the sum of a geometric series. As they work to solve a problem, mathematically proficient students maintain oversight of the process, while attending to the details. They continually evaluate the reasonableness of their intermediate results.

Unit 1 Lessons 3, 4, 5, 6, 7, 10, 11, 14
Unit 2 Lessons 1, 2, 3, 5, 7, 8, 15, 17, 19
Unit 3 Lessons 1, 3, 5, 6, 11
Unit 4 Lessons 1, 2, 10, 11, 12
Unit 5 Lessons 1, 6, 8
Unit 6 Lessons 2, 7, 10
Unit 7 Lessons 1, 3, 6, 8, 10, 11, 13
Unit 8 Lessons 1, 3, 4, 9, 10, 11, 12

Index

Index (continued)

extending, 165–166, 168
growing, 166
in fraction bars, 212
numerical patterns, 50, 137, 165
properties
Associative (addition), 20
Associative (multiplication), 47, 65, 81, 137
Commutative (addition), 20, 137, 140
Commutative (multiplication), 46, 47–48, 137
Distributive, 59–60, 61–62, 75, 137
Identity, 137

Algebraic language, 60, 66, 137–138

Angle Cut-Outs, 298A

Angles, 296–298A, 299–302, 303–304, 305–310, 311–314, 315–316 *See also* **Geometry, angle**

acute, 297–298A, 302, 303–304, 305–306, 309–310, 313, 327–328, 330, 333
angle equations, 311–314, 315–316
classifying, 297–298A, 302, 303, 311–312 333
compose, 311–312, 315
cut-outs, 298A
decompose, 313–314, 316
draw and describe, 296–298, 300–302, 304, 305, 310, 312–313
measuring, 299–302, 303–304, 311–313
naming, 296, 298, 307
obtuse, 297–298A, 302, 303–304, 305–306, 309–310, 313, 327–328, 330, 333
real world examples, 302, 315–316
reflex, 303
right, 297–298A, 299, 301–302, 303, 305–306, 309–310, 311, 313, 320–322, 327–328, 330–332, 333–334A
straight, 298A, 299, 301, 303–304, 311–313, 316

turns in a circle, 299, 303–304
vertex of, 296

Area, 45–46, 196–198, 200, 201–202

formulas, 196–197
of rectangles, 45–46, 51–52, 196–198, 200

Area models

division and, 99, 103–104, 107, 111, 115, 119
fractions and, 231
multiplication and, 45–46, 48, 51–52, 55, 57–58, 59–60, 61, 65–66, 73–74, 75, 81–82, 83

Arrays, 3–4, 45–46, 48

area and, 45, 197
columns, 45
dot, 3–4, 73–74
factor pairs and, 161–162
multiplication strategy, 45–46, 48, 73–74
rows, 45
units, 48

Assessment

Assessment Resources, 37–42, 91–96, 129–134, 169–174, 203–208, 241–246, 287–292, 341–346
Summative Assessment
Unit Review and Test, 37–42, 91–96, 129–134, 169–174, 203–208, 241–246, 287–292, 341–346

Associative Property

of Addition, 20
of Multiplication, 46, 47–48, 81, 137

B

Bar graph, 152

analyze, 36, 152
comparisons using, 152

horizontal, 35

make, 35

scale, 35

vertical, 152

Break apart drawings, 25, 140

C

California Common Core Standards, S27–S34

Centimeter, 177–179, 195–196

Circles. *See also* **Graphs, circle**

angles and, 299, 303–304, 315

Common denominator, 266–268

Commutative Property

of addition, 20, 137, 140

of multiplication, 46, 47–48, 67, 137

Compare. *See also* **Inequality**

decimals, 279–280, 283–284

fractions, 217–218, 226, 248A–250, 252–254, 255–256, 265–268

whole numbers, 10, 13

Comparison

bars, 145–146, 147–150

language, 145, 147

problems, 145–146, 147–150, 151–152, 155–156, 233

Comparison problems, 145–146, 147–150, 151–152, 155–156, 168, 233

Comparison situations

addition and subtraction, 147, 150, 151–152

language, 145, 147

more or fewer, 147–150

multiplication and division, 145–146, 149–150, 151–152

use a bar graph, 152

use a pictograph, 151

write comparison statements, 146, 147–149

Compose

angles, 311–312. *See also* Decompose, angles

fractions, 211, 213, 219–220, 225, 227–228. *See also* Decompose, fractions

numbers, 3–6, 6A–8, 11–12, 15–16, 17–18, 31, 161. *See also* Decompose, numbers

quadrilaterals, 329–330. *See also* Decompose, quadrilaterals

triangles, 327–328. *See also* Decompose, triangles

Composite number, 162, 164

Content Overview

Unit 1, 1–2, 21–22

Unit 2, 43–44

Unit 3, 97–98

Unit 4, 135–136

Unit 5, 175–176

Unit 6, 209–210

Unit 7, 247–248, 271–272

Unit 8, 293–294, 317–318

Cup, 193–194

Customary measurement. *See* **Measurement, customary**

D

Data Analysis. *See also* **Graphs**

analyze data

from a bar graph, 35–36, 152

from a line plot, 186, 230, 240, 269–270

from a pictograph, 151

G

Gallon, 193

Geometry

angle, 296–298, 299–302, 303–304,
305–306, 311–314, 315–316
  acute, 297–298A, 302, 303–304,
    305–306, 309–310, 313, 327–328,
    330, 333
  classifying, 297–298A, 302, 303,
    311–312, 333
  cut outs, 298A
  naming, 296, 298, 307
  obtuse, 297–298A, 302, 303–304, 305–
    306, 309–310, 313, 327–328, 330,
    333
  real world examples, 302, 315–316
  reflex, 303
  right, 297–298A, 299, 301–302,
    303, 305–306, 309–310, 311,
    313, 320–322, 327–328, 330–332,
    333–334A
  straight, 298A, 299, 301, 303–304,
    311–313, 316
  vertex of, 296
lines, 295, 319–322, 331–332
line segment, 295, 319–322, 331–332
patterns in, 166, 168
point, 295–296, 331
ray, 296, 299–302, 304, 312
symmetry, 335–338
  draw lines, 336, 338
  identify lines, 335, 337
two-dimensional figures
  circle. *See also* Graphs, circle
    angles and, 299, 303–304, 315
  parallelogram, 324–326, 327–330
  perimeter, 195, 197–198, 200, 201–202
  polygon, 331, 333–334A

quadrilaterals, 323–326A, 327–330,
  333–334A, 339
  classify, 324, 326, 326A, 333–334A
  compose, 329–330
  decompose, 327–328
  draw, 325
  name, 324
  parallelogram, *See* Geometry,
    two-dimensional figures,
    parallelogram
  rectangle, 52, 65, 81, 195–198, 200,
    201–202, 324–326A, 327, 329,
    330, 337, 339
  rhombus, 324–326A, 327, 330
  square, 324–326A, 327
  trapezoid, 324–326A, 328, 339
triangle
  acute, 305–306, 309–310, 327–328,
    330
  classify, 305–310, 327–328, 330
  equilateral, 307–310, 330, 332
  isosceles, 307–310, 330–332
  obtuse, 305–306, 309–310, 327–328,
    330
  right, 305–306, 309–310, 327–328,
    330–332
  scalene, 307–310, 331
  sorting, 309, 333–334A

Glossary, S13–S25

Gram, 183–184

Graphs

bar, 35–36, 152
  make, 35
circle, 315
comparisons using, 151–152
  pictograph, 151
  vertical bar, 152
horizontal bar, 35–36
line plot, 186, 230, 240, 269–270

© Houghton Mifflin Harcourt Publishing Company

© Houghton Mifflin Harcourt Publishing Company

estimate to check, 28

find mistakes, 27, 28

fractions, 219–222, 225–228, 237–240

inverse operations, 25, 140

methods

Ungrouping, 23–24

money, 33–34

multidigit, 23–30, 36

patterns, 23

related to addition. *See* Subtraction, inverse operations

related to division, 103–104

repeated, 103

types, 31, 147–149

units of time, 187

from zeros, 23–24

Sum, 140

Symbols, 30, 137

+, 137

=, 139

> and <, 10, 217

for multiplication, 137

Symmetry. *See* **Geometry, symmetry**

Symmetry Around the Ones, 281

T

Technology

calculator, 200

Tens, 3, 9

Tenth, 273, 277–278, 282

Time, 185–188

across midnight, 188

add and subtract units, 187–188

elapsed time, 187–188, 223

unit conversions, 185

Transitivity, 178

Triangle, 305–310, 327–332

acute, 305–306, 309–310, 327–328, 330

classify, 309–310, 333, 334A

equilateral, 307–310, 327–328, 330

identify, 305–310, 327–328, 330

isosceles, 307–310, 327–328, 330

name, 305–310, 327–330, 327–328, 330

obtuse, 305–306, 309–310, 327–328, 330

from quadrilaterals, 327–330

right, 305–306, 309–310, 327–328, 330–332

scalene, 307–310, 327–328, 330

sorting, 309–310, 333, 334A

Two-dimensional figures. *See* **Geometry, two-dimensional figures**

Two-step problems, 29, 153–154

U

Ungroup, 23–24, 188

Unit

choosing, 178

measurement, 177–183, 189–193, 195–196

time, 185

Unit fractions, 211–212, 217–218, 231, 235, 257–258

Unit Review and Test, 37–42, 91–96, 129–134, 169–174, 203–208, 241–246, 287–292, 341–346

V

Variable, 29, 137–138, 141–158

Vertex

of angle, 296, 302, 307, 312, 331–332

Nutrition for Nursing
Review Module Edition 4.0

Contributors

Audrey Knippa, MS, MPH, RN, CNE
Nursing Education Coordinator and
   Content Project Leader

Sheryl Sommer, PhD, MSN, RN
Director, Nursing Curriculum and
   Education Services

Brenda Ball, MEd, BSN, RN
Nursing Education Specialist

Lois Churchill, MN, RN
Nursing Education Specialist

Carrie B. Elkins, DHSc, MSN, PHCNS, BC
Nursing Education Specialist

Mary Jane Janowski, MA, BSN, RN
Nursing Resource Specialist

Karin Roberts, PhD, MSN, RN, CNE
Nursing Education Coordinator

Mendy G. Wright, DNP, MSN, RN
Nursing Education Specialist

Derek Prater, MS Journalism
Lead Product Developer and Editorial Project Leader

Erika A. Archer, BS Education, Foreign Language
Product Developer

Johanna Barnes, BA Journalism
Product Developer

Chris Crawford, BS Journalism
Product Developer

Hilary E. Groninger, BS Journalism
Product Developer

Megan E. Herre, BS Journalism
Product Developer

Amanda Lehman, BA English
Product Developer

Joanna Shindler, BA Journalism
Product Developer

Brant L. Stacy, BS Journalism, BA English
Product Developer

Consultants

Penny Fauber, PhD, RN

Gale P. Sewell, MSN, RN, CNE

INTELLECTUAL PROPERTY NOTICE

IMPORTANT NOTICE TO THE READER

USER'S GUIDE

Welcome to the Assessment Technologies Institute® Nutrition for Nursing Review Module Edition 4.0. The mission of ATI's Content Mastery Series® review modules is to provide user-friendly compendiums of nursing knowledge that will:

- Help you locate important information quickly.

- Assist in your remediation efforts.

- Provide exercises for applying your nursing knowledge.

- Facilitate your entry into the nursing profession as a newly licensed RN.

Organization

This review module is organized into units covering principles of nutrition, clinical nutrition, and alterations in nutrition. Chapters within these units conform to one of three organizing principles for presenting the content:

- Nursing concepts

- Procedures

- Disorders

Nursing concepts chapters begin with an overview describing the central concept and its relevance to nursing. Subordinate themes are covered in outline form to demonstrate relationships and present the information in a clear, succinct manner.

Procedures chapters include an overview describing the procedure covered in the chapter. These chapters will provide you with nursing knowledge relevant to each procedure, including indications, client outcomes, nursing actions, and complications.

Disorders chapters include an overview describing the disorder(s) and the relation to nutrition. These chapters cover assessment and nutritional guidelines and nursing interventions, including preventive and therapeutic nutrition.

Application Exercises

Questions are provided at the end of each chapter so you can practice applying your knowledge. The Application Exercises include both NCLEX-style questions, such as multiple-choice and multiple-select items, and questions that ask you to apply your knowledge in other formats, such as short-answer and matching items. After the Application Exercises, an answer key is provided, along with rationales for the answers.

NCLEX® Connections

To prepare for the NCLEX-RN, it is important for you to understand how the content in this review module is connected to the NCLEX-RN test plan. You can find information on the detailed test plan at the National Council of State Boards of Nursing's Web site: https://www.ncsbn.org/. When reviewing content in this review module, regularly ask yourself, "How does this content fit into the test plan, and what types of questions related to this content should I expect?"

To help you in this process, we've included NCLEX Connections at the beginning of each unit and with each question in the Application Exercises Answer Keys. The NCLEX Connections at the beginning of each unit will point out areas of the detailed test plan that relate to the content within that unit. The NCLEX Connections attached to the Application Exercises Answer Keys will demonstrate how each exercise fits within the detailed content outline.

These NCLEX Connections will help you understand how the detailed content outline is organized, starting with major client needs categories and subcategories and followed by related content areas and tasks. The major client needs categories are:

- Safe and Effective Care Environment
  - Management of Care
  - Safety and Infection Control
- Health Promotion and Maintenance
- Psychosocial Integrity
- Physiological Integrity
  - Basic Care and Comfort
  - Pharmacological and Parenteral Therapies
  - Reduction of Risk Potential
  - Physiological Adaptation

An NCLEX Connection might, for example, alert you that content within a unit is related to:

- Basic Care and Comfort
  - Nutrition and Oral Hydration
    - Manage the client who has an alteration in nutritional intake.

Icons

Icons are used throughout the review module to draw your attention to particular areas. Keep an eye out for these icons:

 This icon indicates an Overview, or introduction, to a particular subject matter. Descriptions and categories will typically be found in an Overview.

 This icon is used for the Application Exercises and the Application Exercises Answer Keys.

 This icon is used for NCLEX connections.

This icon is used for gerontological content. When you see this icon, take note of information that is specific to aging or the care of older adult clients.

This icon is used for content related to safety. When you see this icon, take note of safety concerns or steps that nurses can take to ensure client safety and a safe environment.

 This icon indicates that a media supplement, such as a graphic, an animation, or a video, is available. If you have an electronic copy of the review module, this icon will appear alongside clickable links to media supplements. If you have a hardcopy version of the review module, visit www.atitesting.com for details on how to access these features.

Feedback

ATI welcomes feedback regarding this review module. Please provide comments to: comments@ atitesting.com.

Table of Contents

Unit 3   Alterations in Nutrition

UNIT 1: PRINCIPLES OF NUTRITION

- Sources of Nutrition
- Ingestion, Digestion, Absorption, and Metabolism
- Nutrition Assessment
- Guidelines for Healthy Eating
- Food Safety
- Cultural, Ethnic, and Religious Influences
- Nutrition Across the Lifespan

NCLEX® CONNECTIONS

When reviewing the chapters in this unit, keep in mind the relevant sections of the NCLEX® outline, in particular:

CLIENT NEEDS:
HEALTH PROMOTION AND MAINTENANCE

Relevant topics/tasks include:
- Aging Process
  - Provide care and education that meets the special needs of the preschool client ages 1 year to 4 years.
- Ante/Intra/Postpartum and Newborn Care
  - Provide prenatal care and education.
- Health and Wellness
  - Identify the client's health-oriented behaviors.

CLIENT NEEDS:
BASIC CARE AND COMFORT

Relevant topics/tasks include:
- Nutrition and Oral Hydration
  - Calculate the client's intake and output.
  - Initiate calorie counts for clients.
  - Apply knowledge of mathematics to client nutrition.

UNIT 1	PRINCIPLES OF NUTRITION
Chapter 1	Sources of Nutrition

Overview

- Nutrients absorbed in the diet determine, to a large degree, the health of the body. Deficiencies or excesses can contribute to a poor state of health. Essential nutrients are those that the body cannot manufacture, and the absence of essential nutrients can cause deficiency diseases.

- Components of nutritive sources are:

  o Carbohydrates and fiber

  o Protein

  o Lipids (fats)

  o Vitamins

  o Minerals and electrolytes

  o Water

- Carbohydrates, fats, and proteins are all energy-yielding nutrients.

- Dietary Reference Intakes (DRIs), are developed by the Institute of Medicine's Food and Nutrition Board, and are the most commonly used source on nutrient allowances for healthy individuals. Formerly known as the Recommended Dietary Allowances (RDAs), the DRIs are comprised of four reference values: RDAs, Estimated Average Requirements (EARs), Adequate Intakes (AIs), and Tolerable Upper Intake Levels (ULs).

Carbohydrates and Fiber

- All carbohydrates are organic compounds composed of carbon, hydrogen, and oxygen (CHO). The main function of carbohydrates is to provide energy for the body.

  o The average minimum amount of carbohydrates needed to fuel the brain is 130 g/day. Median carbohydrate intake is 200 to 330 g/day among men and 180 to 230 g/day among women, and the acceptable macronutrient distribution range for carbohydrates is 45% to 65% of calories.

  o Carbohydrates provide energy for cellular work, and help to regulate protein and fat metabolism. They are essential for normal cardiac and central nervous system (CNS) functioning.

- ○ Carbohydrates are classified according to the number of saccharide units making up their structure:
  - ■ Monosaccharides are simple carbohydrates (glucose, fructose).
  - ■ Disaccharides are simple carbohydrates (sucrose, lactose).
  - ■ Polysaccharides are complex carbohydrates (starch, fiber, glycogen).
- ○ As complex carbohydrates are ingested and broken down, they are easily absorbed in the intestine and into the bloodstream where they are stored in the liver and muscles for energy needs.
- ○ The body absorbs 80% to 95% of carbohydrates. Absorption occurs mainly in the small intestine using pancreatic and intestinal enzymes.
- ○ Glycogen is the stored carbohydrate energy source found in the liver and muscles. It is a vital source of backup energy.
- ○ Carbohydrates provide 4 cal/g of energy.
- ○ Fiber is categorized as a carbohydrate, but it does not yield energy for the body.
  - ■ Dietary fiber is the substance in plant foods that is indigestible. Types are: pectin, gum, cellulose, and mucilage.
  - ■ Fiber is important for proper bowel elimination. It adds bulk to the feces and stimulates peristalsis to ease elimination.
  - ■ Studies show fiber helps to lower cholesterol and lessen the incidence of intestinal cancers.

TYPES OF CARBOHYDRATES			
TYPE	MONOSACCHARIDES	DISACCHARIDES	POLYSACCHARIDES
Example/(Sources)	Glucose (corn syrup), fructose (fruits), galactose (milk sugar broken down)	Sucrose (table sugar, molasses), lactose (milk sugar), maltose (sweeteners)	Starches (grains, legumes, root vegetables), fiber (indigestible plant parts)
Function	Basic energy for cells	Energy, aids calcium and phosphorus absorption (lactose)	Energy storage (starches), digestive aid (fiber)

Proteins

- • Proteins are provided by plant and animal sources. They are formed by linking amino acids in various combinations for specific use by the body.
  - ○ There are three types of proteins: complete, incomplete, and complementary. Each is obtained from the diet in various ways.
    - ■ Complete proteins, generally from animal sources, contain all of the essential amino acids (there are nine essential amino acids).

- Incomplete proteins, generally from plants (grains, nuts, legumes, vegetables, fruits), do not contain all of the essential amino acids.

- Complementary proteins are those food sources that when eaten together, provide all the essential amino acids.

○ Proteins have many metabolic functions (tissue building and maintenance, balance of nitrogen and water, backup energy, support of metabolic processes [nitrogen balance, transportation of nutrients, other vital substances], support of the immune system).

○ Three main factors influence the body's requirement for protein:

- Tissue growth needs.

- Quality of the dietary protein.

- Added needs due to illness.

○ The recommended dietary requirement of protein for adults is 10% of intake, or 46 g/day for women and 56 g/day for men.

○ Undernutrition may lead to protein malnourishment, which can lead to kwashiorkor or marasmus. These serious disorders are caused by a lack of protein ingestion, or the metabolism resulting in a cachectic (wasting) state.

○ Protein provides 4 cal/g of energy.

Lipids

- The chemical group of fats is called lipids, and they are available from many sources (dark meat, poultry skin, dairy foods, and added oils [margarine, butter, shortening, oils, lard]).

○ Fat is an essential nutrient for the body. It serves as a concentrated form of energy for the body (second to carbohydrates) and supplies important tissue needs (hormone production, structural material for cell walls, protective padding for vital organs, insulation to maintain body temperature, covering for nerve fibers, aid in the absorption of fat-soluble vitamins).

○ Fats are divided into the following categories: triglycerides, phospholipids, sterols, saturated fats, unsaturated fats, polyunsaturated fats, and essential fatty acids.

- Triglycerides (the chemical name for fats) are the primary form of fat in food. They combine with glycerol to supply energy to the body, allow fat-soluble vitamin transport, and form adipose tissue that protects the body.

- Phospholipids are derived from triglycerides. They are important to cell membrane structure.

- Cholesterol belongs to the chemical substance group called sterols. It is necessary for cell membrane stability and the production of certain hormones and bile salts for digestion. If cholesterol is consumed in excess, it can build up in the tissues causing congestion and increasing the risk for cardiovascular disease.

- Saturated fats are of animal origin. Unsaturated fats are usually from plant sources and help reduce health risks (notable exceptions are coconut and palm oil).

- Essential fatty acids, made from broken down fats, must be supplied by the diet. Essential fatty acids, including omega-3 and omega-6, are used to support blood clotting, blood pressure, inflammatory responses, and many other metabolic processes.

- Linoleic acid is an important essential fatty acid and is found primarily in polyunsaturated vegetable oils.

○ Generally, no more than 20% to 35% of total calories should come from fat (10% or less from saturated fat sources).

- A diet high in fat is linked to cardiovascular disease, hypertension, and diabetes mellitus.

- The exception is for children under 2 years of age, who need a higher amount of fat to form brain tissue.

○ Conversely, a diet with less than 10% fat cannot supply adequate amounts of essential fatty acids and results in a cachectic (wasting) state.

○ The majority of lipid metabolism occurs after fat reaches the small intestine, where the gallbladder secretes concentrated bile and acts as an emulsifier to break fat into smaller particles. At the same time, the pancreas secretes pancreatic lipase which breaks down fat. The small intestine secretes an enzyme for further breakdown. The muscles, liver, and adipose tissue cause the release of fatty acids, and the liver produces lipoproteins to carry lipids.

- Very Low Density Lipoproteins (VLDL) carry triglycerides to the tissues.

- Low Density Lipoproteins (LDL) carry cholesterol to the tissues.

- High Density Lipoproteins (HDL) remove excess cholesterol from the tissues. HDL is considered "good" cholesterol.

○ Lipids provide 9 cal/g of energy and are the densest form of stored energy.

Vitamins

- Vitamins are organic substances required for many enzymatic reactions. The main function of vitamins is to be a catalyst for metabolic functions and chemical reactions.

○ There are 13 essential vitamins, each having a specialized function.

○ The two classes of vitamins are:

- Water-soluble – Vitamins C and B-complex

- Fat-soluble – Vitamins A, D, E, and K

○ Vitamins yield no usable energy for the body.

- Water-Soluble Vitamins

  o Vitamin C (ascorbic acid) aids in tissue building and metabolic reactions (wound and fracture healing, collagen formation, adrenaline production, iron absorption, conversion of folic acid, cellular adhesion).

    - Vitamin C is found in citrus fruits (oranges, lemons), tomatoes, peppers, green leafy vegetables, and strawberries.

    - Stress and illness increase the need for vitamin C.

    - Severe deficiency causes scurvy, a hemorrhagic disease with diffuse tissue bleeding, painful limbs/joints, weak bones, and swollen gums/loose teeth.

  o B-complex vitamins have many functions in cell metabolism. Each one has a varied duty. Many partner with other B vitamins for metabolic reactions. Most affect energy, metabolism, and neurological function. Sources for B vitamins almost always include green leafy vegetables and unprocessed or enriched grains.

    - Thiamin (B_1) is necessary for proper digestion, peristalsis, and providing energy to the smooth muscles, glands, the CNS, and blood vessels.

      □ Deficiency results in beriberi, gastrointestinal symptoms, and cardiovascular problems.

      □ Food sources are widespread in almost all plant and animal tissues, especially meats, grains, and legumes.

    - Riboflavin (B_2) is required for growth and tissue healing.

      □ Deficiency results in cheilosis (manifestations include scales and cracks on lips and mouth), smooth/swollen red tongue, and dermatitis particularly in skin folds.

      □ Dietary sources include milk, meats, and green leafy vegetables.

    - Niacin (B_3) aids in the metabolism of fats, glucose, and alcohol.

      □ Deficiency causes pellagra (manifestations include sun-sensitive skin lesions, and gastrointestinal and neurologic symptoms).

      □ Sources include beef liver, nuts, legumes, whole grain and enriched breads and cereals.

    - Pantothenic acid (B_5) is involved in biological reactions (energy production, catabolism, and synthesis of fatty acids, phospholipids, cholesterol, steroid hormones, the neurotransmitter acetylcholine).

      □ Deficiency results in anemia and CNS changes. However, a deficiency is unlikely due to the diverse availability in foods.

      □ Rich sources include organ meats (liver, kidney), egg yolk, avocados, cashew nuts and peanuts, brown rice, soy, lentils, broccoli, and milk.

- Pyridoxine (B_6) is needed for cellular function and synthesis of hemoglobin, neurotransmitters, and niacin.
  - Deficiency causes anemia and CNS disturbances.
  - High intake of supplements may cause sensory neuropathy.
  - Widespread food sources include organ meats and grains.
- Biotin serves as a coenzyme used in fatty acid synthesis, amino acid metabolism, and the formation of glucose.
  - Deficiency is rare, but results in neurological symptoms (depression, fatigue) and rashes on the skin, especially the face ("biotin deficient face").
  - Widespread food sources include eggs, milk, and dark green vegetables.
- Folate (folic acid is the synthetic form) is required for hemoglobin and amino acid synthesis, cellular reproduction, and prevention of neural tube defects in utero.
  - Deficiency causes megaloblastic anemia, CNS disturbances, and fetal neural tube defects (spina bifida and anencephaly). It is important that all women of child-bearing age get an adequate amount of folate due to neural tube formation occurring early in gestation, often before a woman knows she is pregnant.
  - Folate occurs naturally in a variety of foods including liver, dark-green leafy vegetables, citrus fruits, whole-grain products, and legumes.
- Cobalamin (B_{12}) is necessary for the production of red blood cells.
  - Deficiency causes pernicious anemia and is seen mostly in strict vegetarians (B_{12} is found solely in foods of animal origin), and those with the absence of intrinsic factor needed for the absorption of B_{12}.
  - Sources include beef liver, shellfish, and fortified grains.

WATER-SOLUBLE VITAMINS AT A GLANCE			
VITAMINS	MAJOR ACTIONS	MAJOR SOURCES	DEFICIENCY
Ascorbic Acid Vitamin C	Antioxidant, tissue building, iron absorption	Citrus fruits and juices, vegetables	Scurvy, decreased iron absorption, bleeding gums
Thiamin B_1	Muscle energy, GI support, CV support	Meats, grains, legumes	Beriberi, altered digestion, CNS and CV problems
Riboflavin B_2	Growth, energy, tissue healing	Milk, meats, green leafy vegetables	Skin eruptions, cracked lips, red swollen tongue
Niacin B_3	Energy and protein metabolism/ cellular metabolism	Liver, nuts, legumes	Pellagra, skin lesions, GI and CNS symptoms, dementia

WATER-SOLUBLE VITAMINS AT A GLANCE			
VITAMINS	**MAJOR ACTIONS**	**MAJOR SOURCES**	**DEFICIENCY**
Pantothenic Acid B_5	Fatty acid metabolism, cell synthesis, heme production	Organ meats, egg yolk, avocados, broccoli	Anemia, CNS changes
Pyridoxine B_6	Cellular function, heme and neurotransmitter synthesis	Organ meats, grains	Anemia, CNS hyper-irritability, dermatitis
Folate	Synthesis of amino acids and hemoglobin, lower neural tube defect in fetus	Liver, green leafy vegetables, grains, legumes	Megaloblastic anemia, CNS disturbance
Cobalamin B_{12}	Hemoglobin Synthesis, fatty acid metabolism	Organ meats, clams, oysters, grains	Pernicious anemia, GI symptoms, poor muscle coordination

- Fat-Soluble Vitamins
  - All fat-soluble vitamins have the possibility for toxicity due to their ability to be stored in the body for long periods of time.
  - Absorption of fat-soluble vitamins is dependent on the body's ability to absorb dietary fat.
    - Fat digestion can be interrupted by any number of conditions, particularly those that affect the secretion of fat-converting enzymes, and conditions of the small intestine. Clients with cystic fibrosis, celiac disease, Crohn's disease, or intestinal bypasses are at risk for deficiencies.
  - Clients with liver disease should be careful not to take more than the daily recommendations of fat-soluble vitamins, as levels can build up.
  - Vitamin A (retinol, beta-carotene) contributes to vision health, tissue strength and growth, and embryonic development.
    - Care should be taken when administered to pregnant clients as some forms have teratogenic effects on the fetus.
    - Deficiency results in vision changes, xerophthalmia (dryness and thickening of the conjunctiva), and changes in epithelial cells (especially in the mouth and vaginal mucosa).
    - Food sources include fish liver oils, egg yolks, butter, cream, and dark yellow/orange fruits and vegetables (carrots, yams, apricots, squash, cantaloupe).
  - Vitamin D (calciferol) assists in the utilization of calcium and phosphorus, and aids in skin repair.
    - Sunlight enables the body to synthesize vitamin D.
    - Deficiency results in bone demineralization, and extreme deficiency results in rickets. Clients on glucocorticoid therapy may require additional amounts. Excess consumption may cause hypercalcemia.
    - Food sources include fortified milk, cod liver oil, and eggs.

- ○ Vitamin E (tocopherol) is an antioxidant that helps to preserve muscles and red blood cells, and maintains the myelin sheath that insulates nerve cells.
  - ■ Deficiency results in hemolytic anemia and affects the nerve fibers that influence walking and vision.
  - ■ Food sources include vegetable oils and certain nuts.
- ○ Vitamin K (menaquinone, phylloquinone) assists in blood clotting and bone maintenance.
  - ■ Deficiency results in increased bleeding time.
  - ■ Used as an antidote for excess anticoagulants (warfarin [Coumadin]).
  - ■ Vitamin K is found in some oils, liver, and green leafy vegetables (spinach, broccoli, cabbage). The typical American diet provides adequate amounts.

FAT-SOLUBLE VITAMINS AT A GLANCE			
VITAMINS	MAJOR ACTIONS	MAJOR SOURCES	DEFICIENCY
Vitamin A	Normal vision, tissue strength, growth and tissue healing	Orange/yellow colored foods, liver, dairy	Reduced night vision, dry/thick eyes, mucosa changes
Vitamin D	Maintain serum calcium and phosphorus, aid in bone development	Fish, fortified dairy products, sunlight	Low serum calcium, fragile bones, rickets
Vitamin E	Protects cells from oxidation	Vegetable oils, grains, nuts, dark green vegetables	Hemolytic anemia, CNS changes
Vitamin K	Normal blood clotting (prothrombin production), aids in bone metabolism	Green leafy vegetables, eggs, liver	Increased bleeding times

Minerals and Electrolytes

- • Minerals are available in an abundance of food sources and are used at every cellular level for metabolic exchanges.
  - ○ Minerals are divided into major and trace.
    - ■ Major minerals occur in larger amounts in the body.
    - ■ Trace elements, also called micronutrients, are required by the body in amounts of less than 100 mg/day.

- ○ The seven major minerals are: calcium, phosphorus, sodium, potassium, magnesium, chloride, and sulfur.

- ○ The ten trace elements are: iron, iodine, zinc, copper, manganese, chromium, cobalt, selenium, molybdenum, and fluoride.

- ○ Electrolytes are electrically charged minerals that cause physiological reactions that maintain homeostasis. The most commonly monitored electrolytes are: sodium, potassium, chloride, calcium, and magnesium. They affect many disease processes.

MAJOR MINERALS AT A GLANCE					
MINERAL	MAJOR ACTIONS	MAJOR SOURCES	SYMPTOMS OF DEFICIENCY	SYMPTOMS OF EXCESS	NURSING IMPLICATIONS
Sodium (Na)	Maintains fluid volume, allows muscle contractions, cardiovascular support	Table salt, added salts, processed foods, butter	Muscle cramping, cardiac changes	Fluid retention, hypertension, CVA	Monitor ECG, edema, and blood pressure.
Potassium (K)	Maintains fluid volume inside/outside cells, muscle action, blood pressure, cardiovascular support	Oranges, dried fruits, tomatoes, avocados, dried peas, meats, broccoli, bananas	Dysrhythmias, muscle cramps, confusion	Dysrhythmias (caused by supplements, potassium-sparing diuretics, ACE inhibitors, inadequate kidney function, diabetes)	Monitor ECG and muscle tone. PO tabs irritate the GI system. Give with meals.
Chloride (Cl)	Bonds to other minerals (esp. sodium) to facilitate cellular actions and reactions, fluid balance	Table salt	Rare	In concert with sodium, results in high blood pressure	Monitor sodium levels.
Calcium (Ca)	Bones/teeth, cardiovascular support, blood clotting, nerve transmission	Dairy, broccoli, kale, grains, egg yolks	Osteoporosis, tetany, Chvostek's and Trousseau's signs, ECG changes	Constipation, kidney stones	Monitor ECG and muscle tone. Give PO tabs with vitamin D.

MAJOR MINERALS AT A GLANCE					
MINERAL	MAJOR ACTIONS	MAJOR SOURCES	SYMPTOMS OF DEFICIENCY	SYMPTOMS OF EXCESS	NURSING IMPLICATIONS
Magnesium (Mg)	Bone nourishment, catalyst for many enzyme reactions, nerve/muscle function, CV support	Green leafy vegetables, nuts, grains, meat, milk	Weakness, dysrhythmias, tetany, seizure, reduced blood clotting, eclampsia	Diarrhea, kidney stones, decreased muscle control, CV changes	Incompatible with some antibiotics. Give PO, 2 hr apart.
Phosphorus (P)	Energy transfer of RNA/DNA, acid-base balance, bone and teeth formation	Dairy, peas, soft drinks, meat, eggs, some grains	Calcium level changes, muscle weakness	Skeletal porosity, decreased calcium levels, must stay in balance with calcium	Evaluate the use of antacids (note type) and the use of alcohol.
Sulfur (S)	A component of vitamin structure, by-product of protein metabolism	Dried fruits (dates, raisins, apples), meats, red and white wines	Only seen in severe protein malnourishment, found in all protein-containing foods	Toxicity has a very low risk	Sulfur levels are not usually monitored.

- ○ Select Trace Minerals
  - ■ Iodine is used for synthesis of thyroxine, the thyroid hormone that helps regulate metabolism. Iodine is taken up by the thyroid. When iodine is lacking, the thyroid gland enlarges creating a goiter.
    - □ Grown food sources vary widely and are dependent on the iodine content of the soil in which they were grown.
    - □ Seafood provides a good amount of iodine. Table salt in the United States is fortified with iodine, so deficiencies are not as prevalent.
    - □ The RDA is 100 to 150 mcg for adults.
  - ■ Iron is responsible for hemoglobin formation/function, cellular oxidation of glucose, antibody production, and collagen synthesis.
    - □ The body "scavenges" unused iron from dying red blood cells and stores it for later use.
    - □ Iron supplements may cause constipation, nausea, vomiting, diarrhea, and teeth discoloration (liquid form). They should be taken with food to avert gastrointestinal symptoms, and nurses should encourage fresh fruits, vegetables, and a high-fiber diet.
    - □ Supplements that are unneeded can become toxic.

□   Intramuscular injections are caustic to tissues and must be administered by Z-track method.

□   Food sources include organ meats, egg yolks, whole grains, and green leafy vegetables.

□   Vitamin C increases the absorption of iron.

□   The greatest need for iron is the newborn who is not breastfed, and for females during the menstruating years.

- Fluoride forms a bond with calcium and thus accumulates in calcified body tissue (bones and teeth). Water with added fluoride protects against dental cavities. Nurses should instruct clients who prefer to drink bottled water that they may need fluoride treatments from their dentist.

Water

- Water is the most basic of nutrients. The body can maintain itself for several days or weeks on its food stores of energy, but it cannot survive without water/hydration for more than a few days. Water makes up the largest portion of our total body weight and is crucial for all fluid and cellular functions.

  o   Fluid balance is essential for optimum health and bodily function.

  o   The balance of fluid is a dynamic process regulated by the release of hormones.

  o   To maintain a balance between intake and output, intake should approximate output. The minimum daily total fluid output in healthy adults is 1,500 mL. Therefore, the minimum daily amount of water needed is 1,500 mL.

  o   Under normal conditions, recommended adult fluid intake is 3 to 4 L/day for men and 2 to 3 L/day for women. It is recommended that half be from water.

  o   Additional hydration may be required for athletes, persons with fever/illness (vomiting, diarrhea), and those in hot climate conditions.

  o   Young children and older adults dehydrate more rapidly.

  o   Clients who cannot hold down fluid or must withhold fluids in preparation for a procedure may be hydrated with intravenous fluids.

  o   Water leaves the body via the kidneys, skin, lungs, and feces. The greatest elimination is through the kidneys. Other loss factors to be considered include: bleeding, vomiting, and rapid respirations. Persistent vomiting can quickly dehydrate a person.

  o   A balanced input/output ratio is almost 1:1. Nurses should consider the health status and individual needs of the client.

  o   Assessment for proper hydration should include skin turgor, mental status, orthostatic blood pressures, urine output and concentration, and moistness of mucous membranes.

  o   Thirst is a late sign of the need for hydration, especially in older adults.

  o   Some individuals may have an aversion to drinking water, and should be encouraged to explore other options (fresh fruits, fruit juices, flavored gelatin, frozen treats, soups).

  o   Caffeinated drinks have a diuretic effect and should not be substituted for other drinks.

CHAPTER 1: SOURCES OF NUTRITION

 Application Exercises

1. A nurse is educating a client who is taking iron supplements about foods which aid in iron absorption. Which of the following food choices indicates an understanding of the teaching?

    A. Baked potato

    B. Orange juice

    C. Milk

    D. Green beans

2. Clients who are unable to be out in the sunlight can increase their intake of vitamin D by consuming which of the following foods?

    A. Tacos and rice

    B. Hamburgers and fried potatoes

    C. Ham and Brussels sprouts

    D. Eggs and fortified milk

3. An older adult client is prescribed warfarin (Coumadin), an anticoagulant, due to a previous heart attack. Due to the clotting effects associated with vitamin K, the nurse should advise the client to limit the intake of which of the following food choices?

    A. Orange juice

    B. Broccoli

    C. Ice cream

    D. Chicken

4. Match the following electrolytes and minerals to their food sources.

ELECTROLYTE		FOOD
_____	Potassium	A. Nuts
_____	Sodium	B. Tomatoes
_____	Calcium	C. Canned soup
_____	Magnesium	D. Yogurt

5. Match the following health problems with their associated nutrient deficiencies.

HEALTH PROBLEM		NUTRIENT DEFICIENCY
_____	Dysrhythmias	A. Vitamin C
_____	Scurvy	B. Potassium
_____	Pernicious anemia	C. Folate
_____	Megaloblastic anemia	D. Vitamin B_{12}

CHAPTER 1: SOURCES OF NUTRITION

 Application Exercises Answer Key

1. A nurse is educating a client who is taking iron supplements about foods which aid in iron absorption. Which of the following food choices indicates an understanding of the teaching?

   A. Baked potato

   B. Orange juice

   C. Milk

   D. Green beans

   Vitamin C aids in the absorption of iron, and orange juice is a good source of vitamin C. A baked potato, green beans, and milk do not aid in the absorption of iron.

    NCLEX® Connection: Basic Care and Comfort, Nutrition and Oral Hydration

2. Clients who are unable to be out in the sunlight can increase their intake of vitamin D by consuming which of the following foods?

   A. Tacos and rice

   B. Hamburgers and fried potatoes

   C. Ham and Brussels sprouts

   D. Eggs and fortified milk

   Sunlight helps to synthesize vitamin D, so clients need egg yolks and fortified milk which are both good sources of vitamin D. The other food choices do not provide vitamin D.

    NCLEX® Connection: Health Promotion and Maintenance, Health Promotion/Disease Prevention

3. An older adult client is prescribed warfarin (Coumadin), an anticoagulant, due to a previous heart attack. Due to the clotting effects associated with vitamin K, the nurse should advise the client to limit the intake of which of the following food choices?

   A. Orange juice

   B. Broccoli

   C. Ice cream

   D. Chicken

   Broccoli is a green leafy vegetable and is a good source of vitamin K. The client should avoid excess vitamin K as it has a negative response to warfarin effects.

    NCLEX® Connection: Basic Care and Comfort, Nutrition and Oral Hydration

4. Match the following electrolytes and minerals to their food sources.

	ELECTROLYTE	FOOD
__B__	Potassium	A. Nuts
__C__	Sodium	B. Tomatoes
__D__	Calcium	C. Canned soup
__A__	Magnesium	D. Yogurt

(N) NCLEX® Connection: Basic Care and Comfort, Nutrition and Oral Hydration

5. Match the following health problems with their associated nutrient deficiencies.

	HEALTH PROBLEM	NUTRIENT DEFICIENCY
__B__	Dysrhythmias	A. Vitamin C
__A__	Scurvy	B. Potassium
__D__	Pernicious anemia	C. Folate
__C__	Megaloblastic anemia	D. Vitamin B_{12}

(N) NCLEX® Connection: Basic Care and Comfort, Nutrition and Oral Hydration

UNIT 1	PRINCIPLES OF NUTRITION
Chapter 2	Ingestion, Digestion, Absorption, and Metabolism

Overview

- Ingestion is the process of consuming food by the mouth, and moving through the digestive system.

- Digestion is a systemic process that includes the breakdown and absorption of nutrients.

- Absorption occurs as components of nutrients pass through the digestive system into the bloodstream and lymphatic system.

    o Medication absorption can be affected by food intake. It is important for nurses to be aware of food and medication absorption.

    o Nurses should assess liver and kidney functioning to determine adequacy prior to medication administration.

- Metabolism is the sum of all chemical processes that occur on a cellular level to maintain homeostasis. Nutrients from food must enter a cell in order for metabolism to occur.

    o Metabolism is comprised of two processes: catabolism, the breaking down of substances with the resultant release of energy, and anabolism, the use of energy to build or repair substances.

    o Energy nutrients are metabolized to provide carbon dioxide, water, heat, and adenosine triphosphate (ATP).

    o Excess energy nutrients are stored: Glucose is converted to glycogen and stored in the liver and muscle tissue; surplus glucose is converted to fat; glycerol and fatty acids are reassembled into triglycerides and stored in adipose tissue; and amino acids make body proteins. The liver removes excess amino acids and utilizes the residue to form glucose or store it as fat.

    o Body cells first use available ATP for growth and repair, then utilize glycogen and stored fat.

Metabolic Rate

- Metabolic rate refers to the speed at which food energy is burned. Basal metabolic rate (BMR), also called resting energy expenditure (REE), refers to the amount of energy used when the body is at rest.

- BMR is primarily affected by lean body mass and hormones. Body surface area, age, and gender are minor factors as they relate to body mass index (BMI).

FACTORS AFFECTING BMR	INCREASE	DECREASE
Lean, muscular body build	X	
Short, overweight body build		X
Starvation/malnutrition		X
Exposure to extreme cold	X	
Prolonged stress	X	
Rapid growth periods (infancy, puberty)	X	
Pregnancy	X	
Lactation	X	
Over 60 years of age		X
Physical conditioning	X	

- In general, men have a higher metabolic rate than women because of their higher amount of body muscle and decreased amount of fat.

- Thyroid function tests may be used as an indirect measure of BMR.

- Acute stress causes an increase in metabolism, blood glucose levels, and protein catabolism.

  o The major nutritional concern during acute stress is protein deficiency as stress hormones break down protein at a very rapid rate.

  o Protein deficiency increases the risk of complications from severe trauma or critical illness (skin breakdown, delayed wound healing, infections, organ failure, ulcers, impaired drug tolerance).

  o Protein requirements may be increased to 2.0 g/kg of body weight depending on the client's age and prior nutritional status.

  o Inadequate protein intake prevents the body from adapting to physiologic stress.

- Alcohol is more quickly metabolized and absorbed than nutrients. Alcohol metabolism changes liver cells and reduces the liver's ability to metabolize fat. Alcoholics suffer from protein-energy malnutrition, generally consuming about 75% of energy requirements resulting in low to normal albumin levels.

- Any catabolic illness (surgery, extensive burns) increases the body's requirement for calories to meet the demands of an increased BMR.

THE FOLLOWING CONDITIONS AFFECT METABOLIC RATE:		
CONDITION	INCREASES METABOLISM	DECREASES METABOLISM
Fever	X	
Involuntary muscle tremors, as in shivering or Parkinson's	X	
Hypothyroidism		X
Hyperthyroidism	X	
Cancer	X	
Cardiac failure	X	
Some anemias	X	
Hypertension	X	
Chronic obstructive pulmonary disease	X	
Burns	X	
Surgery/wound healing	X	
HIV/AIDS	X	

SEVERAL MEDICATIONS AFFECT THE BODY'S RATE OF METABOLISM:		
MEDICATION	INCREASES BMR	DECREASES BMR
Somatropin (Genotropin)	X	
Prednisone (Deltasone)	X	
Hydrocortisone (Cortef)	X	
Epinephrine hydrochloride	X	
Levothyroxine sodium (Synthroid)	X	
Glucagon	X	
Ephedrine sulfate	X	
Amitriptyline (Elavil)		X

Nitrogen Balance

- Nitrogen balance refers to the difference between the daily intake and excretion of nitrogen. It is also an indicator of tissue integrity. A healthy adult experiencing a stable weight is in nitrogen equilibrium, also known as neutral nitrogen balance.

- Positive nitrogen balance indicates that the intake of nitrogen exceeds excretion. Specifically, the body builds more tissue than it breaks down. This normally occurs during periods of growth: infancy, childhood, adolescence, pregnancy, and lactation.

- Negative nitrogen balance indicates that the excretion of nitrogen exceeds intake. The individual is receiving insufficient protein and the body is breaking down more tissue than it is building, as seen in illness, trauma, immobility, and malnutrition.

- Clinical signs of negative nitrogen balance are not immediately evident. Decreased muscle tissue, impaired organ function, and increased susceptibility to infection are late signs.

Nursing Assessments/Data Collection

- Weight and history of recent weight patterns

- Medical history for diseases that affect metabolism and nitrogen balance

- Extent of traumatic injuries, as appropriate

- Fluid and electrolyte status

- Abnormal laboratory values: albumin, transferrin, glucose, and creatinine

- Clinical signs of malnutrition: pitting edema, hair loss, and wasted appearance

- Medication side effects that can affect nutrition

- Usual 24 hr diet intake

- Use of nutritional supplements, vitamins, and minerals

- Use of alcohol, caffeine, and nicotine

Nursing Interventions

- Provide adequate calories and high quality protein. Strategies to increase protein and caloric content include:

  o Add skim milk powder to milk (double strength milk).

  o Substitute whole milk for water in recipes.

  o Add cheese, peanut butter, chopped hard-cooked eggs, or yogurt to foods.

  o Dip meats in eggs or milk and coat with bread crumbs before cooking.

- Monitor food intake.

- Monitor fluid intake and output.

CHAPTER 2: INGESTION, DIGESTION, ABSORPTION, AND METABOLISM

(A) Application Exercises

1. Explain why a client experiencing a fever requires an increased calorie intake.

2. A nurse is caring for a client on the medical surgical unit. She understands that certain disease processes affect metabolic demands. Which of the following diseases decreases metabolism?

    A. Cardiac failure

    B. Cancer

    C. Hypothyroidism

    D. Chronic obstructive pulmonary disease

3. A nurse is caring for a malnourished surgical client. Discuss the rationale for why the client is at risk for delayed wound healing.

4. List the appropriate food choices for a client who is immobilized because of bilateral femur and tibia fractures.

CHAPTER 2: INGESTION, DIGESTION, ABSORPTION, AND METABOLISM

 Application Exercises Answer Key

1. Explain why a client experiencing a fever requires an increased calorie intake.

A fever increases metabolic demand. Thus, more calories should be ingested.

 NCLEX® Connection: Health Promotion and Maintenanace, Health Promotion/Disease Prevention

2. A nurse is caring for a client on the medical surgical unit. She understands that certain disease processes affect metabolic demands. Which of the following diseases decreases metabolism?

    A. Cardiac failure

    B. Cancer

    C. Hypothyroidism

    D. Chronic obstructive pulmonary disease

Hypothyroidism causes a decreased metabolic demand. Cancer, cardiac failure, and chronic obstructive pulmonary disease increase the metabolic demand. Thus, more calories are indicated.

 NCLEX® Connection: Health Promotion and Maintenance, Health Promotion/Disease Prevention

3. A nurse is caring for a malnourished surgical client. Discuss the rationale for why the client is at risk for delayed wound healing.

Protein deficiency (malnutrition, stress of surgery) increases the risk for delayed wound healing.

 NCLEX® Connection: Basic Care and Comfort, Nutrition and Oral Hydration

4. List the appropriate food choices for a client who is immobilized because of bilateral femur and tibia fractures.

Nutrient-dense, high-quality protein foods are appropriate (milk shakes, yogurt, eggs, turkey, chicken, lean beef, orange juice, strawberries, whole grains, dark green leafy vegetables).

NCLEX® Connection: Basic Care and Comfort, Nutrition and Oral Hydration

UNIT 1	PRINCIPLES OF NUTRITION
Chapter 3	Nutrition Assessment

Overview

- Nurses play a key role in assessing the nutritional needs of clients.

  - Nurses monitor and intervene with clients requiring acute and chronic nutritional care.

  - The family's nutritional habits must be considered and incorporated into a client's individual plan of care.

  - Nurses should take an active role in surveying and teaching community groups regarding nutrition.

- A collaborative multidisciplinary approach provides the best outcomes for the client.

  - Physical assessment data is collected by providers and nurses.

  - Comprehensive nutritional assessments are completed by registered dieticians.

  - Nurses monitor and evaluate interventions provided to clients.

- A client's physical appearance can be deceiving.

  - A client with a healthy weight and appearance can be malnourished.

  - Cultural, social, and physical norms must be part of a client's assessment.

- Even with adequate client education, personal preferences can be an overriding factor to successful nutritional balance.

Diet History

- A diet history is an assessment of usual foods, fluids, and supplements. Components include:

  - Time, type, and amount of food eaten for breakfast, lunch, dinner, and snacks.

  - Time, type, and amount of fluids consumed throughout the day including water, health drinks, coffee/tea, carbonated beverages, and beverages with caffeine.

  - Type, amount, and frequency of "special foods" (celebration foods, movie foods).

  - Typical preparation of foods and fluids (coffee with sugar, fried foods).

  - Number of meals eaten away from home (at work or school).

  - Type of normal diet (lacto-ovo-vegetarian, 2 g sodium/low-fat diet).

- Foods avoided due to allergy or preference.

- Frequency and dose/amount of medications or nutritional supplements taken daily.

- Satisfaction with diet over a specified time frame (last 3 months, year).

Assessment Tools to Determine Nutritional Status

- A physical assessment is performed by the provider or nurse to identify indicators of inadequate nutrition. However, signs and symptoms may be caused by other processes, diseases, or conditions. Symptoms include:

  - Hair that is dry or brittle, or skin that has dry patches.

  - Poor wound healing or sores.

  - Lack of subcutaneous fat or muscle wasting.

  - Abnormal cardiovascular measurements (heart rate and rhythm, blood pressure).

  - General weakness or impaired coordination.

- Anthropometric Tools

  - Weight

    - Weigh at the same time of day wearing similar clothing to ensure accurate weight readings.

    - Daily fluctuations are generally indicative of water weight changes.

    - Percentage weight change calculation (weight change over a specified time):

      $$\frac{\text{usual weight} - \text{present weight}}{\text{usual weight}} \times 100$$

      - 1% to 2% in 1 week indicates a significant weight loss.

      - 7.5% in 3 months indicates a significant weight loss.

    - "Ideal" body weight based on height (plus or minus 10% depending on frame size).

      - For males, 48 kg (106 lb) for the first 152 cm (5 ft) of height, and 2.7 kg (6 lb) for each additional 2.5 cm (1 inch).

      - For females, 45 kg (100 lb) for the first 152 cm (5 ft) of height, and 2.3 kg (5 lb) for each additional 2.5 cm (1 inch).

  - Height

    - Young children and infants should be measured lying on a firm, flat surface.

- o Body Mass Index (BMI)
    - Normal/healthy weight is indicated by a BMI of 18.5 to 24.9.
    - Overweight is defined as an increased body weight in relation to height. It is indicated by a BMI of 25 to 29.9.
    - Obesity is an excess amount of body fat. It indicated by a BMI greater than or equal to 30.
    - BMI = weight (kg) ÷ height (m²)
- Clinical Values
    - o Fluid Intake and Output (I&O)
    - o Normal daily range
    - o Adults 2,000 to 3,000 milliliters (2 to 3 liters) per day
    - o Total average output 2,300 to 2,600 milliliters per day
    - o Protein levels are commonly measured by serum albumin levels. Many non-nutritional factors (injury or renal disease), interfere with this measure for protein malnutrition.
    - o Prealbumin (thyroxin-binding protein) is a more susceptible measure used to assess critically ill clients who are at a higher risk for malnutrition. This test reflects more acute changes as opposed to gradual changes.

CLINICAL LABORATORY TESTS	NORMAL	MODERATE DEPLETION
Albumin	3.5 to 5.0 g/dL	2.1 to 2.7 g/dL
Prealbumin	23 to 43 mg/dL	5 to 9 mg/dL

Risk Factors for Inadequate Nutrition

- Biophysical Factors
    - o Medical disease/conditions/treatment/ (hypertension, HIV/AIDS, surgery)
    - o Genetic predisposition (lactose intolerance, osteoporosis)
    - o Age
- Psychological Factors
    - o Mental illness (clinical depression)
    - o Excessive stress
    - o Negative self-concept
    - o Use of comfort foods

- Socioeconomic Factors

  - Poverty

  - Alcohol and drug abuse

  - Fad or "special" diets

  - Food preferences: cultural, ethnic, or religious

- Impact of Risk Factors on Nutritional Status

  - The following are examples of how risk factors can affect nutritional status.

    - A client is edematous and requires treatment with a diuretic and low-sodium diet. Diuretics can cause sodium and potassium imbalances. A low-sodium diet may be unappetizing and cause inadequate consumption. Salt substitutes in moderation may be used to add flavor.

    - Osteoporosis has many modifiable risk factors (calcium and vitamin D intake, inactive lifestyle, cigarette smoking, alcohol intake). Altering these risk factors can affect nutritional status in a positive manner.

    - Poor self-concept may cause a client to avoid needed foods and nutrients, or to overeat.

    - A client practices a traditional cultural foodway (see Chapter 5) that is high in meat proteins and fats. These foods can put the client's nutritional status at risk.

CHAPTER 3: NUTRITION ASSESSMENT

(A) Application Exercises

Scenario: An adolescent female client recently broke her wrist and is at the eating disorder clinic for a twice-a-week appointment. The nurse smells a strong odor of cigarette smoke on her clothes. Her slender mother anxiously states, "The ER doctor said the cast weighs 10 oz. She is now using her broken wrist as an excuse to spend more time in her bed or on the couch." She currently weighs 50 kg (110 lb) and is 170 cm (67 in) tall.

1. Determine the client's BMI.

2. Outline what the nurse should teach the client regarding her risk for osteoporosis.

3. Which of the following laboratory values suggests moderate protein deficiency for an acutely ill client?

    A. Serum albumin, 3.5 g/dL

    B. Serum prealbumin, 5 mg/dL

    C. Serum albumin, 4.5 g/dL

    D. Serum prealbumin, 10 mg/dL

4. A nurse is performing a nutritional assessment on a client. Which of the following client findings is suggestive of malnutrition? (Select all that apply.)

    _____ Poor wound healing

    _____ Dry hair

    _____ Blood pressure 130/80 mm Hg

    _____ Weak hand grips

    _____ Impaired coordination

5. Describe a recording tool that a client should use to gather information needed to analyze his nutritional intake.

6. Develop one specific question to ask a client for each of the following diet history components.

DIET HISTORY COMPONENT	CLIENT QUESTION
Time, type, and amount of food eaten for breakfast, lunch, dinner, and snacks	
Time, type, and amount of fluids consumed throughout the day (water, health drinks, coffee/tea, carbonated beverages, beverages with caffeine)	
Type, amount, and frequency of "special foods" (celebration foods, movie foods)	
Typical preparation of foods and fluids (coffee with sugar, fried foods)	
Number of meals eaten away from home	
Type of normal diet (lacto-ovo-vegetarian, 2 g sodium/low-fat diet)	
Foods avoided due to allergy or preference	
Frequency and dose/amount of medications or nutritional supplements taken daily	
Satisfaction with diet over a specified time frame (last 3 months, year)	

CHAPTER 3: NUTRITION ASSESSMENT

 Application Exercises Answer Key

Scenario: An adolescent female client recently broke her wrist and is at the eating disorder clinic for a twice-a-week appointment. The nurse smells a strong odor of cigarette smoke on her clothes. Her slender mother anxiously states, "The ER doctor said the cast weighs 10 oz. She is now using her broken wrist as an excuse to spend more time in her bed or on the couch." She currently weighs 50 kg (110 lb) and is 170 cm (67 in) tall.

1. Determine the client's BMI.

$$170 \text{ cm} = 1.7 \text{ m}$$

$$BMI = \frac{\text{weight (kg)}}{\text{height (m}^2)}$$

$$= \frac{50}{1.7^2} = \frac{50}{2.89} = 17.3$$

 NCLEX® Connection: Health Promotion and Maintenance, Health and Wellness

2. Outline what the nurse should teach the client regarding her risk for osteoporosis.

Osteoporosis runs in families and the client's mother is slender. Therefore, the client might have an increased risk for osteoporosis.

Cigarette smoking may increase the incidence of osteoporosis, or make it worse. Smoking cessation should be encouraged with a community or medical referral.

There is an increased risk for osteoporosis due to inactivity and weight-bearing exercises should be planned.

Weight loss can cause a decreased intake of dietary calcium and vitamin D. The client's diet should be evaluated for a possible increase in dietary calcium and vitamin D.

NCLEX® Connection: Health Promotion and Maintenance, High Risk Behaviors

3. Which of the following laboratory values suggests moderate protein deficiency for an acutely ill client?

> A. Serum albumin, 3.5 g/dL
> B. **Serum prealbumin, 5 mg/dL**
> C. Serum albumin, 4.5 g/dL
> D. Serum prealbumin, 10 mg/dL

> A serum prealbumin level of 5 mg/dL is indicative of a moderate depletion of protein. The serum prealbumin test, also known as thyroxin-binding protein, is the most sensitive to acute changes in protein nutrition. Serum albumin levels reflect slow changes in serum protein levels, not acute serum protein changes. A serum albumin of 3.5 g/dl and 4.5 g/dL is within the normal range. A serum prealbumin of 10 mg/dL is indicative of a mild depletion of protein.

 NCLEX® Connection: Basic Care and Comfort, Nutrition and Oral Hydration

4. A nurse is performing a nutritional assessment on a client. Which of the following client findings is suggestive of malnutrition? (Select all that apply.)

> | X | **Poor wound healing** |
> | X | **Dry hair** |
> | | Blood pressure 130/80 mm Hg |
> | X | **Weak hand grips** |
> | X | **Impaired coordination** |

> Poor wound healing, dry hair, weak hand grips, and impaired coordination describe changes reflective of malnutrition. A blood pressure value of 130/80 mm Hg is a normal cardiovascular finding and is not associated with malnutrition.

 NCLEX® Connection: Health Promotion and Maintenance, High Risk Behaviors

5. Describe a recording tool that a client should use to gather information needed to analyze his nutritional intake.

> Diet log: Record all foods, times, and portions of items consumed in the last 3 days, week, or month.

> Diet recall: List all foods and fluids consumed in the past 24 hr.

 NCLEX® Connection: Basic Care and Comfort, Nutrition and Oral Hydration

6. Develop one specific question to ask a client for each of the following diet history components.

DIET HISTORY COMPONENT	CLIENT QUESTION
Time, type, and amount of food eaten for breakfast, lunch, dinner, and snacks	"Tell me what time you usually eat breakfast and what you eat. I'll give you an example: I typically eat at 7 a.m. and have either two pieces of buttered toast and 8 oz of orange juice, or 1 cup of hot oatmeal with half a banana and 10 oz of non-fat milk."
Time, type, and amount of fluids consumed throughout the day (water, health drinks, coffee/tea, carbonated beverages, beverages with caffeine)	"Describe what type of fluid you drink throughout the day and what size of glass or cup you use." "Tell me what you drink for breakfast, lunch, and dinner." "How many cups of coffee do you drink a day?" "Do you drink carbonated beverages?"
Type, amount, and frequency of "special foods" (celebration foods, movie foods)	"When you go to the movie theater, what do you buy to eat and drink? What size do you buy?" "When you are celebrating something special with your family, what special foods do you eat?"
Typical preparation of foods and fluids (coffee with sugar, fried foods)	"Do you like your meat and chicken dishes baked, broiled, pan fried, deep-fat fried, or barbecued?" "Do you salt your foods when you eat or cook?" "How much sugar do you use each day?"
Number of meals eaten away from home	"How many times do you go out to eat each week?" "Do you pack your lunch from home or buy your lunch at or near your workplace?"
Type of normal diet (lacto-ovo-vegetarian, 2 g sodium/low-fat diet)	"Do you eat a special diet, like a low-fat diet?" "Do you eat both vegetables and meat?" "Are you a vegan?" "Do you eat Kosher?"
Foods avoided due to allergy or preference	"Are there any foods that you are allergic to?" "Does any food give you a rash, make you itch, or cause your tongue or throat to swell?" "Is there any type of food that you will not eat? What is it?"
Frequency and dose/amount of medications or nutritional supplements taken daily	"Please list the time and amount of all medications that you use daily." "Do you use any supplements, health food tablets, herbs, or diet supplements? Which ones and how often?"
Satisfaction with diet over a specified time frame (last 3 months, year)	"Are you happy with the way you have been eating for the last 3 months?" "Have you changed the foods you eat over the last year? Why?"

(N) **NCLEX® Connection: Health Promotion and Maintenance, High Risk Behaviors**

UNIT 1	PRINCIPLES OF NUTRITION
Chapter 4	Guidelines for Healthy Eating

Overview

- Nutrition is vital to maintaining optimal health. Healthy food choices and controlling weight are important steps in promoting health and reducing risk factors for disease.

- Nurses should encourage favorable nutritional choices, and can serve as informational resources for clients regarding guidelines for healthy eating.

- Established guidelines for healthy eating that clients and nurses can refer to include the Dietary Guidelines for Americans and *MyPyramid* (the Food Guide Pyramid), along with a number of condition or system specific guidelines.

The Dietary Guidelines for Americans

- The U.S. Department of Agriculture (USDA) and the U.S. Department of Health and Human Services (HHS) publish the Dietary Guidelines for Americans jointly every 5 years. It provides research-based advice concerning food intake and physical activity for healthy Americans over 2 years of age. The updates can be found at http://www.cnpp.usda.gov/DietaryGuidelines.htm or http://www.health.gov/dietaryguidelines/

- The Dietary Guidelines for Americans advocates healthy food selections: a variety of fiber-rich fruits and vegetables, whole grains, low-fat or fat-free milk and milk products, lean meats, poultry, fish, legumes, eggs, and nuts. Recommendations include:

  ○ Balance energy intake with energy expenditure by selecting a wide variety of foods, and limiting saturated and transaturated fat, sugars, sodium, and alcohol.

  ○ Establish exercise routines to promote cardiovascular health, muscle strength and endurance, and psychological well-being.

  ○ Increase consumption of fiber-rich fruits and vegetables to a minimum of five servings per day in order to decrease risk factors for certain cancers. The vitamin and mineral content of these foods may decrease the risk of DNA damage and cancer.

  ○ Choose monounsaturated and polyunsaturated fats from fish, lean meats, nuts, and vegetable oils. Fat intake may average 30% of total caloric intake with less than 10% from saturated fats.

  ○ Limit sugar and starchy foods to decrease the occurrence of dental caries.

  ○ Consume less than 2,300 mg of salt per day (about 1 tsp) by limiting most canned and processed foods. Prepare foods without adding salt.

- o Drink alcohol in moderation: up to one drink per day for women and two per day for men, as appropriate. Certain medical conditions, medication therapies, and physical activities preclude the use of alcohol.

- o Follow food safety guidelines when preparing, cooking, and storing food. Avoid consumption of raw eggs and unpasteurized milk and juices.

The Food Guide Pyramid

- • The USDA sponsors a Web site that promotes healthy food choices balanced with physical activity (www.MyPyramid.gov). The pyramid is based on the current USDA dietary guidelines, and is a tool to help individuals identify daily amounts of foods based on criteria (age, gender, activity level). The five food groups represented are grains, vegetables, fruit, dairy, and meat and beans.

View Media Supplement: Food Pyramid (Image)

FOOD GROUP	RECOMMENDED SERVINGS (2,000 CALORIE DIET)	REPRESENTATIVE FOODS
Grains	6 oz	Whole grain breads, cereals, rice, pasta One slice bread = 1 oz 1 cup cereal = 1 oz ½ cup cooked pasta = 1 oz
Vegetables	2 ½ cups (raw, cooked, or juice)	Broccoli, carrots, dry beans and peas, corn, potatoes, tomatoes
Fruits	2 cups	One small banana, orange, ¼ cup dried apricots
Milk	3 cups (2 cups for children ages two to eight)	2% milk, yogurt, cheese
Meat and Beans	5 ½ oz	Beef, poultry, eggs, kidney beans, soy beans, fish, nuts and seeds, peanut butter One small chicken breast = 3 oz One egg = 1 oz ¼ cup dried cooked beans = 1 oz
Oils	6 tsp	Canola oil, corn oil, olive oil, nuts, olives, some fish

- • The steps of the Food Pyramid can serve as a reminder to balance calorie intake with suitable activity:

- o Engage in physical activity for 30 min most days of the week.

- o In order to prevent weight gain, 60 min of moderate intensity physical activity per day may be necessary.

- o Children and teenagers should be physically active for 60 min/day.

Strategies for Weight Control

- Assess body mass index (BMI) to determine an estimate of overall body fat. Normal BMI range is 18.5 to 24.9. A BMI of 30 or more places an adult at an increased risk for cardiovascular disease, hypertension, type 2 diabetes mellitus, and dyslipidemia.

- A physically fit person has strength, flexibility, cardiopulmonary endurance, and muscular endurance.

- Encourage increased physical activity as the first step to becoming physically fit, and for the maintenance of energy balance. Although aerobic exercise burns more calories, 20 min of low and moderate intensity exercise burns more fat.

- To lose 1 lb of body fat per week, an adult must have an energy deficit of 3,500 calories (500 cal/day).

- Based on the Food Pyramid, adequate nutrition maintains energy balance, while increased physical activity promotes and maintains weight loss.

- Monitor progress toward a healthy lifestyle through a daily log of food intake and physical activity.

Food Labels

- The Food and Drug Administration (FDA) requires certain information be included with packaged foods and beverages. The information is included on the Nutrition Facts label or food label, which is often a boxed label found on foods and beverages. Food labels must include single serving size, number of servings in the package, percent of daily values, and the amount of each nutrient in one serving.

- Nutrients included on the food label:
  - Calories
  - Calories from Fat
  - Total Fat
  - Saturated Fat
  - Trans Fat
  - Cholesterol
  - Sodium
  - Total Carbohydrates
  - Dietary Fiber
  - Sugars
  - Protein
  - Vitamin A
  - Vitamin C
  - Calcium
  - Iron

- Clients should be taught to read food labels properly to ensure individual nutritional needs are met, and healthy choices are made.

 **View Media Supplement:** Understanding Food Labels (Video)

Strategies for Promotion of Specific Areas of Health

- Healthy Hearts

  - Limit saturated fat to 10% of calories and cholesterol to 300 mg/day.

  - For individuals with elevated low density lipoproteins (LDL), the American Heart Association (AHA) recommends increasing monounsaturated fats and soluble fiber.

- Healthy Nervous Systems

  - Normal functioning of the nervous system depends on adequate levels of the B-complex vitamins, especially thiamin, niacin, and vitamins B_6 and B_{12}.

  - Calcium and sodium are important regulators of nerve responses. Consuming the recommended servings from the grain and dairy food groups provides these nutrients.

- Healthy Bones

  - Consuming the recommended servings from the Food Pyramid's dairy group supplies the calcium, magnesium, and phosphorus necessary for bone formation, and vitamin D that aids in the absorption of calcium and phosphorus.

  - Weight-bearing physical activity is essential to decrease the risk of osteoporosis.

- Good Bowel Function

  - Normal bowel functioning depends on adequate fluid intake and 25 g/day of fiber for women, and 38 g/day for men.

  - The minimum number of servings from the Food Pyramid's fruit, vegetable, and grain food groups (specifically whole grains) provides the essential nutrients.

- Cancer Prevention

  - A well-balanced diet using the Food Pyramid and a healthy weight are guidelines to prevent cancer.

  - Increase high-fiber plant-based foods.

  - Limit saturated and polyunsaturated fat, while emphasizing foods with monounsaturated fat or omega-3 fatty acids (nuts and fish).

  - Limit sodium intake.

  - Avoid excess alcohol intake.

  - Include regular physical activity.

CHAPTER 4: GUIDELINES FOR HEALTHY EATING

 Application Exercises

Scenario: A nurse is discussing nutrition with a client who has a BMI of 34 and is receptive to health education. The client recorded the following menu for three breakfasts last week:

Two scrambled eggs

Two slices of bacon

One slice of toast with butter

½ cup orange juice

1. What recommendations should be shared with the client in regard to the Dietary Guidelines for Americans?

2. What teaching should be provided concerning the client's BMI and physical activity?

3. To decrease risk factors for common health problems, nurses should encourage an increased intake of which foods?

4. What is the recommended daily fat intake?

5. What is the recommended daily intake of salt?

6. Match the following:

_____ Healthy heart	A. Calcium, vitamin D, and weight-bearing exercise
_____ Healthy bones	B. Fluid, fiber, and exercise
_____ Good bowel function	C. Limit saturated fat to 10% of total caloric intake

CHAPTER 4: GUIDELINES FOR HEALTHY EATING

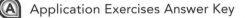 Application Exercises Answer Key

Scenario: A nurse is discussing nutrition with a client who has a BMI of 34 and is receptive to health education. The client recorded the following menu for three breakfasts last week:

Two scrambled eggs

Two slices of bacon

One slice of toast with butter

½ cup orange juice

1. What recommendations should be shared with the client in regard to the Dietary Guidelines for Americans?

The client may need to reduce saturated fat in the diet. Egg yolks, bacon, and butter are all high in saturated fat and cholesterol. The client did have a high-quality protein (egg white) and one serving of fruit.

 NCLEX® Connection: Health Promotion and Maintenance, Disease Prevention

2. What teaching should be provided concerning the client's BMI and physical activity?

Normal BMI range is 18.5 to 24.9. The client is at risk for cardiovascular disease, hypertension, elevated triglycerides with a low concentration of high density lipoproteins, and diabetes. The client should start an exercise program that will include low- to moderate-intensity exercise each day, after consulting with a health care provider.

 NCLEX® Connection: Health Promotion and Maintenance, Health and Wellness

3. To decrease risk factors for common health problems, nurses should encourage an increased intake of which foods?

High-fiber foods (fruits and vegetables) should be encouraged. The nurse should also encourage limiting saturated fat intake.

 NCLEX® Connection: Health Promotion and Maintenance, Health Promotion/Disease Prevention

4. What is the recommended daily fat intake?

Fat intake should comprise 30% of total caloric intake with less than 10% from saturated fat.

 NCLEX® Connection: Health Promotion and Maintenance, Health and Wellness

5. What is the recommended daily intake of salt?

Less than 2,300 mg/day.

 NCLEX® Connection: Health Promotion and Maintenance, Health and Wellness

6. Match the following:

C	Healthy heart	A. Calcium, vitamin D, and weight-bearing exercise
A	Healthy bones	B. Fluid, fiber, and exercise
B	Good bowel function	C. Limit saturated fat to 10% of total caloric intake

 NCLEX® Connection: Health Promotion and Maintenance, Health and Wellness

UNIT 1	PRINCIPLES OF NUTRITION
Chapter 5	Food Safety

Overview

- Food safety is an important concept in nursing. It is essential to provide clients with the necessary education regarding food safety and food-medication interactions.

- Food safety concerns (preventing aspiration of food, reducing the risk of foodborne illness, assessing for food allergies, understanding food-medication interactions.)

Food Safety

- Ingestion of food poses a risk of aspiration in some circumstances.

  - To minimize the risk of aspiration, food should only be consumed by individuals who are conscious and have an intact gag or swallow reflex.

  - For clients with a known risk of aspiration (following a stroke or a procedure involving anesthesia of the esophagus), it is important for nurses to monitor the client's ability to swallow prior to eating.

- Food safety requires:

  - Proper food storage.

  - Proper handling.

  - Proper preparation guidelines.

- Proper food storage guidelines include:

  - Fresh meat: 1 to 2 days at 40° F or cooler.

  - Fish: 1 to 2 days at 40° F or cooler.

  - Dairy products: Store in the refrigerator for 5 days for milk, and 3 to 4 weeks for cheese.

  - Eggs: Store in the refrigerator for 3 weeks in shell, and 1 week for hard-boiled.

  - Fruits and vegetables: Keep for 3 to 5 days; citrus fruits and apples, 1 week or longer.

  - Pantry items: Store in a dry, dark place at room temperature.

  - Canned goods: Store 1 year or longer at room temperature.

- Proper handling is simple:

  ○ Wash hands and surfaces frequently, and before handling food.

  ○ Separate foods to avoid cross-contamination.

- Proper preparation guidelines include:

  ○ Cook food to the proper temperature (roasts and steaks, 145° F; chicken, 180° F; ground beef, 160° F).

  ○ Products that contain eggs must be cooked to 160° F.

- It is important to understand packaging labels:

  ○ Sell-by date is the final recommended day of sale.

  ○ Use-by date is how long the product will maintain top quality.

  ○ Expiration date is the final day the product should be used or consumed.

Foodborne Illness

- Foodborne illnesses occur due to improper storage of food products and unsafe handling. In order to decrease the incidence of foodborne illnesses, primary education should be conducted by nurses. Proper handing and preparation is simple and includes performing frequent hand hygiene. It is important to refrigerate food products when necessary, and to avoid cross contamination when preparing food. Food should be heated to adequate temperatures to kill unwanted bacteria. These basic principles can prevent the occurrence of foodborne illnesses.

- Foodborne illnesses pose the greatest risk to children, older adults, and immunocompromised and pregnant clients.

- Common Foodborne Illnesses

  ○ Salmonella

    ▪ Salmonella occurs due to undercooked or raw meat, poultry, eggs, fish, fruit, and dairy products. Common symptoms include headache, fever, abdominal cramping, diarrhea, nausea, and vomiting. This condition can be fatal.

  ○ Escherichia coli 0157:H7

    ▪ Raw or undercooked meat, especially hamburger can cause this foodborne pathogen. Symptoms include severe abdominal pain and diarrhea.

  ○ Shigella

    ▪ Poor personal hygiene and improper hand hygiene commonly cause Shigella. Food sources include dairy products and salads. Symptoms are characterized by diarrhea.

- ○ Listeria monocytogenes

  - ■ Soft cheese, raw milk products, undercooked poultry, meat, seafood, and vegetables are sources that can cause the illness. Listeria monocytogenes causes significant problems for newborns, pregnant clients, and immunocompromised clients. Onset of symptoms include sudden fever, diarrhea, headache, back pains, and abdominal discomfort. It can lead to stillbirth or miscarriage in the pregnant client.

Food Allergies

- Nutritional assessments include identification of food allergies.

  - ○ Milk, peanuts, fish, eggs, and wheat are the most common food allergies reported by clients.

  - ○ Common reactions and reportable symptoms may include nausea, vomiting, dyspnea, itching, dizziness, and headache. Some reactions are severe and can cause anaphylaxis.

Food-Medication Interactions

- Foods and medications can interact in the body in ways that alter the intended action of medications. The composition and timing of food intake should be considered in relation to medication use.

- Foods can alter the absorption of medications:

  - ○ Decreased absorption: Food can decrease the rate and extent of absorption.

    - ■ Reducing the rate of absorption alters the onset of peak effects.

    - ■ Reducing the extent of absorption reduces the intended effect of the medication.

- Some medications cause gastric irritation. It is important to take certain medications with food to avoid gastric upset (ibuprofen [Advil, Motrin], some antibiotics, amoxicillin [Amoxil], and some anti-depressants, bupropion [Wellbutrin]).

- Certain foods alter the metabolism/actions of medications:

  - ○ Grapefruit juice interferes with the metabolism of many medications resulting in an increased serum level of the medication.

  - ○ Consumption of foods high in vitamin K (green leafy vegetables, eggs, liver) can decrease the anticoagulant effects of warfarin (Coumadin).

  - ○ Foods high in protein, amino acids, and vitamin B_6 can increase the metabolism of the anti-Parkinson's medication levodopa (L-dopa, Sinemet), which decreases the duration of its therapeutic effects.

  - ○ Licorice can cause hyperkalemia (elevated serum potassium). Excess ingestion can be dangerous for clients taking digoxin (Lanoxin), stimulant laxatives, some beta-blockers, ACE inhibitors, some calcium channel blockers, MAO inhibitors, and spironolactone.

- o Tyramine is a naturally occurring amine that is found in many foods and has hypertensive effects similar to other amines (norepinephrine). Tyramine is metabolized by monoamine oxidase (MAO), and clients taking an MAO inhibitor who consume foods high in tyramine may suffer a hypertensive crisis. Foods high in tyramine include aged mature cheese, smoked meats, red wines, and pickled meats.

- o Herbal supplements can cause potential interactions with prescribed medications. It is important that any herbal medication consumed by a client be discussed with the provider.

Nursing Assessments/Data Collection and Interventions

- Nursing assessments should include a complete dietary profile of the client, medications, herbal supplements, baseline knowledge about food safety, and food-medication interactions.

- Nursing interventions should include basic teaching about food safety, and the interactions between food and client medications.

CHAPTER 5: FOOD SAFETY

 Application Exercises

Scenario: A nurse is caring for a client who has begun taking warfarin (Coumadin) for its anticoagulant effects.

1. Foods high in what fat-soluble vitamin can decrease the anticoagulant effects of warfarin (Coumadin)?

2. Which of the following are appropriate food choices for the client? (Select all that apply.)

    _____ Peanut butter sandwich and orange juice

    _____ Leaf lettuce salad

    _____ Carrots and salad dressing

    _____ Liver

    _____ Crackers with cheese

3. The client states he does not like the hospital food and asks if his family can bring food in. What teaching should the nurse provide to the client and his family regarding the types of food that are appropriate?

4. The juice of what citrus fruit can interfere with the metabolism of many medications? What is the result on medication levels?

5. Why are high amounts of protein, vitamin B_6, and amino acids not recommended for clients taking the anti-Parkinson's medication levodopa (L-dopa, Sinemet)?

6. A client picked up her new amoxicillin (Amoxil) prescription at the local pharmacy. What instructions should the nurse expect to see on the label and why?

CHAPTER 5: FOOD SAFETY

 Application Exercises Answer Key

Scenario: A nurse is caring for a client who has begun taking warfarin (Coumadin) for its anticoagulant effects.

1. Foods high in what fat-soluble vitamin can decrease the anticoagulant effects of warfarin (Coumadin)?

   Vitamin K

    NCLEX® Connection: Basic Care and Comfort, Nutrition and Oral Hydration

2. Which of the following are appropriate food choices for the client? (Select all that apply.)

__X__	**Peanut butter sandwich and orange juice**
_____	Leaf lettuce salad
__X__	**Carrots and salad dressing**
_____	Liver
__X__	**Crackers with cheese**

   Foods high in vitamin K (leaf lettuce salad, liver) should be avoided for clients taking Coumadin. The other foods choices are appropriate selections.

    NCLEX® Connection: Basic Care and Comfort, Nutrition and Oral Hydration

3. The client states he does not like the hospital food and asks if his family can bring food in. What teaching should the nurse provide to the client and his family regarding the types of food that are appropriate?

   The nurse should encourage the client to maintain consistent vitamin K intake. Additionally, the nurse should provide the client and family with a list of foods that are high in vitamin K. It should include green leafy vegetables, liver, eggs, and milk.

    NCLEX® Connection: Basic Care and Comfort, Nutrition and Oral Hydration

4. The juice of what citrus fruit can interfere with the metabolism of many medications? What is the result on medication levels?

   Grapefruit juice interferes with the metabolism of many medications and results in increased serum levels of medications.

    NCLEX® Connection: Basic Care and Comfort, Nutrition and Oral Hydration

5. Why are high amounts of protein, vitamin B_6, and amino acids not recommended for clients taking the anti-Parkinson's medication levodopa (L-dopa, Sinemet)?

> **Foods high in protein, vitamin B_6, and amino acids increase the metabolism of levodopa, thus decreasing the duration of its therapeutic effects.**

 NCLEX® Connection: Basic Care and Comfort, Nutrition and Oral Hydration

6. A client picked up her new amoxicillin (Amoxil) prescription at the local pharmacy. What instructions should the nurse expect to see on the label and why?

> **The nurse should expect the label to instruct the client to take the medication with food to avoid gastrointestinal upset.**

 NCLEX® Connection: Health Promotion and Maintenance, Health Promotion /Disease Prevention

| UNIT 1 | PRINCIPLES OF NUTRITION |
| Chapter 6 | Cultural, Ethnic, and Religious Influences |

Overview

- Cultural, ethnic, and religious considerations greatly impact nutritional health. Therefore, it is imperative that nurses gain a greater understanding of cultural needs.

- Cultural traditions impact food choices and routines. Nurses should consider these implications when planning and communicating nutritional goals with clients.

- Acculturation is the process of a cultural, ethnic, or religious group's adopting of the dominant culture's behaviors, beliefs, and values.

- Care must be taken by nurses to avoid demonstrating ethnocentrism, which is the belief that one's own cultural practices are the only correct behaviors, beliefs, attitudes, and values.

Culture and Nutrition

- The degree to which clients follow their cultural, ethnic, or religious group's traditional nutritional practices should guide the nurse's care.

- The first generation members of a family are more likely to follow their traditional foodway (all aspects of an individual's nutritional practices), with subsequent generations incorporating the host culture's food practices through socialization.

- Frequently, the dominant culture's breakfast and lunch foods are eaten, and traditional meals are consumed at dinner and symbolic events (religious holidays, weddings, childbirth).

- To avoid ethnocentrism, nurses should understand that ideas regarding food choices and nutrition vary among cultures. For instance:

  o Beetles and bugs are food items in some cultures.

  o Not all cultures identify with the American ideal of slimness.

  o Milk is not a good source of calcium in many cultures (especially when compared to the Euro-American foodway) due to the high incidence of lactose intolerance.

- Culturally respectful communication is necessary in all forms of client communication, including client education on nutrition.

  o The appropriateness of eye contact and touch, and orientation to time and literacy vary among cultures and can impact communication.

- o   Americanization of traditional foodways may have positive or negative consequences.

- o   New foods are added to the traditional diet.

- o   Food dishes are made in new ways.

- o   Cuisine items may be deleted entirely.

- Religion has a profound influence on foodways, especially since religion crosses geographic boundaries. Implications include:

  - o   Feasting/celebration foods.

  - o   Special food preparations (kosher kitchens in Orthodox Jewish homes).

  - o   Prescriptive guidelines for animal slaughter (Islam and Orthodox Judaism).

  - o   Avoidance of stimulants (coffee, tea, caffeinated soda) by Muslims and Mormons.

  - o   The practice of vegetarianism by Seventh-Day Adventists and some Buddhists.

  - o   Fasting for religious holidays (Ramadan for Muslims, or refraining from meat consumption on Ash Wednesday and Fridays during Lent for Catholics).

- Changes in the American foodway reflect cultural changes in American society and present nutritional challenges. Some trends that have made a significant impact on nutrition include:

  - o   Make it quick.

  - o   Make it easy and add only three to four ingredients, or pop it ready-made into the microwave.

  - o   When all else fails, go to the drive-thru or order in/eat out.

- Paying careful attention to reading labels, adding beneficial side dishes, practicing portion control, and choosing better dine-out options can minimize the detrimental effect of societal changes. These changes result in diets that are high in salt, carbohydrates, fat, refined sugars, and caffeine while providing low amounts of fiber and calcium.

Meeting Nutritional Needs with a Vegetarian Diet

- Individuals following a pure vegetarian diet do not consume animal products of any type, including eggs and all milk products. These diets are often adequate in protein due to the intake of nuts and legumes (dried peas and cooked beans). Vitamin B_{12} and vitamin D supplementation may be needed with a pure vegan diet.

  - o   These individuals require a variety of plant materials in specific combinations in order to ensure essential amino acid intake.

- Individuals following a lactovegetarian diet consume milk products in addition to vegetables. Individuals following a lacto-ovo-vegetarian diet consume milk products and eggs in addition to vegetables.

Selected U.S. Cultural Subgroups

- African American ("Soul Food"): origins in the Caribbean, Central America, East Africa, and West Africa

  - Traditional Foods

    - Rice, grits, cornbread; hominy, okra, greens, sweet potatoes; apples, peaches; buttermilk, pudding, cheddar or American cheese; ham, pork, chicken, catfish, black-eyed peas, red and pinto beans, peanuts; soft drinks, fatback, chitterlings, banana pudding

  - Traditional Food Preparation

    - Frying and cooking with added animal fats (lard, salt pork)

    - Promoting a shared inheritance and loving family

  - Acculturation

    - Increased milk consumption

    - Use of packaged meat, pork preferred

    - Continued low intake of fruit and vegetables

  - Nutritional Health Risks

    - High in fat, protein, and sodium, and low in potassium, calcium, and fiber

    - Low fresh fruit and vegetable intake

    - Substantial weight is equated with good health and prosperity

    - Increased incidence of type 2 diabetes mellitus and hypertension

  - Health Promotion

    - Encourage frying lightly with canola/olive oil instead of animal fats.

    - Introduce fresh fruit and vegetable dishes and decrease meat portions.

    - Suggest dark green leafy vegetables and low-fat cheeses as calcium sources.

    - Associate "good health" with better food choices and portion control.

    - Advise preparing unhealthy soul food items only at special occasions.

- Asian American ("Chinese Food"): origins in the Far East, Southeast Asia, and the Indian subcontinent

  - Traditional Foods

    - Wheat (northern), rice (southern), noodles; fruits, land and sea vegetables, nuts/seeds, soy foods (tofu), nut/seed oils; fish, shellfish, poultry, eggs; sweets; rarely red meats; tea, beer

- o Traditional Food Preparation
  - Fruits and vegetables peeled and raw
  - Stir-frying in oils quickly to retain crispness of vegetables
  - Cutting meat and poultry into bite-sized pieces
  - Cooking with salt, oil, and oil products (spices important)
  - Preventing "imbalances" and indigestion through balance of yin and yang
- o Acculturation
  - Increased use of bread and cereal; rice/wheat staple remains high
  - Utilization of new location's fruit and vegetables with increased use of fruit and salads
  - Increased use of sugar through soft drinks, candy, and desserts
- o Nutritional Health Risks
  - High sodium intake
  - Increased cancer rate as living in the U.S. continues
- o Health Promotion
  - Encourage continued use of plant-based diet and food preparation as generations take on "American foods."
  - Moderate salt intake.
  - Limit sugar-laden foods.
- Latino American ("Mexican Food"): origins in Mexico, Caribbean, and Central and South America
  - o Traditional Foods
    - Rice, maize, tortillas; tropical fruits, vegetables; nuts, beans, legumes; eggs, cheese, seafood, poultry; infrequent sweets and red meat
  - o Traditional Food Preparation
    - Frying and stewing in lard or oil
    - Meats ground or chopped
    - Meat mixed with vegetables and grains, or stuffed (tamales)
    - Heavily spiced with common use of chilies
    - Minimal use of sugar
    - "Hot" and "cold" food choices maintain "balance"

- o Acculturation
  - Increased milk use
  - Decreased meat consumption as mixed meals decline
  - Replacement of maize by wheat in tortillas and breads
  - Decreased bean use and change in rice preparation to plain boiled rice
  - Increased fruit and vegetable intake
  - Added fats in the form of butter or salad dressings on cooked vegetables and side salads
  - Replacement of fruit-based drinks by sugar-laden drinks
- o Nutritional Health Risks
  - Increased incidence of type 2 diabetes mellitus
  - Positive associations with substantial weight
- o Health Promotion
  - Encourage boiling, braising, and baking in place of frying and stewing in lard and oils.
  - Return to traditional corn tortillas.
  - Encourage use of fresh unprocessed/preserved plant-based diet.

CHAPTER 6: CULTURAL, ETHNIC, AND RELIGIOUS INFLUENCES

(A) Application Exercises

Scenario: A nurse is caring for a client recently admitted to the cardiac telemetry unit post myocardial infarction. The client is a business executive who is Euro-American. He states that he doesn't understand why he had a heart attack and says, "I've been eating like my Asian co-workers in China and they are so healthy." When asked how he prepares his Asian cuisine, he states that during the work week he eats a bowl of multigrain cereal for breakfast, and often eats at one of several local Asian restaurants or gets Chinese take-out for lunch and dinner.

1. Discuss the traditional Asian foodway and the benefits of the dietary pattern on the heart.

2. Describe the steps that should be taken to determine the benefits and risks of the client's eating pattern.

3. Describe the major teaching points that should be on the nutritional teaching plan for the client.

4. Identify healthy and unhealthy aspects of the following traditional foodways:

TRADITIONAL FOODWAY	HEALTHY ASPECTS	UNHEALTHY ASPECTS
African American		
Asian American		
Latino American		

5. An ethnocentric approach to filling out a client's menu to provide for more calcium is to

    A. ask the client what he likes to eat.

    B. call the dietician to fill the menu out.

    C. recommend one's own favorite foods.

    D. have the family fill out the menu.

6. A nurse is attending a class on culture and food. Which of the following statements made by the nurse indicates a need for further teaching?

    A. "Clients who practice Roman Catholicism do not drink coffee, tea, or caffeinated sodas."

    B. "By working closely with nutritional services, I can meet the prescribed diet and still follow my client's religious practices."

    C. "Clients who follow the teachings of Islam and Orthodox Judaism eat only specified animals that are slaughtered under strict guidelines."

    D. "Because not all individuals in one country necessarily practice the same religion, I cannot consider ethnicity alone in my plan of care."

CHAPTER 6: CULTURAL, ETHNIC, AND RELIGIOUS INFLUENCES

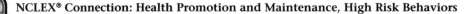 Application Exercises Answer Key

Scenario: A nurse is caring for a client recently admitted to the cardiac telemetry unit post myocardial infarction. The client is a business executive who is Euro-American. He states that he doesn't understand why he had a heart attack and says, "I've been eating like my Asian co-workers in China and they are so healthy." When asked how he prepares his Asian cuisine, he states that during the work week he eats a bowl of multigrain cereal for breakfast, and often eats at one of several local Asian restaurants or gets Chinese take-out for lunch and dinner.

1. Discuss the traditional Asian foodway and the benefits of the dietary pattern on the heart.

   Traditional Asian foodway:

   - **Plant-based diet**

   - **Consume raw fruits and vegetables**

   - **Stir-fry quickly to retain crispness of foods, which retain vitamins**

   - **Use of plant-based oils**

   - **High sodium content of diet from spices and condiments (soy source)**

   - **Major protein sources are plant-based (soy), fish, shellfish, poultry, and nuts**

   - **Rare use of red meats, consumed in small portions**

   - **Moderate portions of all food groups (cultural value on moderation in life)**

   Benefits to heart:

   - **Low cholesterol and lipids**

   - **Generally not overweight**

   NCLEX® Connection: Health Promotion and Maintenance, High Risk Behaviors

2. Describe the steps that should be taken to determine the benefits and risks of the client's eating pattern.

Assess your knowledge of the client's foodway and obtain assistance if necessary.

Set a leisurely and attentive atmosphere for a discussion.

Ask the client to describe 2 days of typical meals, snacks, and fluid consumption during his work week.

Discuss how meals and snacks are prepared.

Discuss portions/amounts of the different foods typically consumed.

Supply written material on traditional Asian foods, food preparations, and portions.

Compare and contrast the traditional Asian foodway with the client's description of his diet.

Explore ways to better closely align the client's diet with the traditional Asian foodway.

Request a dietary consult from the provider.

Provide printed follow-up information from discussion.

(N) NCLEX® Connection: Health Promotion and Maintenance, High Risk Behaviors

3. Describe the major teaching points that should be on the nutritional teaching plan for the client.

Encourage continued high intake of a plant-based diet, decreased salt intake, and adequate calcium intake.

(N) NCLEX® Connection: Health Promotion and Maintenance, Health and Wellness

4. Identify healthy and unhealthy aspects of the following traditional foodways:

TRADITIONAL FOODWAY	HEALTHY ASPECTS	UNHEALTHY ASPECTS
African American	Family involvement	Animal proteins and oils Increased sodium Increased incidence of type 2 diabetes mellitus
Asian American	Plant-based diet Fruits in diet	Increased sodium Risk calcium deficit due to plant base
Latino American	Plant-based diet Fruits in diet Family involvement	Animal proteins and oils Increased incidence of type 2 diabetes mellitus Risk calcium deficit due to lactose intolerance

(N) NCLEX® Connection: Health Promotion and Maintenance, High Risk Behaviors

5. An ethnocentric approach to filling out a client's menu to provide for more calcium is to

   A. ask the client what he likes to eat.

   B. call the dietician to fill the menu out.

   C. recommend one's own favorite foods.

   D. have the family fill out the menu.

   Ethnocentrism is the belief that the dominant or host culture's practices are the only correct behaviors/beliefs. Contacting the dietician, family, or client regarding menu selection is not an ethnocentric approach.

   Ⓝ NCLEX® Connection: Health Promotion and Maintenance, High Risk Behaviors

6. A nurse is attending a class on culture and food. Which of the following statements made by the nurse indicates a need for further teaching?

   A. "Clients who practice Roman Catholicism do not drink coffee, tea, or caffeinated sodas."

   B. "By working closely with nutritional services, I can meet the prescribed diet and still follow my client's religious practices."

   C. "Clients who follow the teachings of Islam and Orthodox Judaism eat only specified animals that are slaughtered under strict guidelines."

   D. "Because not all individuals in one country necessarily practice the same religion, I cannot consider ethnicity alone in my plan of care."

   Stimulants (coffee, tea, caffeinated sodas) are not consumed by Muslims or Mormons. A Roman Catholic cultural practice is not eating meat on Ash Wednesday or Fridays during Lent. The other statements made by the nurse are appropriate and do not require additional cultural education.

   Ⓝ NCLEX® Connection: Health Promotion and Maintenance, Nutrition and Oral Hydration

UNIT 1	PRINCIPLES OF NUTRITION
Chapter 7	Nutrition Across the Lifespan

Overview

- Nutritional needs change as clients pass through the stages of the lifespan, reflecting the physiological changes that clients experience.

- Nurses must address nutritional needs across the lifespan and have a thorough understanding of how needs change. Nurses should focus on planning and implementing dietary plans that meet clients' specific needs.

- The major stages of the lifespan that have specific nutritional needs are:

  ○ Pregnancy and Lactation

  ○ Infancy

  ○ Childhood

  ○ Adolescence

  ○ Adulthood and Older Adulthood

PREGNANCY AND LACTATION

Overview

- Good nutrition during pregnancy is essential for the health of the unborn child.

- Maternal nutritional demands are increased for the development of the placenta, enlargement of the uterus, formation of amniotic fluid, increase in blood volume, and preparation of the breasts for lactation.

- A daily increase of 340 calories is recommended during the second trimester of pregnancy, and an increase of 452 calories is recommended during the third trimester of pregnancy.

- The nutritional requirements of women who are pregnant or lactating involves more than increased caloric intake. Specific dietary requirements for major nutrients and micronutrients should be taught.

Dietary Guidelines During Pregnancy and Lactation

- Achieving an appropriate amount of weight gain during pregnancy prepares a woman for the energy demands of labor and lactation, and contributes to the delivery of a newborn of normal birth weight.

- The recommended weight gain during pregnancy varies for each woman depending on her body mass index (BMI) and weight prior to pregnancy.

  o Recommended weight gain during the first trimester is 2 to 4 lb.

  o Trimesters 2 and 3:

    - Normal weight client – 1 lb/week for a total of 25 to 35 lb.

    - Underweight client – just more than 1 lb/week for a total of 28 to 40 lb.

    - Overweight client – 0.66 lb/week for a total of 15 to 25 lb.

- Lactating women require an increase in daily caloric intake. If the client is breastfeeding during the postpartum period, an additional daily intake of 330 calories is recommended during the first 6 months, and an additional daily intake of 400 calories is recommended during the second 6 months.

Major and Micronutrient Requirements During Pregnancy and Lactation

- Dietary requirements for major nutrients include:

  o Protein should comprise 20% of the daily total calorie intake. The recommended daily allowance (RDA) for protein during pregnancy is 1.1 g/kg/day. Protein is essential for rapid tissue growth of maternal and fetal structures, amniotic fluid, and extra blood volume. Women who are pregnant should be aware that animal sources of protein might contain large amounts of fats.

  o Fat should be limited to 30% of total daily calorie intake.

  o Carbohydrates should comprise 50% of the total daily calorie intake. Ensuring adequate carbohydrate intake allows for protein to be spared and available for the synthesis of fetal tissue.

- The need for most vitamins and minerals increases during pregnancy and lactation. Vitamins are essential for blood formation, the absorption of iron, and the development of fetal tissue. The following table lists the comparative RDAs of major vitamins for women age 19 to 30 during nonpregnancy, pregnancy, and lactation.

RDAS OF MAJOR VITAMINS			
NUTRIENT	NONPREGNANT	PREGNANT	LACTATING
Protein (g)	46	71	71
Vitamin A (mcg)	700	770	1,300
Vitamin C (mg)	75	85	120
Vitamin D (mcg)*	5	5	5
Vitamin E (mcg)	15	15	19
Vitamin K (mcg)*	90	90	90
Thiamin (mg)	1.1	1.4	1.4
Vitamin B$_6$ (mg)	1.3	1.9	2.0

RDAS OF MAJOR VITAMINS			
NUTRIENT	NONPREGNANT	PREGNANT	LACTATING
Folate (mcg)	400	600	500
Vitamin B$_{12}$ (mcg)	2.4	2.6	2.8
Calcium (mg)*	1,000	1,000	1,000
Iron (mg)	18	27	9

*Values represent adequate intakes (AIs).

Source: Food and Nutrition Information Center. *Dietary Reference Intakes (DRI) and Recommended Dietary Allowances (RDA)*. Retrieved April 27, 2009, from www.nal.usda.gov

Additional Dietary Recommendations

- Fluid: 2,000 to 3,000 mL of fluids daily from food and drinks. Preferable fluids include water, fruit juice, or milk. Carbonated beverages and fruit drinks provide little or no nutrients.

- Alcohol: It is recommended that women abstain from alcohol consumption during pregnancy.

- Caffeine: Caffeine crosses the placenta and can affect the movement and heart rate of the fetus. However, moderate use (less than 300 mg/day) does not appear to be harmful.

- Vegetarian diets: Well-balanced vegetarian diets that include dairy products can provide all the nutritional requirements of pregnancy.

- Folic acid intake: It is recommended that 600 mcg per day of folic acid be taken during pregnancy. Current recommendations for lactating clients include 500 mcg of folic acid per day. It is necessary for the neurological development of the fetus and to prevent birth defects. It is essential for maternal red blood cell formation. Food sources include green leafy vegetables, enriched grains, and orange juice.

- Iron can be obtained from dairy products and meats, especially red meats. Consuming foods high in vitamin C aids in the absorption of iron.

Dietary Complications During Pregnancy

- Nausea and constipation are common during pregnancy.

  - For nausea, eat dry crackers or toast. Avoid alcohol, caffeine, fats, and spices. Avoid drinking fluids with meals, and do not take medications to control nausea without checking with the provider.

  - For constipation, increase fluid consumption and include extra fiber in the diet. Fruits, vegetables, and whole grains contain fiber.

- Maternal Phenylketonuria (PKU): This is a maternal genetic disease in which high levels of phenylalanine poses danger to the fetus.

  o It is important for a client to resume the PKU diet at least 3 months prior to pregnancy, and continue the diet throughout pregnancy.

  o The diet should include foods low in phenylalanine. Foods high in protein (fish, poultry, meat, eggs, nuts, dairy products) must be avoided due to high phenylalanine levels.

  o The client's blood phenylalanine levels should be monitored during pregnancy.

  o These interventions will prevent fetal complications (mental retardation, behavioral problems).

Nursing Assessments/Data Collection and Interventions

- Nursing assessments should include a complete profile of the client's knowledge base regarding nutritional requirements during pregnancy.

- Additionally, nurses should review the appropriate and recommended dietary practices for pregnant and lactating women with the client, while providing materials containing this information.

INFANCY

Overview

- Growth rate during infancy is more rapid than any other period of the life cycle. It's important to understand normal growth patterns to determine the adequacy of an infant's nutritional intake.

- Birth weight doubles by 4 to 6 months and triples by 1 year of age. The need for calories and nutrients is high to support the rapid rate of growth.

- Appropriate weight gain averages 150 to 210 g (5 to 7 oz) per week during the first 5 to 6 months.

- An infant grows approximately 2.5 cm (1 in) per month in height the first 6 months, and approximately 1.25 cm (0.5 in) in height per month the last 6 months.

- Head circumference increases rapidly during the first 6 months at a rate of 1.5 cm (0.6 in) per month. The rate slows to 0.5 cm per month for months 6 to 12. By 1 year, head size should have increased by 33%. This is reflective of the growth of the nervous system.

- Breast milk, infant formula, or a combination of the two is the sole source of nutrition for the first 4 to 6 months of life.

- Semi-solid foods should not be introduced before 4 months of age to coincide with the development of head control, the ability to sit, and the back-and-forth motion of the tongue.

- Iron-fortified infant cereal is the first solid food introduced as gestational iron stores begin to deplete around 4 months of age.

- Cow's milk should not be introduced into the diet until after 1 year of age as protein and mineral content stress the immature kidney. A young infant cannot fully digest the protein and fat contained in cow's milk.

Meeting Nutritional Needs

- The American Academy of Pediatrics recommends that infants receive breast milk for the first 6 to 12 months of age. Even a short period of breastfeeding has physiological benefits. If breastfeeding is not possible, the mother should be reassured that commercial formulas can supply the infant with adequate nutrition.

  - Advantages of Breastfeeding

    - Incidence of otitis media (ear infections), and gastrointestinal and respiratory disorders are reduced. This is due to the transfer of antibodies from mother to infant.

    - Carbohydrates, proteins, and fats in breast milk are predigested for ready absorption.

    - Breast milk is high in omega-3 fatty acids.

    - Breast milk is low in sodium.

    - Iron, zinc, and magnesium found in breast milk are highly absorbable.

    - Calcium absorption is enhanced as the calcium-to-phosphorous ratio is 2 to 1.

    - The risk of allergies is reduced.

    - Maternal-infant bonding is promoted.

  - Breastfeeding Teaching Points

    - The newborn is offered the breast immediately after birth and frequently thereafter. There should be eight to 12 feedings in a 24 hr period.

    - The newborn should nurse up to 15 to 20 min per breast. However, educating clients regarding an expected duration of feedings should be avoided. Clients should be educated on how to evaluate when the newborn has completed the feeding by noting the slowing of newborn suckling, a softened breast, or sleeping.

    - Do not offer the newborn any other fluids unless indicated by the provider.

    - The mother's milk supply is equal to the demand of the infant.

    - Eventually, the infant will empty a breast within 5 to 10 min, but may need to continue to suck to meet comfort needs.

    - Frequent feedings (every 2 hr may be indicated) and manual expression of milk to initiate flow may be needed.

    - Expressed milk may be refrigerated in sterile bottles for use within 3 to 5 days, or frozen in sterile containers for 6 months.

- Thaw milk in the refrigerator, it can be stored for 24 hr after thawing. Defrosting or heating in a microwave oven is not recommended as high heat destroys some of milk's antibodies, and may burn the infant's oral mucosa.

- Do not refreeze thawed milk.

- Unused breast milk must be discarded.

- Avoid consuming freshwater fish or alcohol, and limit caffeine.

- Do not take medications unless prescribed by a provider.

- Formula Feeding

  o Commercial infant formulas provide an alternative to breast milk. They are modified from cow's milk to provide comparable nutrients.

  o An iron-fortified formula is recommended by the American Academy of Pediatrics for at least the first 6 months of life or until the infant consumes adequate solid food. After 6 months, formula without added iron may be indicated.

  o Fluoride supplements may be required if an adequate level is not supplied by the water supply.

  o Wash hands prior to preparing formula.

  o Use sterile bottles and nipples.

  o Precisely follow the manufacturer's mixing directions.

  o Bottles of mixed formula or open cans of liquid formula require refrigeration. Do not use if the formula has been left at room temperature for 2 hr or longer. Do not reuse partially emptied bottles of formula.

  o Formula may be fed chilled, warmed, or at room temperature. Always give formula at approximately the same temperature.

  o Hold the infant during feedings with the head slightly elevated to facilitate passage of formula into the stomach. Tilt the bottle to maintain formula in the nipple and prevent the swallowing of air.

  o Do not prop the bottle or put an infant to bed with a bottle. This practice promotes tooth decay.

  o The infant should not drink more than 32 oz of formula per 24 hr period unless directed by a provider.

- Weaning

  o Developmentally, the infant is ready for weaning from the breast or bottle to a cup between 5 to 8 months of age.

  o If breastfeeding is eliminated before 5 to 6 months, a bottle should be provided for the infant's sucking needs.

  o It is best to substitute the cup for one feeding period at a time over a 5 to 7 day period.

  o Nighttime feedings are often the last to disappear.

- o   Never allow a child to take a bottle to bed as this promotes dental caries.

- o   Use the new schedule for a second feeding period and continue at the infant's pace.

- o   The infant may not be ready to wean from the bottle or breast until 12 to 14 months of age.

- Introducing Solid Food

  - o   Solid food should not be introduced before 4 to 6 months of age due to the risk of food allergies and stress on the immature kidneys.

  - o   Indicators for readiness include: voluntary control of the head and trunk, hunger less than 4 hr after vigorous nursing or intake of 8 oz of formula, and interest of the infant.

  - o   Iron-fortified rice cereal should be offered first. Wheat cereals should not be introduced until after the first year.

  - o   New foods should be introduced one at a time over a 5 to 7 day period to observe for signs of allergy or intolerance, which may include fussiness, rash, vomiting, diarrhea, or constipation. Vegetables or fruits are first started between 6 and 8 months of age, and after both have been introduced meats may be added to the diet.

  - o   Delay the introduction of milk, eggs, wheat, and citrus fruits that may lead to allergic reactions in susceptible infants.

  - o   Do not give peanuts or peanut butter due to the risk of a severe allergic reaction.

  - o   The infant may be ready for three meals a day with three snacks by 8 months of age.

  - o   Homemade baby food is an acceptable feeding option. Do not use canned or packaged foods that are high in sodium. Select fresh or frozen foods, and do not add sugars or other seasonings.

  - o   Open jars of infant food may be stored in the refrigerator for up to 24 hr.

  - o   By 9 months of age, the infant should be able to eat table foods that are cooked, chopped, and unseasoned.

  - o   Do not feed the infant honey because of the risk of botulism.

  - o   Appropriate finger foods include: ripe banana, toast strips, graham crackers, cheese cubes, noodles, and peeled chunks of apples, pears, or peaches.

SUGGESTED INTRODUCTION OF FOODS				
BIRTH TO 4 MONTHS	4 TO 6 MONTHS	6 TO 9 MONTHS	9 TO 12 MONTHS	1 YEAR
Breast milk or formula	Iron-fortified rice cereal Vegetables Fruits	Strained meats	Table foods (cooked, chopped, and unseasoned)	Cow's milk

Nutrition-Related Problems

- Colic is characterized by persistent crying lasting 3 hr or longer per day.

  - The cause of colic is unknown, but usually occurs in the late afternoon, more than 3 days per week for more than 3 weeks. The crying is accompanied by a tense abdomen and legs drawn up to the belly.

  - Colic usually resolves by 3 months of age.

  - Breastfeeding mothers should continue nursing, but limit caffeine and nicotine intake.

  - If breastfeeding, eliminating cruciferous vegetables (cauliflower, broccoli, and Brussels sprouts), cow's milk, onion, and chocolate may be helpful.

  - Burping the infant in an upright position or giving warm water may help.

  - Other comforting techniques (swaddling, carrying the infant, rocking, repetitive soft sound) may soothe the infant.

  - Most infants grow and gain weight despite colic.

  - Reassure the parent that colic is transient and does not indicate more serious problems or a lack of parental ability.

- Lactose intolerance is the inability to digest significant amounts of lactose, the predominant sugar of milk, and is due to inadequate lactase, the enzyme that digests lactose into glucose and galactose.

  - Lactose intolerance has an increased prevalence in individuals of Asian, Native American, African, Latino, and Mediterranean descent.

  - Signs and symptoms include: abdominal distention, flatus, and occasional diarrhea.

  - Either soy-based (ProSobee® or Isomil®) or casein hydrolysate (Nutramigen® or Pregestimil®) formulas can be prescribed as alternative formulas for infants who are lactose intolerant.

- Failure to thrive is inadequate gains in weight and height in comparison to established growth and development norms.

  - Assess for signs and symptoms of congenital defects, central nervous system disorders, or partial intestinal obstruction.

  - Assess for swallowing or sucking problems.

  - Identify feeding patterns, especially concerning preparation of formulas.

  - Assess for psychosocial problems, especially parent-infant bonding.

  - Provide supportive nutritional guidance. Usually a high-calorie, high-protein diet is indicated.

  - Provide supportive parenting guidance.

- Diarrhea is characterized by the passage of more than three loose, watery stools over a 24 hr period.

  ○ Overfeeding and food intolerances are common causes of osmotic diarrhea.

  ○ Infectious diarrhea in the infant is commonly caused by rotavirus.

  ○ Mild diarrhea may require no special interventions. Check with the provider for any diet modifications.

  ○ Treatment for moderate diarrhea should begin at home with oral rehydration solutions (Pedialyte®, Infalyte®, ReVital®) or generic equivalents. After each loose stool, 8 oz of solution should be given. Sports drinks are contraindicated.

  ○ Educate parents about the signs and symptoms of dehydration: listlessness, sunken eyes, decreased tears, dry mucous membranes, and decreased urine output.

  ○ Breastfed infants should continue nursing.

  ○ Formula-fed infants usually do not require diluted formulas or special formulas.

  ○ Contact the provider if signs and symptoms of dehydration are present, or if vomiting, bloody stools, high fever, change in mental status, or refusal to take liquids occurs.

- Constipation is the inability or difficulty to evacuate the bowels.

  ○ Constipation is not a common problem for breastfed infants.

  ○ Constipation may be caused by formula that is too concentrated or by inadequate carbohydrate intake.

  ○ Stress the importance of accurate dilution of formula.

  ○ Advise adherence to the recommended amount of formula intake for age.

Nursing Assessments/Data Collection and Interventions

- Nursing assessments should include an assessment of knowledge base of the client regarding nutritional guidelines for infants, normal infant growth patterns, breastfeeding, formula feeding, and the progression for the introduction of solid foods.

- Additionally, nurses should provide education and references for the client regarding each of the assessments listed above.

CHILDHOOD

Overview

- Growth rate slows following infancy.

- Energy needs and appetite vary with the child's activity level.

- Generally, nutrient needs increase with age.

- Attitudes toward food and general food habits are established by 5 years of age.

- Increasing the variety and texture of foods helps the child develop good eating habits.

- Foods like hot dogs, popcorn, peanuts, grapes, raw carrots, celery, peanut butter, tough meat, and candy may cause choking or aspiration.

- Inclusion in family mealtime is important for social development.

- Group eating becomes a significant means of socialization for school-age children.

- The Food Guide Pyramid for Young Children, developed by the United States Department of Agriculture (USDA), is the recommended guide for providing adequate nutrition. Children require the same food groups as adults, but in smaller serving sizes.

Toddlers: 1 to 3 years old

- Nutrition Guidelines

  o Toddlers generally grow 2 to 3 inches in height and gain approximately 5 lb annually.

  o Limit juice to 4 to 6 oz a day.

  o The 1 to 2-year-old child requires whole cow's milk to provide adequate fat for the still growing brain.

  o Food serving size is 1 tbsp for each year of age.

  o Exposure to a new food may need to occur 8 to 15 times before the child develops an acceptance of it.

  o If there is a negative family history for allergies, cow's milk, chocolate, citrus fruits, egg white, seafood, and nut butters may be gradually introduced while monitoring the child for reactions.

  o Toddlers prefer finger foods because of their increasing autonomy. They prefer plain foods to mixtures, but usually like macaroni and cheese, spaghetti, and pizza.

  o Regular meal times and nutritious snacks best meet nutrient needs.

  o Snacks or desserts that are high in sugar, fat, or sodium should be avoided.

  o Children are at an increased risk for choking until 4 years of age.

  o Avoid foods that are potential choking hazards (nuts, grapes, hot dogs, peanut butter, raw carrots, tough meats, popcorn). Always provide adult supervision during snack and mealtimes. During food preparation, cut small bite-sized pieces for easier swallow, and to prevent choking. Do not allow the child to engage in drinking or eating during play activities or while lying down.

- Nutritional Concerns/Risks

  o Iron

    ▪ Iron deficiency anemia is the most common nutritional deficiency disorder in children.

    ▪ Lean red meats provide sources of readily absorbable iron.

- Consuming vitamin C (orange juice, tomatoes) with plant sources of iron (beans, raisins, peanut butter, whole grains) will maximize absorption.
- Milk should be limited to the recommended quantities (24 oz) as it is a poor source of iron and may displace the intake of iron-rich foods.

  o Vitamin D

  - Vitamin D is essential for bone development.
  - Recommended vitamin D intake is the same (5 mcg/day) from birth through age 50. Children require more vitamin D because their bones are growing.
  - Milk (cow, soy) and fatty fish are good sources of vitamin D.
  - Sunlight exposure leads to vitamin D synthesis. Children who spend large amounts of time inside (watching TV, playing video games) are at an increased risk for vitamin D deficiency.
  - Vitamin D assists in the absorption of calcium into the bones.

Preschoolers: 3 to 5 years

- Nutrition Guidelines

  o Preschoolers generally grow 2 to 3 inches in height and gain approximately 5 lb annually.

  o Preschoolers need 13 to 19 g/day of complete protein in addition to adequate calcium, iron, folate, and vitamins A and C.

  o Preschoolers tend to dislike strong-tasting vegetables (cabbage, onions), but like many raw vegetables that are eaten as finger foods.

  o Food jags (ritualistic preference for one food) are common and usually short-lived.

  o Food Pyramid guidelines are appropriate, requiring the lowest number of servings per food group.

  o Food patterns and preferences are first learned from the family, and peers begin influencing preferences and habits at around 5 years of age.

- Nutritional Concerns/Risks

  o Concerns include overfeeding, intake of high-calorie, high-fat, high-sodium snacks, soft drinks, and juices, and inadequate intake of fruits and vegetables.

  - Be alert to the appropriate serving size of foods (1 tbsp per year of age).
  - Avoid high-fat and high-sugar snacks.
  - Encourage daily physical activities. .
  - May switch to skim or 1% low-fat milk after 2 years of age.

- o Iron deficiency anemia (see previous information for Toddlers).

- o Lead poisoning is a risk for children under 6 years of age as they frequently place objects in their mouths that may contain lead, and have a higher rate of intestinal absorption.

  - ▪ Feed children at frequent intervals since more lead is absorbed on an empty stomach.

  - ▪ Inadequate intake of calories, calcium, iron, zinc, and phosphorous may increase susceptibility.

School-Age Children: 6 to 12 years

- • Nutrition Guidelines

  - o School-age children generally grow 2 to 3 inches in height and gain approximately 5 lb annually.

  - o Following Food Pyramid recommendations, the diet should provide variety, balance, and moderation.

  - o Young athletes need to meet energy, protein, and fluid needs.

  - o Educate children to make healthy food selections.

  - o Children enjoy learning how to safely prepare nutritious snacks.

  - o Children need to learn to eat snacks only when hungry, not when bored or inactive.

- • Nutrition Concerns/Risks

  - o Skipping breakfast occurs in about 10% of children.

    - ▪ Optimum performance in school is dependent on a nutritious breakfast.

    - ▪ Children who regularly eat breakfast tend to have an age appropriate BMI.

  - o Overweight/obesity affects at least 20% of children.

    - ▪ Greater psychosocial implications exist for children than adults.

    - ▪ Overweight children tend to be obese adults.

    - ▪ Prevention is essential: Encourage healthy eating habits, decrease fats and sugars (empty-calorie foods), and increase the level of physical activity.

    - ▪ A weight-loss program directed by a health care provider is indicated for children who are more than 40% overweight.

    - ▪ Praise the child's abilities and skills.

    - ▪ Never use food as a reward or punishment.

Nursing Assessments/Data Collection and Interventions

- • Nursing assessments should include the parent's knowledge base of the child's nutritional requirements, and nutritional concerns with regard to age. Nurses should provide education for the parent and child about nutritional recommendations.

ADOLESCENCE

Overview

- The rate of growth during adolescence is second only to the rate in infancy. Nutritional needs for energy, protein, calcium, iron, and zinc increase at the onset of puberty and the growth spurt.

- The female adolescent growth spurt usually begins at 10 or 11 years of age, peaks at 12 years, and is completed by 17 years. Female energy requirements are less than that of males, as they experience less growth of muscle and bone tissue and more fat deposition.

- The male adolescent growth spurt begins at 12 or 13 years of age, peaks at 14 years, and is completed by 21 years.

- Eating habits of adolescents are often inadequate in meeting recommended nutritional intake goals.

Nutritional Considerations

- Energy requirements average 2,000 cal/day for a 15-year-old female, and 4,000 cal/day for a 15-year-old male.

- The USDA reports that the average U.S. adolescent consumes a diet deficient in folate, vitamins A and E, iron, zinc, magnesium, calcium, and fiber. This trend is more pronounced in females than males.

- Diets of adolescents generally exceed recommendations for total fat, saturated fat, cholesterol, sodium, and sugar.

Nutritional Risks

- Eating and snacking patterns promote essential nutrient deficiencies (calcium, vitamins, iron, fiber) and overconsumption of sugars, fat, and sodium.

  - Adolescents tend to skip meals, especially breakfast, and eat more meals away from home.

  - Foods are often selected from vending machines, convenience stores, and fast food restaurants. These foods are typically high in fat, sugar, and sodium.

  - Carbonated beverages may replace milk and fruit juices in the diet with resulting deficiencies in vitamin C, riboflavin, phosphorous, and calcium.

- Adolescents have an increased need for iron.

  - Females 14 to 18 years of age require 15 mg of iron to support expansion of blood volume and blood loss during menstruation.

  - Males 14 to 18 years of age require 11 mg of iron to support expansion of muscle mass and blood volume.

- Inadequate calcium intake may predispose the adolescent to osteoporosis later in life.

  o During adolescence, 45% of bone mass is added.

  o Normal blood-calcium levels are maintained by drawing calcium from the bones if calcium intake is low.

  o Adolescents require at least 1,300 mg of calcium a day, which may be achieved by 3 to 4 servings from the dairy food group.

- Dieting

  o The stigma of obesity and social pressure to be thin can lead to unhealthy eating practices and poor body image, especially in females.

  o Males are more susceptible to using supplements and high-protein drinks in order to build muscle mass and improve athletic performance. Some athletes restrict calories to maintain or achieve a lower weight.

  o Eating disorders may follow self-imposed crash diets for weight loss.

- Eating disorders (anorexia nervosa, bulimia nervosa, obesity) are on the rise among adolescent clients. These disorders are discussed further in chapter 18 (ATI Mental Health Nursing Review Module).

- Adolescent Pregnancy

  o The physiologic demands of a growing fetus compromise the adolescent's needs for her own unfinished growth and development.

  o Inconsistent eating and poor food choices place the adolescent at risk for anemia, pregnancy-induced hypertension, gestational diabetes, premature labor, spontaneous abortion, and delivery of a newborn of low birth weight.

Nursing Assessments/Data Collection and Interventions

- Nursing assessments should include a determination of the adolescent's:

  o Typical 24 hr food intake.

  o Weight patterns, current weight, and ideal body weight.

  o Attitude about current weight.

  o Use of nutritional supplements, vitamins, and minerals.

  o Medical history and use of prescription medications.

  o Use of over-the-counter medications, street drugs, alcohol, and tobacco.

  o Level of daily physical activity.

- Nurses should assess for signs and symptoms of an eating disorder. This may include an evaluation of the adolescent's laboratory values.

- Nursing assessments should include strategies that promote health for the adolescent.

  o Educate the adolescent on using the Food Pyramid to meet energy and nutrient needs with three regular meals and snacks.

  o Stress the importance of meeting calcium needs by including low-fat milk, yogurt, and cheese in the diet.

  o Educate the adolescent on how to select and prepare nutrient dense snack foods: unbuttered, unsalted popcorn, pretzels, fresh fruit, string cheese, smoothies made with low-fat yogurt, skim milk, or reduced-calorie fruit juice, and raw vegetables with low-fat dips.

  o Encourage participation in vigorous physical activity at least three times a week.

  o Refer pregnant adolescents to the Women, Infant, and Children (WIC) nutrition subsidy program.

  o Provide individual and group counseling for teens with signs and symptoms of eating disorders.

ADULTHOOD AND OLDER ADULTHOOD

Overview

- Nurses should assess the nutritional, physical, and mental health of adults and older adults.

- A balanced diet for all adults consists of 40% to 55% carbohydrate and 10% to 20% fat (with no more than 30% fat).

- The recommended amount for protein is unchanged in adults and older adults, however, many nutrition experts believe that protein requirements increase in older adults.

- Older adults need to reduce total caloric intake. This is due to the decrease in basal metabolic rate that occurs from the decrease in lean body mass that develops with aging.

- Reduced caloric intake predisposes the older adult for development of nutrient deficiencies.

- Regular exercise is encouraged for all adults.

- Older adults may have physical, mental, and social changes that affect their ability to purchase, prepare, and digest foods and nutrients.

- Dehydration is the most common fluid and electrolyte imbalance in older adults. Fluid needs increase with medication-induced fluid losses. Some disease processes necessitate fluid restrictions.

Nutritional Concerns

- A 24 hr dietary intake is helpful in determining the need for dietary education.

- Older adults may have oral problems (ill-fitting dentures, difficulty chewing or swallowing), and a decrease in salivation or poor dental health.

- Older adults have decreased cellular function and reduced body reserves, leading to decreased absorption of B_{12}, folic acid, and calcium, as well as reductions in insulin production and sensitivity.

- Decreased elasticity of blood vessels can lead to hypertension.

- Kidneys (renal) regulate the amount of potassium and sodium in the blood stream. Renal function can decrease as much as 50% in older adults.

- Older adults have a decreased lean muscle mass. Exercise can help to counteract muscle mass loss.

- The loss of calcium can result in decreased bone density in older adults.

- Cell-mediated immunity decreases as an individual ages.

Balanced Diet and Nutrient Needs

- MyPyramid, developed by the USDA, suggests the following daily food intake for adults and older adults who get less than 30 min of moderate physical activity most days:

MYPYRAMID RECOMMENDATIONS FOR ADULTS						
	MEN			WOMEN		
	19-30	31-50	51+	19-30	31-50	51+
Calories	2,400	2,200	2,000	2,000	1,800	1,600
Fruits	2 cups	2 cups	2 cups	2 cups	1 ½ cups	1 ½ cups
Vegetables	3 cups	3 cups	2 ½ cups	2 ½ cups	2 ½ cups	2 cups
Grains	8 oz	7 oz	6 oz	6 oz	6 oz	5 oz
Meats and Beans	6 ½ oz	6 oz	5 ½ oz	5 ½ oz	5 oz	5 oz
Milk	3 cups	3 cups	3 cups	3 cups	3 cups	3 cups
Oils	7 tsp	6 tsp	6 tsp	6 tsp	5 tsp	5 tsp

Source: United States Department of Agriculture. *MyPyramid.gov*. Retrieved April 30, 2009, from http://www.mypyramid.gov

- Grains: Select whole grains.

- Vegetables: Select orange and dark green leafy vegetables.

- Fruits: Select fresh, dried, canned, or juices. Avoid fruits with added sugar.

- Milk, yogurt, and cheese group: One cup of milk or plain yogurt is equivalent to 1 ½ oz of natural cheese or 2 oz processed cheese.

- Meat and bean group: Includes meat, fish, poultry, dry beans, eggs, and nuts. One ounce equals: 1 oz meat, fish, or poultry (baked, grilled, broiled); ¼ cup cooked dry beans; 1 egg; 1 tbsp peanut butter; or ½ oz nuts. Use lean meats.

- Oils: Use vegetable oils (except palm and coconut). One tbsp of oil equals 3 tsp equivalent; 1 tbsp mayonnaise equals 2 ½ tsp dietary intake; and 1 oz nuts equals 3 tsp oils (except hazelnut, which equals 4 tsp).

- Discretionary calories: From 132 to 362 discretionary calories are permitted per day. These add up quickly and can be from more than one food group.

- Minerals: Calcium requirements increase for older adults as the efficiency of calcium absorption decreases with age.

Ⓖ - Vitamins: Vitamins A, D, C, E, B_6, and B_{12} may be decreased in older adults. Supplemental vitamins are recommended.

Regular Exercise

- All adults should exercise at a moderate or vigorous pace for at least 30 min per day, 3 to 7 days a week.

- Physical activity must increase heart rate to be relevant. Moderate activities include gardening/yard work, golf, dancing, and walking briskly.

- The loss of lean muscle mass is part of normal aging and can be decreased with regular exercise. The loss of lean muscle may be associated with a decrease in total protein and insulin sensitivity.

- Regular exercise can improve bone density, relieve depression, and enhance cardiovascular and respiratory function.

Potential Impact of Physical, Mental, and Social Changes

- Diseases and treatments may interfere with nutrient and food absorption, and utilization.

Ⓖ
  ○ Aging adults are at an increased risk for developing osteoporosis (decreasing total bone mass and deterioration of bone tissue). Adequate calcium and vitamin D intake with regular weight-bearing exercise is important for maximizing bone density.

  ○ Osteoarthritis (OA) causes significant disability and pain in older adult clients. OA can limit mobility and present difficulty in obtaining and preparing proper foods.

  ○ Arthritis can interfere with the purchase and preparation of foods.

  ○ Alzheimer's disease is a form of dementia commonly seen in clients age 65 and older. This form of dementia causes impairments in memory and judgment that may make shopping, storing, and cooking food difficult.

- Certain medications (diuretics) for hypertension can cause sodium or potassium losses.

- Loss of smell and vision interfere with the interest in eating food.

- BMI should be between 18.5 and 24.9. There is an increased risk for both overweight and underweight older adult clients. Overweight adults are more prone to hypertension, diabetes, and cardiovascular events.

(G) • Older adults may have difficulty chewing, in which case mincing or chopping food is helpful. They may have difficulty swallowing food, and thickened liquids may decrease the risk for aspiration.

• Social isolation, loss of a spouse, and mental deterioration may cause poor nutrition in adult and older adult clients. Encourage socialization and refer to a senior center or program.

• A fixed income may make it difficult for older adults to purchase needed foods. Refer to food programs, senior centers, and food banks. The Meals on Wheels program is available for housebound older adults.

Fluid Intake

• The long-held standard of consuming eight glasses (8 oz) of liquid per day has been tempered by evidence that dehydration is not imminent even when less than 64 oz of fluid is consumed.

• Solid foods provide varying amounts of water, making it possible to get adequate fluid despite low beverage intake.

• For healthy adults, it is generally acceptable to allow normal drinking and eating habits to provide needed fluids.

• Encourage water and natural juices, and discourage drinking only soda pop and other liquids that have caffeine.

Nursing Assessments/Data Collection and Interventions

• Nursing assessments should include a dietary profile of the adult or older adult. Medical history, medication regimen, mobility, social practices, mental status, and financial circumstances are important components of the assessment. Nurses should provide education about proper dietary practices for the adult and older adult, while additionally providing referrals to community agencies when appropriate.

CHAPTER 7: NUTRITION ACROSS THE LIFESPAN

 Application Exercises

Scenario: A nurse is caring for a client who is 6 weeks pregnant and at her first visit to the provider's office.

1. The client is concerned that she will gain too much weight and states that she is going to watch what she eats. The client's BMI and current weight indicate that she falls within the normal range. How much weight should the client expect to gain?

2. The nurse provides the client with guidelines for her major nutrient intake. Match the appropriate percentage of caloric intake with its corresponding nutrient.

_____	Fat	A. 50%
_____	Protein	B. 30%
_____	Carbohydrates	C. 20%

Scenario: A woman who is 7 weeks pregnant states that she is experiencing nausea each morning when she wakes.

3. What actions should the nurse encourage the client to take?

4. Why is folate (folic acid) an important nutrient during pregnancy?

5. How much fluid does a pregnant woman need each day, and what are recommended sources of fluids?

6. A nurse is caring for a mother who gained the recommended amount of weight during her pregnancy and is now breastfeeding. She states that the baby seems hungry all the time, however, the nurse notes that the baby's weight has not changed significantly since her last visit 2 weeks ago. What information is important to share with the client?

7. A nurse is preparing to teach an infant nutrition class in the hospital's obstetrics clinic. The nurse has decided to teach expectant mothers about infant feeding problems. Create a list of questions the mothers may ask and develop an outline of appropriate responses.

8. A new mother has brought her 6-month-old infant in for a routine check-up. The infant's birth weight was 7 lb, 2 oz, head circumference was 35.5 cm (14 in), and length was 48 cm (19 in). Which of the following characteristics should pose a concern? (Select all that apply.)

    _____ Head circumference of 41.5 cm (16 in)

    _____ Weight of 13 lb, 0 oz (5.9 kg)

    _____ Length of 63 cm (24.8 in)

9. Which of the following snack foods are appropriate for toddlers? (Select all that apply.)

_____ Graham crackers

_____ Apple slices

_____ Peeled raisins

_____ Jelly beans

_____ Cheese cubes

10. Explain why adequate vitamin D intake is important for children. Name two sources of vitamin D.

11. List five examples of iron-rich foods.

12. Which of the following foods selected by a teen indicates an understanding of healthy snacks? (Select all that apply.)

_____ Carrot sticks with low-fat ranch dip

_____ Cheese and crackers

_____ Unbuttered popcorn

_____ Frozen low-fat yogurt

_____ Hot dog

13. An adolescent female arrives for a routine physical. Her mother states that she has reported fatigue for the last 6 weeks and that she is having difficulty staying awake during school hours. What is one possible explanation for the adolescent's extreme fatigue? Include rationale.

14. Why is achieving adequate calcium intake important for an adolescent?

15. A 54-year-old female client is newly diagnosed with hypertension. She is taking the diuretic hydrochlorothiazide (HydroDIURIL) for her condition. What information is important to share with her regarding side effects and potential nutrition complications?

CHAPTER 7: NUTRITION ACROSS THE LIFESPAN

 Application Exercises Answer Key

Scenario: A nurse is caring for a client who is 6 weeks pregnant and at her first visit to the provider's office.

1. The client is concerned that she will gain too much weight and states that she is going to watch what she eats. The client's BMI and current weight indicate that she falls within the normal range. How much weight should the client expect to gain?

> **The nurse should explain to the client that good nutrition during pregnancy is essential to the health of the fetus. Maternal nutritional demands are increased for the development of the placenta, amniotic fluid, increased blood volume, and preparation of the breasts for lactation. The nurse should explain that the expected weight gain during the first trimester is 2 to 4 lb and that a woman of normal weight should expect to gain 1 lb/week during the second and third trimesters for a total of 25 to 35 lb.**

NCLEX® Connection: Health Promotion and Maintenance, Ante/ Intra/ Postpartum and Newborn Care

2. The nurse provides the client with guidelines for her major nutrient intake. Match the appropriate percentage of caloric intake with its corresponding nutrient.

B	Fat	A. 50%
C	Protein	B. 30%
A	Carbohydrates	C. 20%

NCLEX® Connection: Health Promotion and Maintenance, Ante/ Intra/ Postpartum and Newborn Care

Scenario: A woman who is 7 weeks pregnant states that she is experiencing nausea each morning when she wakes.

3. What actions should the nurse encourage the client to take?

The nurse should explain that nausea is a common issue during pregnancy. Encourage the client to eat bland foods (toast, dry cereal, crackers) and avoid consuming liquids with meals. Explain that avoiding alcohol, caffeine, and foods that are spicy or high in fat may help as well.

 NCLEX® Connection: Health Promotion and Maintenance, Ante/ Intra/ Postpartum and Newborn Care

4. Why is folate (folic acid) an important nutrient during pregnancy?

Folic acid is essential for the neurological development of the fetus, and helps to prevent birth defects.

 NCLEX® Connection: Health Promotion and Maintenance, Ante/ Intra/ Postpartum and Newborn Care

5. How much fluid does a pregnant woman need each day, and what are recommended sources of fluids?

A woman should drink 1,500 to 2,000 mL of fluids each day. Water, fruit juices, and milk are nutritionally sound choices.

 NCLEX® Connection: Health Promotion and Maintenance, Ante/ Intra/ Postpartum and Newborn Care

6. A nurse is caring for a mother who gained the recommended amount of weight during her pregnancy and is now breastfeeding. She states that the baby seems hungry all the time, however, the nurse notes that the baby's weight has not changed significantly since her last visit 2 weeks ago. What information is important to share with the client?

The nurse should inform the client that lactating women require an increase in their daily caloric intake. For a woman who gained the recommended amount of weight during pregnancy, an additional 500 cal/day is recommended.

 NCLEX® Connection: Health Promotion and Maintenance, Ante/ Intra/ Postpartum and Newborn Care

7. A nurse is preparing to teach an infant nutrition class in the hospital's obstetrics clinic. The nurse has decided to teach expectant mothers about infant feeding problems. Create a list of questions the mothers may ask and develop an outline of appropriate responses.

What are some benefits of breastfeeding?

The incidence of infections is decreased.

Breast milk contains proteins, fats, and carbohydrates that are more easily absorbed by infants.

The risk of developing food allergies is decreased.

Maternal-infant bonding is promoted.

What is colic and what are ways to prevent it?

The cause of colic is unknown, but it usually occurs in the late afternoon hours, more than 3 days per week for more than 3 weeks.

Colic is characterized by crying, a tense abdomen, and the legs drawn up to the belly.

Burping the infant helps to expel swallowed air, thus decreasing gas formation.

Warm water may provide relief.

If breastfeeding, limit caffeine, nicotine, and gas-forming foods.

Reassure the mother that babies will grow and gain weight.

What foods should I feed the baby first?

Feed with formula or breast milk for 4 to 6 months.

Add iron-fortified rice cereal as the first solid food.

Gradually add vegetables, then fruits.

Add strained meats and egg yolk at 6 to 9 months.

Avoid feeding the infant honey and avoid cow's milk until after 1 year of age.

Ⓝ NCLEX® Connection: Health Promotion and Maintenance, Developmental Stages and Transitions

8. A new mother has brought her 6-month-old infant in for a routine check-up. The infant's birth weight was 7 lb, 2 oz, head circumference was 35.5 cm (14 in), and length was 48 cm (19 in). Which of the following characteristics should pose a concern? (Select all that apply.)

   X   **Head circumference of 41.5 cm (16 in)**

   X   **Weight of 13 lb, 0 oz (5.9 kg)**

   _____   Length of 63 cm (24.8 in)

The normal rate of head circumference growth is approximately 1.5 cm (0.6 in) per month. Based on the infant's birth measurements, its head circumference should be around 44.5 cm (17.5 in). Birth weight should at least double by 6 months of age. Based on the infant's birth weight, the current weight should be at least 14 lb, 4 oz (6.5 kg). Based on the infant's length at birth, his current length should be approximately 63 cm (24.8 in). Expected length increase is 2.5 cm (1 in) per month. The nurse's assessment should begin with an inventory of the infant's eating patterns and sources of nutrition. The nurse should provide nutrition counseling as appropriate. Deviations from expected growth patterns may be an indication of an underlying disease process and should be investigated.

 NCLEX® Connection: Health Promotion and Maintenance, Developmental Stages and Transitions

9. Which of the following snack foods are appropriate for toddlers? (Select all that apply.)

   X   **Graham crackers**

   X   **Apple slices**

   _____   Peeled raisins

   _____   Jelly beans

   X   **Cheese cubes**

Graham crackers, cheese cubes, and apple slices are appropriate snack foods for toddlers. Peeled raisins are difficult to chew and pose a choking hazard. Jelly beans are difficult to swallow, pose a choking risk, and are high in sugar content.

 NCLEX® Connection: Health Promotion and Maintenance, Developmental Stages and Transitions

10. Explain why adequate vitamin D intake is important for children. Name two sources of vitamin D.

Vitamin D is essential for the development of healthy bones. It is important in children because their bones are newly formed and continually growing. Vitamin D aids in the absorption of calcium into the bones. Sunlight exposure, milk (cow's, soy), and fatty fish are sources of vitamin D.

 NCLEX® Connection: Health Promotion and Maintenance, Health Promotion /Disease Prevention

11. List five examples of iron-rich foods.

Iron-rich foods include lean red meats, beans, raisins, peanut butter, and whole grains.

 NCLEX® Connection: Health Promotion and Maintenance, Health Promotion /Disease Prevention

12. Which of the following foods selected by a teen indicates an understanding of healthy snacks? (Select all that apply.)

X	**Carrot sticks with low-fat ranch dip**
X	**Cheese and crackers**
X	**Unbuttered popcorn**
X	**Frozen low-fat yogurt**
_____	Hot dog

Carrot sticks with low-fat ranch dip, cheese and crackers, unbuttered popcorn, and frozen low-fat yogurt are healthy snack selections. Hot dogs are not a healthy food choice as they are high in sodium and fat.

 NCLEX® Connection: Health Promotion and Maintenance, Developmental Stages and Transitions

13. An adolescent female arrives for a routine physical. Her mother states that she has reported fatigue for the last 6 weeks and that she is having difficulty staying awake during school hours. What is one possible explanation for the adolescent's extreme fatigue? Include rationale.

The adolescent female may be experiencing iron deficiency anemia. The nurse should explain that adolescent females have an increased need for iron, and deficiency can result from the growth spurt and blood loss from menses.

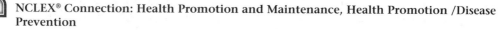 **NCLEX® Connection: Health Promotion and Maintenance, Health Promotion /Disease Prevention**

14. Why is achieving adequate calcium intake important for an adolescent?

Forty-five percent of bone mass is achieved during the adolescent years. Failure to achieve adequate calcium intake leads to the withdrawal of calcium from the bones to maintain adequate blood-calcium levels. This leads to an increased risk of developing osteoporosis later in life.

 NCLEX® Connection: Health Promotion and Maintenance, Health Promotion /Disease Prevention

15. A 54-year-old female client is newly diagnosed with hypertension. She is taking the diuretic hydrochlorothiazide (HydroDIURIL) for her condition. What information is important to share with her regarding side effects and potential nutrition complications?

The nurse should explain that hypertension is a common ailment of aging adults that can be a result of the decrease in the elasticity of blood vessels. Additionally, renal function can decrease up to 50%. The nurse should inform the client that most diuretics, including hydrochlorothiazide, can predispose her to sodium and potassium losses.

 **NCLEX® Connection: Health Promotion and Maintenance, Developmental Stages and Transitions**

UNIT 2: CLINICAL NUTRITION

- Modified Diets
- Enteral Nutrition
- Total Parenteral Nutrition

NCLEX® CONNECTIONS

When reviewing the chapters in this unit, keep in mind the relevant sections of the NCLEX® outline, in particular:

CLIENT NEEDS: BASIC CARE AND COMFORT

Relevant topics/tasks include:
- Nutrition and Oral Hydration
  - Consider the client's choices regarding meeting nutritional requirements and/or maintaining dietary restrictions, including mention of specific food items.
  - Provide client nutrition through continuous or intermittent tube feedings.
  - Evaluate side effects of client tube feedings and intervene, as needed.

UNIT 2	CLINICAL NUTRITION
Chapter 8	Modified Diets

Overview

- Therapeutic nutrition is the role of food and nutrition in the treatment of diseases and disorders.

- The basic diet becomes therapeutic when modifications are made to meet client needs. Modifications may include: increasing or decreasing caloric intake, fiber, or other specific nutrients; omitting specific foods; and modifying the consistency of foods.

- When the gastrointestinal tract is used to provide nourishment, it is referred to as enteral nutrition. Whenever possible, regular oral feedings are preferred.

- Nurses should collaborate with the dietician for nutritional or dietary concerns.

Types of Therapeutic Diets

- Clear Liquid Diet

  o This diet consists of foods that are clear and liquid at room temperature.

  o The clear liquid diet primarily consists of water and carbohydrates. This diet requires minimal digestion, leaves minimal residue, and is non-gas forming. It is nutritionally inadequate and should not be used long term.

  o Indications for a clear liquid diet include acute illness, reduction of colon fecal material prior to certain diagnostic tests and procedures, acute gastrointestinal disorders, and some postoperative recovery.

  o Acceptable foods are water, tea, coffee, fat-free broth, carbonated beverages, clear juices, ginger ale, and gelatin.

  o Caffeine consumption should be limited as it can lead to increased hydrochloric acid and upset stomach.

- Full Liquid Diet

  o Consists of foods that are liquid at room temperature.

  o Full liquid diets offer more variety and nutritional support than a clear liquid diet and can supply adequate amounts of energy and nutrients.

  o Acceptable foods include: all liquids on a clear liquid diet, all forms of milk, soups, strained fruits and vegetables, vegetable and fruit juices, eggnog, plain ice cream and sherbet, refined or strained cereals, and puddings.

- o   If this diet is used more than 2 to 3 days, high-protein and high-calorie supplements may be indicated.

- o   Indications include a transition from liquid to soft diets, postoperative recovery, acute gastritis, febrile conditions, and intolerance of solid foods.

- o   This diet provides oral nourishment for clients having difficulty chewing or swallowing solid foods. Clients with dysphagia (difficulty swallowing) should be cautious with liquids unless they are thickened appropriately.

- o   This diet is contraindicated for clients who have lactose intolerance or hypercholesterolemia. Lactose reduced milk and dairy products should be used when possible.

- **Blenderized Liquid (Pureed) Diet**

  - o   Consists of liquids and foods that have been pureed to liquid form.

  - o   The composition and consistency of a pureed diet varies, depending on the client's needs.

  - o   Pureed diets can be modified with regard to calories, protein, fat, or other nutrients based on the dietary needs of the client.

  - o   Adding broth, milk, gravy, cream, soup, tomato sauce, or fruit juice to foods in place of water provides additional calories and nutritional value.

  - o   Each food is pureed separately to preserve individual flavor.

  - o   Indications for use include clients with chewing or swallowing difficulties, oral or facial surgery, and wired jaws.

- **Soft (Bland, Low-Fiber) Diet**

  - o   A soft diet contains whole foods that are low in fiber, lightly seasoned, and easily digested.

  - o   Food supplements or snacks in between meals are used to add calories.

  - o   Food textures may be smooth, creamy, or crisp. Fruits, vegetables, coarse breads and cereals, beans, and other potentially gas-forming foods are excluded.

  - o   Indications for this diet include clients transitioning between full liquid and regular diets, or those with acute infections, chewing difficulties, or gastrointestinal disorders.

- Mechanical Soft Diet

  ○ A mechanical soft diet is a regular diet that has been modified in texture. The diet composition may be altered for specific nutrient needs.

  ○ This diet includes foods that require minimal chewing before swallowing (ground meats, canned fruits, softly cooked vegetables).

  ○ A mechanical soft diet excludes harder foods (dried fruits, most raw fruits and vegetables, foods containing seeds and nuts).

  ○ Indications for this diet include clients who have limited chewing or swallowing ability; clients with dysphagia, poorly fitting dentures, and who are edentulous (without teeth); clients who have had surgery to the head, neck, or mouth; and clients with strictures of the intestinal tract.

- Regular Diet (Normal or House Diet)

  ○ A regular diet is indicated for clients who do not need dietary restrictions. The diet is adjusted to meet age specific needs throughout the life cycle.

  ○ Many health care facilities offer self select menus for regular diets.

  ○ Dietary modifications to accommodate individual preferences, food habits, and ethnic values can be done without difficulty for the client receiving a regular diet.

Nursing Assessments/Data Collection and Interventions

- Ongoing assessment parameters include daily weights, ordered laboratory values, and an evaluation of a client's nutritional and energy needs and response to diet therapy.

- A client's nutritional intake should be observed and documented. A calorie count may be performed to determine caloric intake and to evaluate adequacy.

- Provide education and support for diet therapy.

- Diet as tolerated is ordered to permit a client's preferences and ability to eat to be considered. Nurses may assess the client for hunger, appetite, and nausea when planning the most appropriate diet, and consult with a dietician.

- Dietary intake is progressively increased (from nothing by mouth to clear liquids to regular diet) following a major surgery. Nurses should assess for the return of bowel function (as evidenced by auscultation of bowel sounds and the passage of flatus) before advancing a client's diet.

- Nurses can increase a client's satisfaction with a hospital diet through courteous delivery, assistance with the tray, displaying a positive attitude toward the diet, and providing education and explanation of the diet.

CHAPTER 8: MODIFIED DIETS

 Application Exercises

Scenario: A 54-year-old female client has returned to her hospital room following an appendectomy. She states that she is hungry, and the provider prescription reads "advance diet as tolerated."

1. Which of the following snack options are appropriate for the client? (Select all that apply.)

_____ Applesauce

_____ Cheese and crackers

_____ Chicken broth

_____ Sherbet

_____ Peanut butter sandwich

_____ Cranberry juice

2. The next day, the client states that she is ready to eat something more substantial. What assessment data is important to obtain before advancing the client's diet?

3. A client has been admitted to the hospital with a diagnosis of acute gastritis. He states that he is starving and hasn't eaten all day. The provider order reads for clear liquids only. The client states that he doesn't want the broth and gelatin that is on his dinner tray. What actions should the nurse take?

4. A client is prescribed a full liquid diet with a minimal caloric requirement. Dietary services performed a calorie count, and it showed that the caloric requirements were not being met with the current diet offerings. List some examples of what should be done to meet the client's current caloric needs without diet progression.

CHAPTER 8: MODIFIED DIETS

 Application Exercises Answer Key

Scenario: A 54-year-old female client has returned to her hospital room following an appendectomy. She states that she is hungry, and the provider prescription reads "advance diet as tolerated."

1. Which of the following snack options are appropriate for the client? (Select all that apply.)

_____	Applesauce
_____	Cheese and crackers
__X__	**Chicken broth**
_____	Sherbet
_____	Peanut butter sandwich
__X__	**Cranberry juice**

> **Clear liquids are an appropriate choice for a postoperative patient. If these choices are tolerated well by the client, the diet should progress to full liquids and eventually solid foods.**

 NCLEX® Connection: Basic Care and Comfort, Nutrition and Oral Hydration

2. The next day, the client states that she is ready to eat something more substantial. What assessment data is important to obtain before advancing the client's diet?

> **Dietary intake should be progressively increased following a major surgery once bowel function has returned. The nurse should verify the client's bowel sounds and the presence of gas or flatus. When diet as tolerated is ordered, the nurse should assess the client for hunger, appetite, and nausea when planning the diet. The nurse should work in conjunction with a dietician when possible.**

 NCLEX® Connection: Basic Care and Comfort, Nutrition and Oral Hydration

3. A client has been admitted to the hospital with a diagnosis of acute gastritis. He states that he is starving and hasn't eaten all day. The provider order reads for clear liquids only. The client states that he doesn't want the broth and gelatin that is on his dinner tray. What actions should the nurse take?

> **The nurse should first acknowledge the client's frustration and explain that clear liquid diets are used for clients with acute gastrointestinal disorders, as the foods included require minimal digestion and are non-gas forming. Reassure the client that he will be continually assessed and that his diet will be advanced when it is deemed appropriate. It may be helpful to ask the client about his preferences for the clear liquid choices so that he feels involved in his care.**

NCLEX® Connection: Basic Care and Comfort, Nutrition and Oral Hydration

4. A client is prescribed a full liquid diet with a minimal caloric requirement. Dietary services performed a calorie count, and it showed that the caloric requirements were not being met with the current diet offerings. List some examples of what should be done to meet the client's current caloric needs without diet progression.

> Pureed diets can fully meet a client's nutritional needs. Substituting liquids for water when preparing the foods can provide additional calories and nutritional value. This includes broth, milk, cream, soup, tomato sauce, and fruit juice. Providing nutritional supplements is another option that will allow the client to obtain adequate caloric and nutrient intake.

Ⓝ NCLEX® Connection: Basic Care and Comfort, Nutrition and Oral Hydration

UNIT 2	CLINICAL NUTRITION
Chapter 9	Enteral Nutrition

Overview

- Enteral nutrition (EN) is used when a client cannot consume adequate nutrients and calories orally, but maintains a partially functional gastrointestinal system.

- EN consists of blenderized foods or a commercial formula administered by a tube into the stomach or small intestine. Enteral feedings most closely utilize the body's own digestive and metabolic routes. EN may augment an oral diet or may be the sole source of nutrition.

Enteral Feeding Routes

- A client's medical status and the anticipated length of time that a tube feeding will be required determine the type of tube used.

  ○ Transnasal tubes extend from the nose to the stomach or small intestine.

    ▪ Nasogastric (NG) tubes are passed from the nose to the stomach.

    ▪ Nasointestinal tubes are passed from the nose to the intestine.

    ▪ These tubes are used short term (less than 3 to 4 weeks).

  ○ An ostomy is a surgically created opening (stoma) made to deliver feedings directly into the stomach or intestines.

    ▪ Gastrostomy tubes are endoscopically or surgically inserted into the stomach. A percutaneous endoscopic gastrostomy (PEG) tube is placed with the aid of an endoscope.

      ☐ Gastrostomy tube feedings are generally well tolerated because the stomach chamber holds and releases feedings in a physiologic manner that promotes effective digestion. As a result, dumping syndrome is usually avoided.

    ▪ Jejunostomy tubes are surgically inserted into the jejunal portion of the small intestine (jejunum).

- Endoscopic or surgical placement is preferred when long-term use is anticipated, or when a nasal obstruction makes insertion through the nose impossible.

- Placement into the stomach stimulates normal gastrointestinal function.

Enteral Feeding Formulas

- Commercial products are preferred over home-blended ingredients because they provide a known nutrient composition, controlled consistency, and bacteriological safety.

- Standard and hydrolyzed formulas are the two primary types of enteral feeding formulas available. They are categorized by the complexity of the proteins included.

  - Standard formulas, also called polymeric or intact, are composed of whole proteins or protein isolates.

    - These formulas require a functioning gastrointestinal tract.

    - Most provide 1.0 to 1.2 cal/mL, but are available in high-protein, high-calorie, and disease-specific formulas.

  - Hydrolyzed formulas, or elemental, are composed of partially digested protein peptides and are referred to as free amino acids.

    - These formulas are used for clients with a partially functioning gastrointestinal tract, or those who have an impaired ability to digest and absorb foods (people with inflammatory bowel disease, short-gut syndrome, cystic fibrosis, pancreatic disorders).

    - Most routine formulas provide 1.0 to 1.2 cal/mL. High calorie formulas provide 1.5 to 2.0 cal/mL. Partially hydrolyzed formulas provide other nutrients in simpler forms that require little or no digestion.

- Tube feedings may be packaged in cans or in pre-filled bags.

  - Pre-filled bags should be discarded every 24 hr or according to facility policy, even if they are not empty.

  - Cans may be used to add formula to a generic bag to infuse via a pump, or for feedings directly from a syringe.

- Factors to consider in determining an appropriate formula include:

  - Caloric density.

  - Water content.

  - Protein density.

  - Osmolality.

  - Fiber and residue content.

  - Presence of other nutrients.

Enteral Feeding Delivery Methods

- The delivery method is dependent on the type and location of the feeding tube, type of formula administered, and the client's tolerance.

  o Continuous drip method: Formula is administered at a continuous rate over a 16 to 24 hr period.

    ■ Infusion pumps help ensure consistent flow rates.

    ■ This method is recommended for critically ill clients because of its association with smaller residual volumes, and a lower risk of aspiration and diarrhea.

    ■ Residual volumes should be measured every 4 to 6 hr.

    ■ Feeding tubes should be flushed with water every 4 hr to maintain patency.

    ■ If the volume of gastric residual exceeds the volume of formula given over the previous 2 hr, it may be necessary to reduce the rate of feeding.

  o Cyclic feedings: Formula is administered at a continuous rate over an 8 to 16 hr time period, often during sleeping hours.

    ■ Often used for transition from total EN to oral intake.

  o Intermittent tube feedings: Formula is administered every 4 to 6 hr in equal portions of 200 to 300 mL over a 30 to 60 min time frame, usually by gravity drip.

    ■ Often used for noncritical clients, home-tube feedings, and clients in rehabilitation.

  o Bolus feedings: A large volume of formula (500 mL maximum, usual volume is 250 to 400 mL) is administered over a short period of time, usually less than 15 min, four to six times daily.

    ■ Bolus feedings are delivered directly into the stomach. They may be poorly tolerated and may cause dumping syndrome.

Indications

- Diagnoses or Clinical Presentations

  o Difficulty with chewing and swallowing

  o Coma

  o Bowel obstruction, fistula, and alterations in upper gastrointestinal tract motility

  o Liver failure

  o Chemotherapy

  o Gastrointestinal malabsorption syndromes and trauma

Nursing Actions

- Preparation of the Client

  - Prior to instilling enteral feeding, tube placement should be verified by radiography. Aspirating gastric contents and measuring pH levels are less reliable methods of verifying placement.

  (M) **View Media Supplement:** Enteral Tube Feeding (Video)

  - Verify the presence of bowel sounds.

  - To maintain feeding tube patency, it should be flushed routinely with warm water.

    - Gastric residuals should be checked every 4 to 6 hr. If the residual volume exceeds the amount of formula given in the previous 2 hr, it may be necessary to consider reducing the rate of the feeding. Residuals should be returned to the stomach as they contain electrolytes, nutrients, and digestive enzymes. Follow the facility policy.

  - The head of the bed should be elevated at least 30° during feedings and for at least 30 min afterward to lessen the risk of aspiration.

  - Begin with a small volume of full-strength formula. Increase volume in intervals as tolerated until the desired volume is achieved.

  - Administer the feeding solution at room temperature to decrease gastrointestinal discomfort.

  - Baseline assessment parameters include:

    - Obtain height, weight, and body mass index (BMI).

    - Monitor serum albumin, hemoglobin, hematocrit, glucose, and electrolyte levels.

    - Evaluate the client's nutritional and energy needs.

    - Verify appropriate gastrointestinal function. Dysfunction of the gastrointestinal tract may indicate a need for alternate forms of nutrition.

- Ongoing Care

  - Monitor daily weights, and daily intake and output.

  - Obtain gastric residuals (every 4 to 6 hr).

  - Monitor electrolyte levels, BUN, creatinine, serum minerals, and CBC as prescribed.

  - Monitor the tube site for signs and symptoms of infection or intolerance (pain, redness, swelling, drainage).

- ○ Monitor the character and frequency of bowel movements.

- ○ Medications may be administered through a feeding tube.

  - Feeding should be stopped prior to administering medications.

  - The tubing should be flushed with water (15 to 30 mL) before and after the medication is given, and between each medication if more than one is given.

  - Liquid medications should be used when possible.

- Interventions

  - ○ Weaning occurs as oral consumption increases. Enteral feedings may be discontinued when the client consumes two-thirds of protein and calorie needs orally for 3 to 5 days.

  - ○ A client who is NPO will require meticulous oral care.

  - ○ A client may require nutritional support service at home for long-term EN. A multidisciplinary team comprised of a nurse, dietician, pharmacist, and the provider, will monitor the weight, electrolyte balance, and overall physical condition of the client.

Complications

- Gastrointestinal Complications

  - ○ Gastrointestinal complications include constipation, diarrhea, cramping, pain, abdominal distention, dumping syndrome, nausea, and vomiting.

- Mechanical Complications

  - ○ Mechanical complications include tube misplacement or dislodgement, aspiration, tube obstruction or rupture, irritation and leakage at the insertion site, and irritation of the nose, esophagus, and mucosa.

  - ○ Nursing Actions

    - Feeding tube obstruction can be prevented by flushing the tube with 20 to 60 mL of warm water after use and every 4 hr, and by avoiding dry products and administering crushed medications. Be sure to include water used to flush the tube in daily intake.

- Metabolic Complications

  - ○ Metabolic complications include dehydration, hyperglycemia, electrolyte imbalances, and overhydration.

- Food Poisoning
  - Bacterial contamination of formula can result in food poisoning.
  - Nursing Actions
    - To avoid bacterial contamination:
      - Wash hands before handling formula or enteral products.
      - Clean equipment and tops of formula cans.
      - Cover and label unused cans with the client's name, room number, date, and time of opening.
      - Refrigerate unused portions promptly for up to 24 hr.
      - Replace the feeding bag and tubing every 24 hr.
      - Fill generic bags with less than 6 hr worth of formula.

CHAPTER 9: ENTERAL NUTRITION

 Application Exercises

Scenario: A nurse is caring for a client who is receiving mechanical ventilation following a recent surgery. The client has a previously placed nasogastric (NG) tube from another institution. The provider order reads to initiate enteral feedings via the NG tube.

1. What data is important to collect before initiating feedings?

2. The enteral tube feeding began at 1000 and has been infusing at a continuous rate of 40 mL/hr. It is now 1400. What actions should the nurse perform? Include rationale.

3. What assessment data should the nurse obtain for the ongoing assessment of a client receiving enteral feedings?

4. Which of the following actions are important in the prevention of bacterial contamination of tube feedings? (Select all that apply.)

_____ Fill the feeding bag with 24 hr worth of formula.

_____ Discard irrigation set after 24 hr.

_____ Leave unused portions in the client's room.

_____ Cover and label any unused portion with the client's name, room number, date, and time opened.

_____ Replace tubing and feeding bag every 48 hr

5. A nurse is preparing a client's 0900 medications. The nurse is to administer 3 separate pills through the client's percutaneous endoscopic gastrostomy (PEG) tube. What actions are appropriate for the nurse to perform?

CHAPTER 9: ENTERAL NUTRITION

 Application Exercises Answer Key

Scenario: A nurse is caring for a client who is receiving mechanical ventilation following a recent surgery. The client has a previously placed nasogastric (NG) tube from another institution. The provider order reads to initiate enteral feedings via the NG tube.

1. What data is important to collect before initiating feedings?

The nurse should first verify the presence of bowel sounds in the client. Then, the placement of the tube should be verified by radiography. Measuring pH levels and aspirating gastric contents are less reliable methods of verifying placement. The nurse should elevate the head of the bed at least 30° during the feeding, and for 30 to 45 min following the feeding. This is done to reduce the risk of aspiration. Lastly, the nurse should obtain baseline assessment data including height, weight, and BMI. Preliminary laboratory values include albumin, hemoglobin, hematocrit, glucose, and electrolyte levels.

 NCLEX® Connection: Basic Care and Comfort, Nutrition and Oral Hydration

2. The enteral tube feeding began at 1000 and has been infusing at a continuous rate of 40 mL/hr. It is now 1400. What actions should the nurse perform? Include rationale.

Feeding tubes should be flushed with 20 to 60 mL of warm water every 4 hr to maintain patency. Residuals should be checked every 4 to 6 hr. Performing these tasks simultaneously allows for less interruption for the client.

 NCLEX® Connection: Basic Care and Comfort, Nutrition and Oral Hydration

3. What assessment data should the nurse obtain for the ongoing assessment of a client receiving enteral feedings?

Clients receiving enteral feedings require careful monitoring to determine the adequacy of the nutrition being received. The nurse should monitor daily weights, and intake and output. The frequency and consistency of bowel movements should be included in output measurements. Serum albumin, hemoglobin, hematocrit, glucose, and electrolyte levels are all indicators of nutritional status and should be monitored. Feeding tube sites, transnasal or surgical, can be sources of irritation or infection for the client. The nurse should monitor the site for any redness, swelling, pain, or drainage and report it to the provider.

 NCLEX® Connection: Basic Care and Comfort, Nutrition and Oral Hydration

4. Which of the following actions are important in the prevention of bacterial contamination of tube feedings? (Select all that apply.)

      _____   Fill the feeding bag with 24 hr worth of formula.

      X   **Discard irrigation set after 24 hr.**

      _____   Leave unused portions in the client's room.

      X   **Cover and label any unused portion with the client's name, room number, date, and time opened.**

      _____   Replace tubing and feeding bag every 48 hr

Feeding bags should be filled with no more than 6 hr worth of formula. Irrigation sets should be changed every 24 hr. Pre-filled bags usually contain enough formula for a 24 hr period. Any unused portion should be covered, properly labeled, and refrigerated. Tubing and feeding should be replaced every 24 hr unless otherwise specified by facility policy.

 NCLEX® Connection: Basic Care and Comfort, Nutrition and Oral Hydration

5. A nurse is preparing a client's 0900 medications. The nurse is to administer 3 separate pills through the client's percutaneous endoscopic gastrostomy (PEG) tube. What actions are appropriate for the nurse to perform?

Medications may be administered through a feeding tube, however they pose a risk for tube obstruction. The nurse should first check with the pharmacist to determine what medications may be available in liquid form. Pills should be thoroughly crushed and diluted before administration. The tube feeding should be stopped before the administration of medications. The tube should be flushed with water (15 to 30 mL) before and after each medication.

NCLEX® Connection: Basic Care and Comfort, Nutrition and Oral Hydration

| UNIT 2 | CLINICAL NUTRITION |
| Chapter 10 | Total Parenteral Nutrition |

Overview

- Parenteral nutrition (PN) is used when a client's gastrointestinal tract is not functioning, or when a client cannot physically or psychologically consume sufficient nutrients orally or enterally.

- Based upon the client's nutritional needs and anticipated duration of therapy, PN can be given as either total parenteral nutrition (TPN) or peripheral parenteral nutrition (PPN).

  - TPN provides a nutritionally complete solution and can be used when caloric needs are very high (more than 2,500 cal/day), when the anticipated duration of therapy is greater than 7 days, or when the solution to be administered is hypertonic (composed of greater than 10% dextrose). It can only be administered in a central vein.

  - PPN can provide a nutritionally complete solution, however, it is administered into a peripheral vein resulting in a limited nutritional value. It is indicated for clients who require short term nutritional support between 2,000 to 2,500 kcal/day. The solution must be isotonic and contain no more than 10% dextrose and 5% amino acids.

Components of Parenteral Nutrition Solutions

- PN includes amino acids, dextrose, electrolytes, vitamins, and trace elements in sterile water.

- Carbohydrate or dextrose solutions are available in concentrations of 5% for PPN and up to 70% for TPN. To avoid hyperglycemia and other complications, dextrose infusions should not exceed 4 to 5 mg/kg/min.

- Electrolytes, vitamins, and trace elements are essential for normal body functions. The amounts added are dependent upon the client's blood chemistry values, and physical assessment findings are used to determine the quantity of electrolytes.

- Lipids (fats) are available in concentrations of 10%, 20%, and 30%. Lipids are a significant source of calories and are used to correct or prevent essential fatty acid deficiency.

  - Lipid emulsions may be added to the solution or administered piggyback or may be given intermittently.

  - Intravenous lipids are contraindicated for clients who have hyperlipidemia or severe hepatic disease.

- Protein is provided as a mixture of essential and non-essential amino acids and is available in concentrations of 3% to 15%.

  - Protein should provide 10% to 20% of total calorie intake.

  - The client's estimated requirements and hepatic and renal function determine the amount of protein provided.

- Medications may be added to PN, and should be added by the pharmacist to avoid incompatibilities. Insulin may be added to reduce the potential for hyperglycemia, and heparin may be added to prevent fibrin buildup on the catheter tip.

Indications

- Diagnoses

  - TPN is commonly used in clients undergoing treatment for cancer, and those suffering from trauma or extensive burns as these conditions are associated with high caloric requirements.

  - PPN may be used when central venous access is not available, or for transition from TPN to enteral or oral intake. It is appropriate for use when PN is needed for less than 7 days, or when caloric needs are less than 2,500 cal/day.

Desired Therapeutic Outcomes

- Evidence supporting the effectiveness of PN includes:

  - Daily weight gain of up to 1 kg/day.

  - Increases in albumin level (normal 3.5 to 5.0 g/dL) and in prealbumin level (normal 23 to 43 mg/dL).

Nursing Actions

- Preparation of the Client

  - Prior to initiating PN, nurses should review the client's weight, BMI, nutritional status, diagnosis, and current laboratory data. This may include: CBC, serum chemistry profile, PT/aPTT, iron, total iron-binding capacity, lipid profile, liver function tests, electrolyte panel, and BUN.

  - Nurse should assess the client's educational needs.

  - An electronic infusion device should be used to prevent the accidental overload of a solution.

- Ongoing Care

  - Nursing care is focused on preventing complications through consistent monitoring. Specific monitoring guidelines vary among health care facilities.

    - Ongoing assessment parameters include: intake and output, daily weights, vital signs, pertinent laboratory values, and ongoing evaluation of the client's underlying condition. This data is used to determine the client's response to therapy and the formulation of the solution to prevent nutrient deficiencies or toxicities.

    - Monitor serum and urine glucose as prescribed. Sliding scale insulin may be prescribed to intervene for hyperglycemia.

    - Flow rate should be monitored carefully:

      - Failure to provide optimal nutritional intake is the result of solutions administered too slowly.

      - Hyperosmolar diuresis can result from an infusion that is too rapid, and can lead to seizures, coma, and death.

    - Monitor for "cracking" of TPN solution. This occurs if the calcium or phosphorous content is high or if poor-salt albumin is added. A "cracked" TPN solution has an oily appearance or a layer of fat on top of the solution and should not be used.

  - Strict aseptic techniques are maintained to reduce the risk of infection. The high dextrose content of PN contributes to bacterial growth.

  - Use sterile technique when changing central line dressing and tubing. The bag and tubing should be changed every 24 hr.

    (M) **View Media Supplement:** Total Parenteral Nutrition (Video)

- Interventions

  - PN should be discontinued as soon as possible to avoid potential complications, but not until the client's enteral or oral intake can provide 60% or more of estimated caloric requirements.

    - Discontinuance should be done gradually to avoid rebound hypoglycemia.

  - Education for clients regarding TPN at home should include aseptic preparation and administration techniques, and criteria to monitor signs and symptoms of infection and complications.

Complications

- Infection and Sepsis

  - Infection and sepsis are evidenced by a fever or elevated WBC count. Infection can result from contamination of the catheter during insertion, contaminated solution, or a long-term indwelling catheter.

- Metabolic Complications

  - Metabolic complications include hyperglycemia, hypoglycemia, hyperkalemia, hypophosphatemia, hypocalcemia, hypoalbuminemia, dehydration, and fluid overload (as evidenced by weight gain greater than 1 kg/day and edema).

- Mechanical Complications

  - Mechanical complications include catheter misplacement, pneumothorax (evidenced by shortness of breath, diminished or absent breath sounds), subclavian artery puncture, catheter embolus, air embolus, thrombosis, obstruction, and bolus infusion.

CHAPTER 10: TOTAL PARENTERAL NUTRITION

 Application Exercises

Scenario: A nurse is caring for a client with a paralytic ileus who is scheduled to begin receiving PPN.

1. What baseline assessment data should the nurse obtain prior to starting the PPN? What assessment data should be included in the ongoing monitoring of the client?

2. After 48 hr of PPN, the client's blood glucose level is 275 mg/dL. The nurse notifies the provider and receives a prescription for insulin to be added to the bag of PPN. Describe the appropriate method for adding medications to PPN therapy. Include rationale.

3. The client's PPN bag has arrived from the pharmacy and is due to be changed at 1800. The nurse notices a layer of fat on the top of the solution. What actions should the nurse take?

4. After 6 days of PPN therapy, the client's bowel sounds have returned and he is consuming 1,700 kcal/day via oral intake. What actions should the nurse anticipate?

CHAPTER 10: TOTAL PARENTERAL NUTRITION

 Application Exercises Answer Key

Scenario: A nurse is caring for a client with a paralytic ileus who is scheduled to begin receiving PPN.

1. What baseline assessment data should the nurse obtain prior to starting the PPN? What assessment data should be included in the ongoing monitoring of the client?

> **Prior to beginning PN, the nurse should review the client's weight, BMI, nutritional status, laboratory values, and current medical diagnosis. Once the PN is started, ongoing assessment parameters should include daily intake and output, daily weights, vital signs, laboratory values, and the client's underlying condition. This data is important because it helps the health care team determine the effectiveness of the PN. If any abnormal values are identified, the PN solution can be modified to address the deficiencies or excesses.**

 NCLEX® Connection: Basic Care and Comfort, Nutrition and Oral Hydration

2. After 48 hr of PPN, the client's blood glucose level is 275 mg/dL. The nurse notifies the provider and receives a prescription for insulin to be added to the bag of PPN. Describe the appropriate method for adding medications to PPN therapy. Include rationale.

> **The nurse should notify the pharmacist responsible for the client's care about the prescription. Medications should be added by the pharmacist to avoid possible incompatibilities with the PN solution.**

 NCLEX® Connection: Basic Care and Comfort, Nutrition and Oral Hydration

3. The client's PPN bag has arrived from the pharmacy and is due to be changed at 1800. The nurse notices a layer of fat on the top of the solution. What actions should the nurse take?

> **The nurse should recognize this as "cracking" of the PPN solution. This can occur if the calcium or phosphorous concentration of the solution is too high, or if poor-salt albumin is used. The solution should not be used and a new solution should be obtained.**

NCLEX® Connection: Basic Care and Comfort, Nutrition and Oral Hydration

4. After 6 days of PPN therapy, the client's bowel sounds have returned and he is consuming 1,700 kcal/day via oral intake. What actions should the nurse anticipate?

> **A PN should be discontinued as soon as possible to avoid complications (infection, electrolyte imbalances, fluid overload). The client is receiving PPN, which is generally recommended for clients who have caloric needs less than 2,500 cal/day. The nurse should expect the PPN to be discontinued as the client is consuming 1,700 kcal/day orally, which is more than the 60% that is recommended for discontinuing PN. It is important to note that discontinuing PN should be done gradually to avoid rebound hypoglycemia.**

NCLEX® Connection: Basic Care and Comfort, Nutrition and Oral Hydration

UNIT 3: ALTERATIONS IN NUTRITION

- Barriers to Adequate Nutrition
- Cardiovascular and Hematologic Disorders
- Gastrointestinal Disorders
- Renal Disorders
- Diabetes Mellitus
- Cancer and Immunosuppression Disorders

NCLEX® CONNECTIONS

When reviewing the chapters in this unit, keep in mind the relevant sections of the NCLEX® outline, in particular:

CLIENT NEEDS: HEALTH PROMOTION AND MAINTENANCE

Relevant topics/tasks include:
- Health Promotion/Disease Prevention
  - Identify risk factors for disease/illness.
- Health Screening
  - Identify risk factors linked to ethnicity.
- High-Risk Behaviors
  - Assist the client to identify behaviors/risks that may impact health.

CLIENT NEEDS: BASIC CARE AND COMFORT

Relevant topics/tasks include:
- Nutrition and Oral Hydration
  - Provide nutritional supplements as needed.
  - Manage the client who has an alteration in nutritional intake.
  - Evaluate the impact of disease/illness on the nutritional status of the client.

CLIENT NEEDS: PHYSIOLOGICAL ADAPTATION

Relevant topics/tasks include:
- Alterations in Body Systems
  - Assess the adaptation of the client to health alteration, illness, and/or disease.
  - Educate the client about managing health problems.
  - Implement interventions to address side/adverse effects of radiation therapy.

UNIT 3	ALTERATIONS IN NUTRITION
Chapter 11	Barriers to Adequate Nutrition

Overview

- Many individuals have difficulty consuming a nutritional or prescribed diet due to factors that create a barrier.

- These factors may relate to an individual's developmental stage, treatment for an alteration in health (cancer, the inability to afford or obtain food related to maintaining a nutritional or special diet), among other factors.

- It is important for nurses to recognize these factors as nutritional education will be ineffective if a client lacks the necessary resources to follow through on recommendations.

- Barriers to client nutrition that nurses commonly have to acknowledge are:

  - Poor dentition or poorly fitting dentures

  - Low socioeconomic status and lack of access

  - Cognitive disorders

  - Altered sensory perception

  - Impairment in swallowing

  - Mechanical fixation of the jaw

  - Lack of knowledge and misinformation about nutrition

Nutritional Barriers and Nursing Interventions

- Poor Dentition or Poorly Fitting Dentures

  - Poor dentition can be a problem for clients across the lifespan.

    - Children who do not have access to dental care or tools (toothbrush, toothpaste) may have caries that impair the ability to chew.

    - Adults who have lost teeth or have teeth that need removal or repair will have an impaired ability to chew.

    - After an adult has their teeth removed, it may be difficult to adjust to dentures.

- o Nursing Care

  - School screenings can help identify children who need dental attention, and can facilitate the referral process.

  - Children should be given information about healthy snacks that are low in sugar content.

  - Children and adults should be encouraged to use a fluoridated tooth paste and have fluoride applied to their teeth.

  - Adults who are admitted to acute or long-term care facilities should have a dental inspection done by a nurse to identify issues that may impact the ability to properly eat.

  - If a barrier is found to exist, a dietician should be consulted so the proper diet is prescribed and nutritional supplements are added as necessary.

- Low Socioeconomic Status and Lack of Access

  - o The lack of money to purchase healthy foods or foods required for a special diet can be a barrier to maintaining a proper diet.

    - Nutritious foods (fresh fruit, vegetables) tend to be more expensive than canned and box foods.

    - Canned and boxed foods are usually high in calories and salt. This is a poor choice for clients on calorie or sodium restricted diets.

    - The lack of money to purchase necessary food can lead to malnutrition or obesity if canned and boxed foods are selected.

    - The lack of transportation to grocery stores is a barrier if the client does not have a car or is not licensed to drive.

  - o Nursing Care

    - Clients should be referred to a dietician who can discuss food options and substitutions that are appropriate.

    - Frozen fruits and vegetables may be an affordable option, and are maintained longer in the freezer.

    - Educate clients on how to read food labels to be aware of nutritional, caloric, and sodium values of the food they are consuming.

    - Contact social services regarding the availability of food or meal delivery to the client's home. Investigate the availability of a nutrition program for older adults that provide a noon meal for a localized community.

- Cognitive Disorders

  ○ Cognitive disorders (dementia, Alzheimer's disease [AD]) may have a significant impact on nutritional status.

    ■ Clients with dementia or AD may experience impairments in memory and judgment making shopping and food selection difficult.

    ■ As dementia and AD progress, clients may refuse to eat or chose a small selection of food that may not provide adequate nutrition.

  ○ Nursing Care

    ■ If the client lives independently, encourage shopping with a friend or family member, and to follow a shopping list.

    ■ Contact social services regarding the availability of food or meal delivery to the client's home.

    ■ If the client lives in a care facility, provide a menu with minimal but nutritious options.

    ■ Serve meals at the same time and in the same location surrounded by the same residents. Keep environmental distractions to a minimum.

    ■ Provide snacks in between meals if meal time intake is inadequate.

    ■ Cut food into small pieces if the client does not chew food well. Remind the client to chew and then swallow. Lightly stroking the chin and throat may help promote swallowing.

- Altered Sensory Perception

  ○ Clients who have an alteration in vision, smell, or taste may find it difficult to either feed themselves or may find food unpalatable.

    ■ Clients with decreased vision will need assistance shopping for food on a regular basis, and with food preparation.

    ■ Clients in a health or long-term care facility will need help with tray setup and location of food on the tray.

    ■ Clients with an altered sense of smell will have an altered sense of taste.

    ■ Clients who are smokers may have a diminished sense of smell.

    ■ Clients on chemotherapy and other types of medications may have an unusual taste in their mouth (metallic taste), masking the real taste of food.

    ■ Clients on chemotherapy may experience nausea and anorexia, resulting in an aversion to food.

  ○ Nursing Care

    ■ Encourage the client with decreased vision to shop with a friend or family member, or have groceries delivered to the house.

    ■ Contact social services regarding availability of food or meal delivery to the client's home.

- Recommend the client with a food aversion to eat foods that are served cool, as they are typically less aromatic and are less likely to precipitate nausea.

- Suggest consuming foods that are spicy or tangy to compensate for the decreased sense of taste.

- Recommend sucking on hard candies, mints, or chewing gum to counteract an unusual taste in the mouth.

- Instruct the client to avoid ingestion of empty calories. If an increase in calories and fluid is desired, milk shakes, juice, and supplements are good options.

- Impairment in Swallowing

  - Clients who have neurological disorders (Parkinson's disease, stroke, had a surgical procedure done on their mouth, throat, epiglottis, larynx) may have difficulty managing food and swallowing without choking.

    - Clients who have a neurological disorder affecting the muscles in their mouth and throat are at risk for aspiration due to delayed swallowing and/or inadequate mastication.

    - Clients with a history of oral cancer may have had part of their lip, tongue, and/or soft palate removed. This significantly affects the ability to masticate and coordinate the development of a bolus of food prior to swallowing.

    - Clients who have had their epiglottis completely or partially removed, or part of their larynx removed, have an anatomical structure removed that previously prevented food from entering the trachea. Unless special precautions are taken, the client will easily aspirate food and fluids consumed.

  - Nursing Care

    - Clients who are at risk for aspiration should be continually monitored during meals, and suction equipment should be immediately available.

    - A dietician should be consulted regarding an appropriate diet for client (thick liquids, pureed, mechanical soft)

    - Thicker fluids should be prescribed, and thin fluids should be thickened with a commercial thickener to the consistency of a nectar, honey, or pudding.

    - Clients who aspirate easily due to surgical alteration of their throat or upper tracheal structures should be taught to tuck their chins when swallowing. Arching the tongue in the back of the throat may help close off the trachea.

- Mechanical Fixation of the Jaw

  - Disorders of the jaw requiring surgery include facial trauma and reconstruction.

    - After fractured bones are realigned, the client's upper and lower jaw may be wired together.

    - The jaw may be immobilized for several weeks.

    - The client may be placed on a liquid diet during this period.

- ○ Nursing Care
    - Encourage the intake of fluids
    - Help the client determine where to insert a straw through the space between the jaws
    - Have the dietician develop a liquid meal plan that includes the necessary nutrients
- Lack of Knowledge and Misinformation about Nutrition
    - ○ Clients who do not have a good understanding about nutritional needs may be subject to over-nutrition, under-nutrition, and/or the ingestion of an inadequate intake of essential nutrients.
        - Clients may not have basic knowledge about nutrition.
        - Information about nutrition may be confusing or misleading.
        - Clients may be drawn to fad diets (which are generally unhealthy) as quick results are promised.
        - Clients can be misled by false advertising.
    - ○ Nursing Care
        - Encourage clients to use dietary guidelines available from governmental and health associations (MyPyramid, the American Heart Association).
        - Assist clients in locating community resources that provide education on nutrition.
        - Perform an assessment of dietary intake.
        - Instruct clients on how to read nutrition fact labels.
        - Provide clients with information on foods that are healthy and portion sizes
        - Warn clients that advertisements may be fraudulent.

CHAPTER 11: BARRIERS TO ADEQUATE NUTRITION

(A) Application Exercises

1. A nurse is caring for several clients in an extended care facility. Which of the following clients should be observed during meals?

   A. A client with decreased vision

   B. A client with Alzheimer's disease

   C. A client who wears dentures

   D. A client with anorexia

2. An older adult client is discharged home after treatment for dehydration and malnutrition. The client lives alone and does not have any family living in town. Which of the following actions should the nurse take to help the client better meet his dietary needs? (Select all that apply.)

   _____ Consult social service for home meal delivery.

   _____ Encourage the client to purchase canned and boxed meals.

   _____ Recommend purchasing frozen fruits and vegetables.

   _____ Recommend drinking a supplement between meals.

   _____ Investigate the availability of an older adult community lunch program.

3. A client recently diagnosed with hypertension has been put on a low sodium diet. Which of the following recommendations should be made regarding food selection when grocery shopping?

   A. Look for foods that are labeled "low fat."

   B. Read the labels prior to purchasing foods.

   C. Consider eating frozen dinners for lunch.

   D. Recommend deli meats and cheese.

4. A nurse is caring for a client who has difficulty swallowing and chokes frequently. Which of the following methods of swallowing should the nurse recommend?

   A. Tip head back when swallowing pills.

   B. Follow each bite with a drink of water.

   C. Tuck the chin when swallowing.

   D. Consume a liquid diet.

CHAPTER 11: BARRIERS TO ADEQUATE NUTRITION

 Application Exercises Answer Key

1. A nurse is caring for several clients in an extended care facility. Which of the following clients should be observed during meals?

A. A client with decreased vision

B. A client with Alzheimer's disease

C. A client who wears dentures

D. A client with anorexia

A client with Alzheimer's disease is at risk for choking due to cognitive deficits that can impair the ability to coordinate mastication with swallowing. The client may need reminders to swallow, or have their throat stroked when swallowing. The client with decreased vision will need help with tray setup but should be able to eat independently. The client with dentures should be able to eat independently. The client with anorexia may need encouragement to eat and several small meals a day, but observation during the meal is unnecessary.

 NCLEX® Connection: Basic Care and Comfort, Nutrition and Oral Hydration

2. An older adult client is discharged home after treatment for dehydration and malnutrition. The client lives alone and does not have any family living in town. Which of the following actions should the nurse take to help the client better meet his dietary needs? (Select all that apply.)

   X   **Consult social service for home meal delivery.**

          Encourage the client to purchase canned and boxed meals.

   X   **Recommend purchasing frozen fruits and vegetables.**

   X   **Recommend drinking a supplement between meals.**

   X   **Investigate the availability of an older adult community lunch program.**

All of the options would be appropriate to help this client meet his dietary needs except for recommending canned and boxed meals. These meals are usually high in calories, sodium, and nitrites that are not nutritionally sound.

 NCLEX® Connection: Health Promotion and Maintenance, Health Promotion/ Disease Prevention

3. A client recently diagnosed with hypertension has been put on a low sodium diet. Which of the following recommendations should be made regarding food selection when grocery shopping?

    A. Look for foods that are labeled "low fat."

    B. Read the labels prior to purchasing foods.

    C. Consider eating frozen dinners for lunch.

    D. Recommend deli meats and cheese.

The client should be encouraged to read the labels on all foods prior to purchase. Frozen dinners and deli meats and cheese are typically high in sodium and should be avoided. Eating low fat foods will not provide a benefit for clients who need to restrict their sodium intake.

 NCLEX® Connection: Basic Care and Comfort, Nutrition and Oral Hydration

4. A nurse is caring for a client who has difficulty swallowing and chokes frequently. Which of the following methods of swallowing should the nurse recommend?

    A. Tip head back when swallowing pills.

    B. Follow each bite with a drink of water.

    C. Tuck the chin when swallowing.

    D. Consume a liquid diet.

The client should tuck the chin when swallowing rather than tipping the head back. Thin fluids (water) are harder to control and should be thickened prior to drinking.

 NCLEX® Connection: Basic Care and Comfort, Nutrition and Oral Hydration

UNIT 3	ALTERATIONS IN NUTRITION
Chapter 12	Cardiovascular and Hematologic Disorders

@ Overview

- Nurses must gain an awareness of nutritional needs for clients with cardiovascular and hematologic disorders. It is important to explore dietary needs with the client and recommend modifications in relationship to the disease process. Understanding the role of primary and secondary prevention is essential to successful treatment.

- Specific nutritional considerations are covered in this chapter for:

  o Coronary heart disease

  o Hypertension

  o Heart failure

  o Myocardial infarction

  o Anemia

- Cardiovascular diseases are the leading cause of death in the United States. Coronary heart disease (CHD) is the single leading cause of death.

Assessment/Data Collection

- Coronary Heart Disease

  o Hypercholesterolemia is a major risk factor for developing CHD. CHD is caused by atherosclerosis, a process of damage and cholesterol deposits on the blood vessels of the heart.

    ▪ High density lipoprotein (HDL) cholesterol is "good" cholesterol as it removes cholesterol from the serum and takes it to the liver.

    ▪ Low density lipoprotein (LDL) cholesterol is "bad" cholesterol as it transports cholesterol out of the liver and into the circulatory system, where it can form plaques on the coronary artery walls.

    ▪ Evidence has demonstrated that a diet high in cholesterol and saturated fats greatly increases the risk of developing heart disease.

- Anemia
  - Iron Deficiency Anemia
    - Symptoms
      - Fatigue
      - Lethargy
      - Pallor of nail beds
      - Intolerance to cold
    - Children with low iron intake can experience short attention spans and display poor intellectual performance before anemia begins.
  - Vitamin B_{12} Deficiency Anemia
    - Gastrointestinal Symptoms
      - Glossitis (inflamed tongue)
      - Anorexia
      - Indigestion
      - Weight loss
    - Neurological Symptoms
      - Paresthesia (numbness) of hands and feet
      - Decreased proprioception (sense of body position)
      - Poor muscle coordination
      - Increasing irritability
      - Delirium
  - Folic Acid Deficiency Anemia
    - Manifestations include mental confusion, fainting, fatigue, and gastrointestinal distress.
    - Symptoms of folic acid deficiency anemia mimic those for vitamin B_{12} deficiency anemia except for the neurological symptoms.

Nutritional Guidelines and Nursing Interventions

- Coronary Heart Disease
  - Preventative Nutrition
    - Consuming a low-fat, low-cholesterol diet can reduce the risk of developing CHD. The Therapeutic Lifestyle Change (TLC) diet is designed to be a user friendly eating guide to encourage dietary changes.
    - Daily cholesterol intake should be less than 200 mg.

- Conservative use of red wine may reduce the risk of developing CHD.

- Increasing fiber and carbohydrate intake, avoiding saturated fat, and decreasing red meat consumption can decrease the risk for developing CHD.

- Homocysteine is an amino acid. Elevated homocysteine levels can increase the risk of developing CHD. Deficiencies in folate and possibly vitamins B_6 and B_{12} may increase homocysteine levels.

○ Therapeutic Nutrition

- Secondary prevention efforts for CHD are focused on lifestyle changes that lower LDL. These include a diet low in cholesterol and saturated fats, a diet high in fiber, exercise and weight management, and smoking cessation.

- Daily cholesterol intake should be less than 200 mg/day. Saturated fat should be limited to less than 7% of daily caloric intake.

- To lower cholesterol and saturated fats, instruct the client to:
  □ Trim visible fat from meats.
  □ Limit red meats and choose lean meats (turkey, chicken).
  □ Remove the skin from meats.
  □ Broil, bake, or steam foods, and avoid frying foods.
  □ Use low-fat or nonfat milk, cheese, and yogurt.
  □ Use spices in place of butter or salt to season foods.
  □ Avoid trans fat as it increases LDL. Partially hydrogenated products contain trans fat.
  □ Read labels.

- Encourage the client to consume a high-fiber diet. Soluble fiber lowers LDL.
  □ Oats, beans, fruits, vegetables, whole grains, barley, and flax are good sources of fiber.

- Encourage the client to exercise.
  □ Instruct the client on practical methods for increasing physical activity (encourage the client to take the stairs rather than the elevator).
  □ Provide the client with references for local exercise facilities.

- Instruct the client to stop all use of tobacco products.

- The recommended lifestyle changes represent a significant change for many clients.
  - Provide support to the client and family.
  - Encourage the client's family to participate in the changes to ease the transition for the client.
  - Explain why the diet is important.
  - Aid the client in developing a diet that is complementary to personal food preferences and lifestyle. A food diary may be helpful.
  - Instruct the client that occasional deviations from the diet are reasonable.

- Hypertension
  - Hypertension is a significant risk factor for developing CHD, a myocardial infarction, and stroke.
  - Hypertension is a sustained elevation in blood pressure.
  - Therapeutic Nutrition
    - The Dietary Approaches to Stopping Hypertension (DASH) diet is a low-sodium, high-potassium, and high-calcium diet that has proven to lower blood pressure and cholesterol.
      - Lower sodium intake (a daily intake of less than 2,400 mg is recommended).
      - Foods high in sodium include: canned soups and sauces, potato chips, pretzels, smoked meats, seasonings, and processed foods.
      - Include low-fat dairy products to promote calcium intake.
      - Include fruits and vegetables rich in potassium (apricots, bananas, tomatoes, potatoes).
    - Limit alcohol intake.
    - Encourage the client to read labels and educate the client about appropriate food choices.
    - Other lifestyle changes include exercising, weight loss, and smoking cessation.

- Heart Failure
  - Heart failure is characterized by the inability of the heart to maintain adequate blood flow throughout the circulatory system. It results in excess sodium and fluid retention, and edema.
  - Therapeutic Nutrition
    - Reduce sodium intake.
    - Monitor (and possibly restrict) fluid intake.

- Myocardial Infarction (MI)

  o An MI occurs when there is an inadequate supply of oxygen to the myocardium. Frequently an MI occurs because of atherosclerosis.

  o After an MI, it is necessary to reduce the myocardial oxygen demands related to metabolic activity.

  o Therapeutic Nutrition

    ▪ A liquid diet is best for the first 24 hr after the infarction.

    ▪ Caffeine should be avoided as it stimulates the heart and increases heart rate.

    ▪ Small, frequent meals are indicated.

    ▪ Counsel the client about recommendations for a heart-healthy diet.

- Anemia

  o Anemia results from either a reduction in the number of red blood cells (RBCs) or in hemoglobin, the oxygen-carrying component of blood. Anemia can result from a decrease in RBC production, an increase in RBC destruction, or a loss of blood.

    ▪ The body requires iron, vitamin B_{12}, and folic acid to produce red blood cells.

    ▪ Iron deficiency anemia is the most common nutritional disorder in the world. It affects approximately 10% of the U.S. population, especially older infants, toddlers, adolescent girls, and pregnant women.

    ▪ From childhood until adolescence, iron intake tends to be marginal.

    ▪ Pernicious anemia is the most common form of vitamin B_{12} deficiency. It is caused by lack of intrinsic factor, a protein that helps the body absorb vitamin B_{12}. Risk factors include gastric surgery, gastric cancer, Helicobacter pylori, and age greater than 50. Clients with pernicious anemia require vitamin B_{12} injections.

  o Iron deficiency anemia can result from poor intestinal absorption, blood loss, and inadequate consumption.

    ▪ Sources of Iron

      □ Beef liver

      □ Red meat

      □ Fish

      □ Poultry

      □ Tofu

      □ Dried peas and beans

      □ Whole grains

      □ Dried fruit

- Iron-Fortified Foods

    □ Infant formula (acceptable alternative or supplement to breastfeeding)

    □ Infant cereal (usually the first food introduced to infants)

    □ Ready-to-eat cereals

- Vitamin C facilitates the absorption of iron (promote consumption).

- Caution: Medicinal iron overdose is the leading cause of accidental poisoning in small children and can lead to acute iron toxicity.

○ Vitamin B_{12} deficiency anemia results from a failure to absorb vitamin B_{12} (pernicious anemia) or inadequate intake.

- Natural Sources of Vitamin B_{12}

    □ Fish

    □ Meat

    □ Poultry

    □ Eggs

    □ Milk

- People over the age of 50 are urged to consume most of their vitamin B_{12} requirement from supplements or fortified food.

- Vegans need supplemental B_{12}.

○ Folic acid deficiency anemia is caused by poor nutrition, malabsorption (Crohn's disease), and drug use.

- Folic Acid Sources

    □ Green leafy vegetables

    □ Dried peas and beans

    □ Liver

    □ Seeds

    □ Orange juice

    □ Cereals and breads fortified with folic acid

- If the client is unable to obtain an adequate supply of folic acid, supplementation may be necessary.

CHAPTER 12: CARDIOVASCULAR AND HEMATOLOGIC DISORDERS

 Application Exercises

1. A nurse is caring for a client who experienced a myocardial infarction at 0300. The client asks, "What is the difference between good cholesterol and bad cholesterol?" How should the nurse respond?

2. Describe the DASH diet and its indications for use.

3. What general dietary recommendations are appropriate for the prevention and control of CHD?

Scenario: A nurse is caring for a 13-year-old female client. She states that she has been feeling tired and is having trouble maintaining her attention span in school. Further assessment yields that she began menstruating 6 months ago.

---

4. These symptoms are indicative of what condition?

5. The nurse should provide what education regarding iron intake?

---

6. A 57-year-old male client is seen for his annual physical. He states that he has felt fatigued over the last 6 weeks and has experienced numbness in his hands. These symptoms are indicative of what condition?

7. Which of the following foods are good sources of vitamin B_{12}? (Select all that apply.)

    _____ Beef liver

    _____ Broccoli

    _____ Salmon

    _____ Apples

    _____ Eggs

    _____ Yogurt

CHAPTER 12: CARDIOVASCULAR AND HEMATOLOGIC DISORDERS

 Application Exercises Answer Key

1. A nurse is caring for a client who experienced a myocardial infarction at 0300. The client asks, "What is the difference between good cholesterol and bad cholesterol?" How should the nurse respond?

The nurse should explain that good cholesterol is known as HDL and it removes cholesterol from the bloodstream and transports it to the liver. LDL is known as bad cholesterol and it transports cholesterol into the bloodstream where it is readily available to form artery plaques (atherosclerosis).

 NCLEX® Connection: Health Promotion and Maintenance, Health Promotion /Disease Prevention

2. Describe the DASH diet and its indications for use.

The DASH diet is a low-sodium, high-potassium, and high-calcium diet that aids in the lowering of blood pressure and cholesterol. Clients should restrict their sodium intake to less than 2,400 mg/day. Avoiding canned soups, sauces, and salty snacks (potato chips, smoked meats, processed foods) contributes to lower sodium consumption. Tomatoes, bananas, and apricots are high-potassium foods. Calcium sources should be from low-fat dairy products and other calcium-fortified foods. Reading food labels will aid the client in identifying the appropriate food choices.

 NCLEX® Connection: Health Promotion and Maintenance, Health and Wellness

3. What general dietary recommendations are appropriate for the prevention and control of CHD?

In general, clients should consume a diet that is low in fat (especially saturated fats) low in sodium, and low in cholesterol. High-fiber foods positively contribute to cardiac health. Red wine can be consumed in moderation. Clients should be encouraged to maintain a healthy weight, exercise, and discontinue tobacco use.

 NCLEX® Connection: Health Promotion and Maintenance, Health Promotion /Disease Prevention

Scenario: A nurse is caring for a 13-year-old female client. She states that she has been feeling tired and is having trouble maintaining her attention span in school. Further assessment yields that she began menstruating 6 months ago.

4. These symptoms are indicative of what condition?

> The client's symptoms are indicative of iron deficiency anemia. Fatigue and nail bed pallor are two signs of iron deficiency anemia. Additionally, iron deficiency anemia is prevalent among adolescent girls, and can result from blood loss experienced during menstruation.

 NCLEX® Connection: Health Promotion and Maintenance, High Risk Behaviors

5. The nurse should provide what education regarding iron intake?

> The nurse should explain that iron deficiency is common among adolescent females, and instruct the client to recognize signs and symptoms. The nurse should encourage the client to incorporate iron-rich foods (meats, fish, beans, whole grains, dried fruit) into her diet to achieve adequate iron intake.

 NCLEX® Connection: Basic Care and Comfort, Nutrition and Oral Hydration

6. A 57-year-old male client is seen for his annual physical. He states that he has felt fatigued over the last 6 weeks and has experienced numbness in his hands. These symptoms are indicative of what condition?

> Vitamin B_{12} deficiency anemia

 NCLEX® Connection: Health Promotion and Maintenance, High Risk Behaviors

7. Which of the following foods are good sources of vitamin B_{12}? (Select all that apply.)

__X__	**Beef liver**
_____	Broccoli
__X__	**Salmon**
_____	Apples
__X__	**Eggs**
__X__	**Yogurt**

> The above selected foods are good dietary sources of vitamin B_{12}. Broccoli and apples are not an adequate source of vitamin B_{12}.

 NCLEX® Connection: Basic Care and Comfort, Nutrition and Oral Hydration

UNIT 3	ALTERATIONS IN NUTRITION
Chapter 13	Gastrointestinal Disorders

Overview

- Nurses must gain an awareness of nutritional needs for clients with gastrointestinal disorders. It is important to explore dietary needs with the client and recommend modifications in relationship to the disease process. Understanding the role of primary and secondary prevention is essential to successful treatment.

- Specific nutrition considerations covered in this chapter are:

  - Nausea and Vomiting
  - Anorexia
  - Constipation
  - Diarrhea
  - Dysphagia
  - Dumping Syndrome
  - Gastroesophageal Reflux Disease
  - Gastritis
  - Peptic Ulcer Disease
  - Lactose Intolerance
  - Ileostomies and Colostomies
  - Diverticulosis and Diverticulitis
  - Inflammatory Bowel Disease
  - Cholecystitis
  - Pancreatitis
  - Liver Disease

- Nutrition therapy for gastrointestinal disorders is generally aimed at minimizing or preventing symptoms.

- For some gastrointestinal disorders, nutrition therapy is the foundation of treatment.

Assessment/Data Collection

- Assess if the client is experiencing any of the following symptoms:

    o Difficulty chewing or swallowing

    o Nausea or vomiting

    o Diarrhea

    o Weight changes

    o Changes in eating patterns or bowel habits

- Assess if the client uses:

    o Tobacco

    o Alcohol

    o Caffeine

    o Over-the-counter medications for gastrointestinal symptoms

    o Nutritional supplements

Nutritional Guidelines and Nursing Interventions

- General Gastrointestinal Considerations

    o Monitor gastrointestinal parameters.

      ▪ Weight and weight changes

      ▪ Laboratory values

      ▪ Bowel sounds

    o Low-fiber diets avoid foods that are high in residue content (whole-grain breads and cereals, raw fruits and vegetables).

      ▪ Diets low in fiber reduces the frequency and volume of fecal output and slow transit time of food through the digestive tract.

      ▪ Low-fiber diets are used short term for:

        □ Diarrhea.

        □ Acute diverticulitis.

        □ Malabsorption syndromes.

        □ Preparation for bowel surgery.

- ○ High-fiber diets focus on foods containing more than 5 g of fiber per serving. A diet high in fiber helps:
    - Increase stool bulk.
    - Stimulate peristalsis.
    - Prevent constipation.
    - Protect against colon cancer.
- Nausea and Vomiting
    - ○ Potential causes of nausea and vomiting include: decreased gastric acid secretion; decreased gastrointestinal motility; bacterial or vital infection; increased intracranial pressure; liver, pancreatic, and gall bladder disorders; or side effects of some medications.
    - ○ The underlying cause of nausea and vomiting should be investigated.
    - ○ Once the client's symptoms subside, begin with clear liquids followed by full liquids, and advance the diet as tolerated.
    - ○ Low-fat carbohydrate foods (crackers, toast, oatmeal, bland fruit) are usually well tolerated.
    - ○ Other interventions include:
        - Clients should avoid liquids with meals as they promote a feeling of fullness.
        - Promote good oral hygiene with mouthwash and ice chips.
        - Elevate the head of the bed.
        - Discourage heated and spicy foods.
        - Serve foods at room temperature or chilled
        - Avoid high fat foods if they contribute to nausea
- Anorexia
    - ○ Anorexia is defined as a lack of appetite. It is a common symptom for numerous physical conditions and is a side effect of certain medications. It is not the same as anorexia nervosa.
    - ○ Provide small, frequent meals and avoid high-fat foods to help maximize the intake of clients who are anorexic.
    - ○ Provide liquid supplements between meals to improve protein and calorie intake.

- Constipation

  o Clients with constipation have difficult or infrequent passage of stools, which may be hard and dry.

  o Causes include: irregular bowel habits, psychogenic factors, inactivity, chronic laxative use or abuse, obstruction, medications, and inadequate consumption of fiber and fluid.

  o Encourage exercise and a diet high in fiber (25 g/day for women and 38 g/day for men), and promote adequate fluid intake to help alleviate symptoms.

- Diarrhea

  o May cause significant losses of potassium, sodium, and fluid. It may lead to nutritional complications

  o Common causes of diarrhea include emotional and physical stress, gastrointestinal disorders, malabsorption disorders, and infections and certain drug therapies.

  o Nutrition therapy varies with the severity and duration of diarrhea. A liberal fluid intake to replace losses is needed.

- Dysphagia

  o Dysphagia is an alteration in the client's ability to swallow.

  o Causes include: obstruction, inflammation, and certain neurological disorders.

  o Modifying the texture of foods and the consistency of liquids may enable the client to achieve proper nutrition.

  o Clients with dysphagia are at an increased risk of aspiration. Place the client in an upright or high-Fowler's position to facilitate swallowing.

  o Provide oral care prior to eating to enhance the client's sense of taste.

  o Clients with dysphagia should be referred to a speech therapist for evaluation.

  o Dietary modifications are based on the specific swallowing limitations experienced by the client.

  o Allow adequate time for eating, utilize adaptive eating devices, and encourage small bites and thorough chewing.

  o Avoid thin liquids and sticky foods.

  o Nutritional supplements may be indicated if nutritional intake is deemed inadequate.

- Dumping Syndrome

  o This occurs as a complication of gastric surgeries that inhibit the ability of the pyloric sphincter to control the movement of food into the small intestine.

    ▪ "Dumping" results in nausea, distention, cramping pains, and diarrhea within 15 min after eating.

    ▪ Weakness, dizziness, rapid heartbeat, and hypoglycemia may occur.

- Small, frequent meals are indicated.

- Consumption of protein and fat at each meal is indicated.

- Avoid food that contains concentrated sugars.

- Restrict lactose intake.

- Consume liquids 1 hr before or after eating instead of during meals (dry diet).

- Gastroesophageal Reflux Disease (GERD)

  - GERD occurs as the result of the lower esophagus causing gastric secretions to move up the esophagus. This leads to indigestion and heartburn.

  - Encourage weight loss for overweight clients.

  - Avoid large meals and bedtime snacks.

  - Avoid trigger foods (citrus fruits and juices, spicy foods, carbonated beverages).

  - Avoid items that reduce lower esophageal sphincter (LES) pressure, including:

    - Fatty foods

    - Caffeine

    - Chocolate

    - Alcohol

    - Cigarette smoke

    - Peppermint and spearmint flavors

- Gastritis

  - Gastritis is characterized by inflammation of the gastric mucosa.

  - Causes include food poisoning, radiation therapy, metabolic stress, and excessive alcohol use.

  - Symptoms include vomiting, bleeding, and hematemesis (vomiting of blood).

  - Avoid eating frequent meals and snacks, as they promote increased gastric acid secretion.

  - Avoid alcohol, cigarette smoking, aspirin and other non-steroidal anti-inflammatory drugs (NSAIDs), coffee, black pepper, spicy foods, and caffeine.

- Peptic Ulcer Disease (PUD)

  o PUD is characterized by an erosion of the mucosal layer of the stomach or duodenum.

  o This may be caused by a bacterial infection with Helicobacter pylori or the chronic use of NSAIDs (aspirin, ibuprofen).

  o Avoid eating frequent meals and snacks as they promote increased gastric acid secretion.

  o Avoid coffee, alcohol, caffeine, aspirin and other NSAIDs, cigarette smoking, black pepper, and spicy foods.

- Lactose Intolerance

  o Lactose intolerance results from an inadequate supply of lactase, the enzyme that digests lactose.

  o Symptoms include distention, cramps, flatus, and diarrhea.

  o Clients should be encouraged to avoid or limit their intake of foods high in lactose (milk, cheese, ice cream, cream soups, sour cream, puddings, chocolate, coffee creamer).

- Ileostomies and Colostomies

  o An ostomy is a surgically created opening on the surface of the abdomen from either the end of the small intestine (ileostomy) or from the colon (colostomy).

  o Fluid and electrolyte maintenance is the primary concern for clients with ileostomies and colostomies.

  o The colon absorbs large amounts of fluid, sodium, and potassium.

  o Nutrition therapy begins with liquids only and is slowly advanced based upon client tolerance.

  o Advise the client to consume a diet that is high in fluids and soluble fiber.

  o Encourage the client to avoid foods that cause gas (beans, eggs, carbonated beverages), stomal blockage (nuts, raw carrots, popcorn), and foods that produce odor (eggs, fish, garlic).

  o Additional calories and protein are needed to promote healing of the stoma site.

  o Clients require emotional support due to their altered body image.

- Diverticulosis and Diverticulitis

  o Diverticula are pouches that protrude from the wall of the intestine.

  o Diverticulosis is a condition characterized by the presence of diverticula.

  o Diverticulitis is the inflammation that occurs when fecal matter becomes trapped in the diverticula.

  o A high-fiber diet may prevent diverticulosis and diverticulitis by producing stools that are easily passed, thus decreasing pressure within the colon.

- During acute diverticulitis, a low-fiber diet is prescribed in order to reduce bowel stimulation.

- Avoid foods with seeds or husks (corn, popcorn, berries, tomatoes).

- Clients require instruction regarding diet adjustment based on the need for an acute intervention or preventive approach.

- Inflammatory Bowel Disease

  - Crohn's disease (regional enteritis) and ulcerative colitis are chronic, inflammatory bowel diseases characterized by periods of exacerbation and remission.

  - Symptoms include nausea, vomiting, abdominal cramps, fever, fatigue, anorexia, and weight loss.

  - Nutrition therapy is focused on providing nutrients in forms that the client can tolerate.

  - Generally diets are low in fiber to minimize bowel stimulation.

  - Total parenteral nutrition (TPN) may be indicated for clients who are severely ill during the acute phase of the illness.

- Cholecystitis

  - Cholecystitis is characterized by inflammation of the gallbladder.

  - The gallbladder stores and releases bile that aids in the digestion of fats.

  - Fat intake should be limited to reduce stimulation of the gallbladder.

  - Other foods that may cause problems include coffee, broccoli, cauliflower, Brussels sprouts, cabbage, onions, legumes, and highly seasoned foods.

  - The diet is individualized to the client's needs and tolerance.

  - No diet modifications are necessary for healthy people with asymptomatic gallstones.

- Pancreatitis

  - Pancreatitis is an inflammation of the pancreas.

  - The pancreas is responsible for secreting enzymes needed to digest fats, carbohydrates, and proteins.

  - Nutritional therapy for acute pancreatitis involves reducing any pancreatic stimulation. The client is prescribed to have nothing by mouth (NPO), and a nasogastric tube is inserted to suction gastric contents.

  - TPN may be used until oral intake is resumed.

  - Nutritional therapy for chronic pancreatitis usually includes a low-fat, high-protein, and high-carbohydrate diet. It may include providing supplements of vitamin C and B-complex vitamins.

- Liver Disease
  - The liver is involved in the metabolism of almost all nutrients.
  - Disorders affecting the liver include cirrhosis, hepatitis, and cancer.
  - Malnutrition is common with liver disease.
  - Protein needs are increased to promote a positive nitrogen balance and to prevent a breakdown of the body's protein stores.
  - Carbohydrates are generally not restricted, as they are an important source of calories.
  - Caloric requirements may need to be increased based upon an evaluation of the client's stage of disease, weight, and general health status.
  - Multivitamins (especially vitamins B, C, and K) and mineral supplements may be necessary.
  - Alcohol should be eliminated.

CHAPTER 13: GASTROINTESTINAL DISORDERS

 Application Exercises

1. Match the gastrointestinal disorders listed below with the appropriate dietary recommendations.

_____ Dysphagia	A. The client should remain NPO and TPN may be utilized.
_____ GERD	B. Low-fiber diet during the acute phase.
_____ Nausea and vomiting	C. Low-fat diet to decrease stimulation of the gallbladder.
_____ Dumping syndrome	D. High-fiber diet is a preventative measure.
_____ Pancreatitis	E. Increase protein intake to avoid utilizing bodily stores.
_____ Diverticulitis	F. Modify the texture of foods and the consistency of liquids.
_____ Cholecystitis	G. Low-fat carbohydrate foods (crackers, toast, oatmeal).
_____ Diverticulosis	H. Small, frequent meals are indicated for this postoperative complication.
_____ Liver disease	I. Avoid large meals, eating late, alcohol, caffeine, and smoking.

2. Provide a summary of the dietary recommendations for clients with gastrointestinal disorders affecting the mucosa of the stomach (PUD, gastritis).

3. What dietary recommendations should a nurse anticipate sharing with a client with inflammatory bowel disease?

CHAPTER 13: GASTROINTESTINAL DISORDERS

 Application Exercises Answer Key

1. Match the gastrointestinal disorders listed below with the appropriate dietary recommendations.

F	Dysphagia	A. The client should remain NPO and TPN may be utilized.
I	GERD	B. Low-fiber diet during the acute phase.
G	Nausea and vomiting	C. Low-fat diet to decrease stimulation of the gallbladder.
H	Dumping syndrome	D. High-fiber diet is a preventative measure.
A	Pancreatitis	E. Increase protein intake to avoid utilizing bodily stores.
B	Diverticulitis	F. Modify the texture of foods and the consistency of liquids.
C	Cholecystitis	G. Low-fat carbohydrate foods (crackers, toast, oatmeal).
D	Diverticulosis	H. Small, frequent meals are indicated for this postoperative complication.
E	Liver disease	I. Avoid large meals, eating late, alcohol, caffeine, and smoking.

 NCLEX® Connection: Basic Care and Comfort, Nutrition and Oral Hydration

2. Provide a summary of the dietary recommendations for clients with gastrointestinal disorders affecting the mucosa of the stomach (PUD, gastritis).

Clients with gastrointestinal disorders affecting the mucosa of the stomach should avoid eating frequent meals as it promotes the secretion of gastric acid, irritating the affected areas. Clients should be encouraged to avoid NSAIDs, alcohol, caffeine, smoking, coffee, and spicy foods.

NCLEX® Connection: Health Promotion and Maintenance, Health Promotion/ Disease Prevention

3. What dietary recommendations should a nurse anticipate sharing with a client with inflammatory bowel disease?

Based upon a review of the symptoms associated with inflammatory bowel disease, the client should be encouraged to:

During periods of exacerbation

- Consume foods low in fiber to minimize bowel stimulation.

- Avoid alcohol, caffeine, and cold and carbonated beverages as they are stimulants.

- Consume foods high in protein and calories to restore weight and nutrient deficiencies.

- Consume small, frequent meals to help maximize absorption.

During periods of remission

- Consume a well-balanced diet that is well tolerated by the client.

(N) NCLEX® Connection: Health Promotion and Maintenance, Health Promotion /Disease Prevention

UNIT 3	ALTERATIONS IN NUTRITION
Chapter 14	Renal Disorders

Overview

- Nurses must gain an awareness of nutritional needs for clients with renal disorders. It is important to explore dietary needs with the client and recommend modifications in relationship to the disease process. Understanding the role of primary and secondary prevention is essential to successful treatment.

- Specific nutritional considerations covered in this chapter are:

    o Pre-End Stage Renal Disease

    o End Stage Renal Disease

    o Acute Renal Failure

    o Nephrotic Syndrome

    o Nephrolithiasis (Kidney Stones)

- The kidneys have two basic functions: maintaining normal blood volume and excreting waste products.

    o Renal damage and/or loss of renal function has profound effects on the nutritional state.

    o Urea is a waste byproduct of protein metabolism, and urea levels rise with renal disease. Monitoring protein intake is paramount for clients with renal disease

- Short-term renal disease requires nutritional support for healing rather than dietary restrictions.

- Dietary recommendations are dependent upon the stage of renal disease.

Assessment/Data Collection

- Pre-end stage renal disease (pre-ESRD) is distinguished by an increase in serum creatinine. Signs and symptoms include fatigue, back pain, and appetite changes.

- Signs and symptoms of end stage renal disease (ESRD) include fatigue, decreased alertness, anemia, decreased urination, headache, and weight loss.

- Signs and symptoms of acute renal failure (ARF) include a decrease in urination, decreased sensation in the extremities, swelling of the lower extremities, and flank pain. It is characterized by rising blood levels of urea and other nitrogenous wastes.

- The most pronounced manifestation of nephrotic syndrome is edema. Other manifestations include hypoalbuminemia, hyperlipidemia, and blood hypercoagulation.

- The passing of a kidney stone is characterized by sudden, intense pain that is typically located in the flank and is unrelieved by position changes Diaphoresis and nausea and vomiting are common, and there may be blood in the urine. Approximately 80% of stones contain calcium.

Nutritional Guidelines and Nursing Interventions

- General Renal Considerations

  o Monitor renal parameters for clients who have renal disorders.

    - Nurses should monitor the client's weight daily or as frequently as prescribed. Weight is an indicator of fluid status, which is a primary concern for clients.

    - Monitor the client's fluid intake and encourage compliance with fluid restrictions.

    - Nurses should monitor urine output. Placement of an indwelling urinary catheter may be necessary for accurate measurement.

    - Monitor for signs and symptoms of constipation. Fluid restrictions predispose clients to constipation.

  o Explain to clients why dietary changes are necessary. Ultimately, alterations in the intake of protein, calories, sodium, potassium, phosphorus, and other vitamins will be necessary.

  o Provide support for the client and family.

- Pre-End Stage Renal Disease (pre-ESRD)

  o Pre-ESRD, or diminished renal reserve/renal insufficiency, is a predialysis condition characterized by an increase in serum creatinine.

  o Therapeutic Nutrition

    - Goals of nutritional therapy for pre-ESRD are to:

      □ Control blood glucose levels and hypertension, which are both risk factors.

      □ Help preserve remaining renal function by limiting the intake of protein and phosphorus.

    - Restricting phosphorus intake slows the progression of renal disease.

      □ High levels of phosphorus contribute to calcium and phosphorus deposits in the kidneys.

    - Protein restriction is essential for clients with pre-ESRD.

      □ Slows the progression of renal disease.

      □ Too little protein results in the breakdown of body protein. Protein intake must be carefully determined.

- Dietary recommendations for pre-ESRD:
  - Restrict sodium intake to maintain blood pressure.
  - The recommended daily protein intake is 0.6 to 1.0 g/kg of ideal body weight.
  - Limit meat intake to <5 to 6 oz/day for most men and < 4 oz/day for most women.
  - Limit dairy products to ½ cup per day.
  - Limit high-phosphorus foods (peanut butter, dried peas and beans, bran, cola, chocolate, beer, some whole grains) to one serving or less per day.
  - Caution clients to use vitamin and mineral supplements only when recommended by a health care provider.

- End Stage Renal Disease (ESRD)
  - ESRD, or chronic renal failure, occurs when the glomerular filtration rate (GFR) is less than 25 mL/min, the serum creatinine level steadily rises, or dialysis or transplantation is necessary.
  - Therapeutic Nutrition
    - The goal of nutritional therapy is to maintain appropriate fluid status, blood pressure, and blood chemistries.
      - A high-protein, low-phosphorus, low-potassium, low-sodium (2 to 4 g/day), fluid-restricted diet is recommended.
      - Vitamin D and calcium are nutrients of concern.
    - Potassium intake is dependent upon the client's laboratory values, which should be closely monitored.
    - Sodium and fluid allowances are determined by blood pressure, weight, serum electrolyte levels, and urine output.
    - Achieving a well-balanced diet based on the above guidelines is difficult. The National Renal Diet provides clients with a list of appropriate food choices.
    - Protein needs increase once dialysis has begun as protein and amino acids are lost in the dialysate.
      - Fifty percent of protein intake should come from biologic sources (eggs, milk, meat, fish, poultry, soy).
      - Adequate calories (35 kcal/kg of body weight) should be consumed to maintain body protein stores.
    - Phosphorus must be restricted.
      - A high protein requirement leads to an increase in phosphorus intake.
      - Phosphate binders must be taken with all meals and snacks.

- Vitamin D deficiency occurs as the kidneys are unable to convert vitamin D to its active form.
  - This alters the metabolism of calcium, phosphorus, and magnesium, leading to hyperphosphatemia, hypocalcemia, and hypermagnesemia.
  - Calcium supplements will likely be required since foods high in phosphorus (which are restricted) are also high in calcium.

- Acute Renal Failure (ARF)

  - ARF is an abrupt, rapid decline in renal function. It is usually caused by trauma, sepsis, poor perfusion, or medications. ARF can cause hyponatremia, hyperkalemia, hypocalcemia, and hyperphosphatemia.

  - Therapeutic Nutrition

    - Diet therapy for ARF is dependent upon the phase of ARF and its underlying cause. Protein, calories, fluids, potassium, and sodium need to be individualized according to the phase of ARF, and adjusted as improvement develops.

- Nephrotic Syndrome

  - Nephrotic syndrome results in the leakage of serum proteins into the urine.

  - Therapeutic Nutrition

    - Nutritional therapy goals include minimizing edema, replacing lost nutrients, and minimizing renal damage.

    - Dietary recommendations indicate sufficient protein and low-sodium intake.

- Nephrolithiasis (Kidney Stones)

  - Preventative Nutrition

    - Excessive intake of protein, sodium, calcium, and oxalates (rhubarb, spinach, beets) may increase the risk of stone formation.

  - Therapeutic Nutrition

    - Increasing fluid consumption is the primary intervention for the treatment and prevention of renal calculi. At least 8 to 12 oz (240 to 360 mL) of fluid, preferably water should be consumed before bedtime as urine becomes more concentrated at night.

CHAPTER 14: RENAL DISORDERS

 Application Exercises

1. A nurse is providing teaching for a client who has a history of calcium-based kidney stones. Which of the following should the nurse include in the teaching?

    A. Avoid drinking fluids at bedtime.

    B. Drink 12 oz of water at bedtime.

    C. Include an adequate intake of milk products in the diet

    D. Exclude tomatoes and whole grains from diet.

2. A nurse is preparing to discharge a client who has pre ESRD. Which of the following should be included in the instructions? (Select all that apply.)

    _____ Limit sodium intake

    _____ Limit the intake of meat

    _____ Limit carbohydrate intake

    _____ Limit the intake of dairy products

    _____ Limit the intake of fat

3. A nurse is completing the initial assessment of a client. Her past medical history indicates that the client has a history of ESRD and undergoes dialysis three times per week. What initial and ongoing assessment data should the nurse collect?

CHAPTER 14: RENAL DISORDERS

 Application Exercises Answer Key

1. A nurse is providing teaching for a client who has a history of calcium-based kidney stones. Which of the following should the nurse include in the teaching?

    A. Avoid drinking fluids at bedtime.

    B. Drink 12 oz of water at bedtime.

    C. Include an adequate intake of milk products in the diet

    D. Exclude tomatoes and whole grains from diet.

    The client should drink water at bedtime to promote dilution of the urine during the night. Milk products should be avoided as they are high in calcium and may contribute to the formation of calcium stones. Tomatoes and whole grains should be included in the diet as they increase the acidity of urine and decrease stone formation.

 NCLEX® Connection: Health Promotion and Maintenance, Health Promotion/Disease Prevention

2. A nurse is preparing to discharge a client who has pre ESRD. Which of the following should be included in the instructions? (Select all that apply.)

    <u> X </u>   **Limit sodium intake**

    <u> X </u>   **Limit the intake of meat**

    <u>   </u>   Limit carbohydrate intake

    <u> X </u>   **Limit the intake of dairy products**

    <u>   </u>   Limit the intake of fat

    Sodium is limited to avoid fluid retention. The intake of proteins which includes dairy products and meats are limited to prevent uremia. The client should consume adequate carbohydrates and fats to prevent breakdown of body proteins by catabolism.

 NCLEX® Connection: Health Promotion and Maintenance, Health Promotion/Disease Prevention

3. A nurse is completing the initial assessment of a client. Her past medical history indicates that the client has a history of ESRD and undergoes dialysis three times per week. What initial and ongoing assessment data should the nurse collect?

    The nurse should monitor the following:

    •   **Daily weights.**

    •   **Intake and output.**

    •   **Signs of constipation.**

    •   **BUN, creatinine, and electrolytes.**

    All of the above are important indicators of renal function.

 NCLEX® Connection: Basic Care and Comfort, Nutrition and Oral Hydration

UNIT 3	ALTERATIONS IN NUTRITION
Chapter 15	Diabetes Mellitus

Overview

- Nurses must gain an awareness of nutritional needs for clients with diabetes mellitus. It is important to explore dietary needs with the client and recommend modifications in relationship to the disease process. Understanding the role of primary and secondary prevention is essential to successful treatment.

- Diabetes mellitus inhibits the body's production and/or utilization of insulin. This results in above-normal glucose levels and health complications including heart disease, blindness, and renal failure.

  ○ Glucose is the body's primary source of energy, and insulin is needed to assist the body in using glucose.

  ○ The goal of treatment is to assist the client in making the appropriate lifestyle changes and nutritional choices necessary to control blood glucose levels.

  ○ Achieving proper nutrition and meeting specific dietary needs is essential in controlling the effects of diabetes mellitus.

  ○ Blood glucose levels are used to diagnose diabetes.

- Types of Diabetes Mellitus

  ○ Type 1 Diabetes Mellitus

    ▪ Autoimmune, genetically linked disease.

    ▪ Characterized by the absence of insulin which damages or destroys beta cells of the pancreas.

    ▪ Usually occurs in individuals under the age of 30 with a normal or below normal weight.

  ○ Type 2 Diabetes Mellitus

    ▪ Result of genetic and environmental factors.

    ▪ Characterized by abnormal patterns of insulin secretion and decreased cellular uptake of glucose (insulin resistance).

    ▪ Usually occurs in individuals over the age of 40.

    ▪ Obesity and sedentary lifestyle are risk factors.

- o Gestational Diabetes Mellitus (GDM)

    - Glucose intolerance that is recognized during pregnancy.

    - Usually occurs during the 2nd and 3rd trimesters.

    - Occurs only during pregnancy and typically resolves after delivery.

    - Characterized by increased insulin resistance and increased insulin antagonists.

    - Many women with GDM develop type 2 diabetes mellitus later in life.

    - Blood glucose control is important for preventing damage to the fetus in women with pre-existing diabetes mellitus who are pregnant or those with GDM.

Assessment/Data Collection

- Hypoglycemia is an abnormally low blood glucose level.

    - o It results from taking too much insulin, inadequate food intake, delayed or skipped meals, extra physical activity, or consumption of alcohol without food.

    - o Blood glucose levels of 70 mg/dL or less require immediate action.

    - o Symptoms include mild shakiness, mental confusion, sweating, palpitations, headache, lack of coordination, blurred vision, seizures, and coma.

- Hyperglycemia is an abnormally high blood glucose level.

    - o It results from an imbalance among food, medication, and activity.

    - o Symptoms include blood glucose greater than 250 mg/dL, ketones in urine, polydipsia (excessive thirst), polyuria (excessive urination), hyperventilation, dehydration, fruity odor to breath, and coma.

Nutritional Guidelines and Nursing Interventions

- Hypoglycemia

    - o Clients with hypoglycemia should be instructed to take 15 to 20 g of a readily absorbable carbohydrate, including:

        - Two or three glucose tablets (5 g each).

        - Five Lifesavers™/hard candies.

        - ½ cup (4 oz) juice or regular soda.

        - 1 tbsp of honey or brown sugar.

    - o Retest the blood glucose in 15 min. If it is 70 to 75 mg/dL, repeat the above steps. Once levels normalize, give an additional 15 g if the next meal is more than 1 hr away.

- Hyperglycemia
  - Clients with symptoms of hyperglycemia should:
    - Immediately consult a health care provider, or go to the emergency department.
    - Take medication if forgotten.
    - Consider modifications to insulin or oral diabetic medications.
  - Long-term implications of untreated or inadequately treated hyperglycemia include blindness, kidney failure, dyslipidemia, hypertension, neuropathy, microvascular disease, and limb amputation.
  - Somagyi's phenomenon is morning hyperglycemia in response to overnight hypoglycemia. Providing a bedtime snack and appropriate insulin dose will prevent hypoglycemia.
  - Dawn phenomenon is an elevation of blood glucose around 0500 to 0600. It results from an overnight release of growth hormone, and is treated by increasing the amount of insulin provided during the overnight hours.
- General Nutritional Guidelines
  - Coronary heart disease (CHD) is the leading cause of death among clients with diabetes. Therefore, clients with diabetes are encouraged to follow a diet that is high in fiber and low in saturated fat, trans fat, and cholesterol.
  - Dietary intake should be individualized. General guidelines include:
    - Encourage the client to consume complex carbohydrates found in grains, fruits, and vegetables.
    - Carbohydrates and monounsaturated fats combined should account for 60% to 70% of total calories.
    - Saturated fat should account for less than 10% of total calories. If LDL is greater than 100 mg/dL, the saturated fat should be limited to less than 7% of intake.
    - Promote fiber intake (beans, vegetables, oats, whole grains).
    - Protein should comprise 15% to 20% of total caloric intake. Protein intake may need to be reduced in clients with diabetes and renal failure.
  - Encourage clients with diabetes mellitus to eliminate all tobacco use.
  - Limit alcohol intake and consuming food with alcohol consumption.
  - Vitamin and mineral requirements are unchanged for clients who have diabetes. Supplements are recommended for identified deficiencies. Deficiencies in magnesium and potassium can aggravate glucose intolerance.
  - Artificial sweeteners are acceptable. Saccharin crosses the placenta and should be avoided during pregnancy.
  - Cultural and personal preferences should be considered in planning food intake.

- o According to the American Diabetes Association and the American Dietetic Association, daily nutritional requirements are based on the needs of each client. The dietitian will work with the client to develop meal planning that will meet the client's needs. This is based on healthy food choices. The goal of therapy is to maintain blood glucose levels as close to normal range as possible.

- o The dietitian will instruct the client on various dietary methods including exchange list and carbohydrate counting.

- o Using the exchange list as a guide for meal planning allows for the incorporation of three basic food groups: meats, carbohydrates, and fats. This dietary regimen will assist the client in maintaining a blood glucose level within a target range. Each client will have a recommended amount of daily exchanges within each group based on the client's needs.

- o Carbohydrate counting focuses on counting total grams of carbohydrates in each food item. Each client will be prescribed a number of grams of carbohydrates for each meal and daily snacks. The dietitian will determine needs of the individual and provide instructions for reading food labels and counting carbohydrate amounts in food selections.

- Other Nursing Interventions

  - o Encourage exercise. Blood glucose levels and medication dosages should be closely monitored.

  - o Encourage weight loss.

    - ▪ Weight loss is especially encouraged in clients with type 2 diabetes mellitus as it can decrease insulin resistance, improve glucose and lipid levels, and lower blood pressure.

  - o Clients should be encouraged to perform self-monitoring of blood glucose levels.

    - ▪ Strict control of glucose levels can reduce or postpone complications (retinopathy, nephropathy, neuropathy).

  - o Clients should be encouraged to receive regular evaluations from the provider.

  - o Client education and support should be provided for:

    - ▪ Self-monitoring of blood glucose.

    - ▪ Dietary and activity recommendations.

    - ▪ Signs, symptoms, and treatment of hypoglycemia and hyperglycemia.

    - ▪ Long-term complications of diabetes.

    - ▪ Psychological implications.

  - o Children with diabetes will require parental support, guidance, and participation. Dietary intake must provide for proper growth and development.

CHAPTER 15: DIABETES MELLITUS

(A) Application Exercises

1. A nurse is caring for a 7-year-old child who is newly diagnosed with type 1 diabetes mellitus. His mother expresses concern regarding the implications of the diabetes, which she does not fully understand. What information is important to share with the client?

2. Which of the following symptoms suggest hypoglycemia in a client with diabetes mellitus? (Select all that apply.)

   _____   Fruity odor to breath
   _____   Confusion
   _____   Vomiting
   _____   Shakiness
   _____   Sweating

3. A nurse is caring for a 53-year-old client with diabetes mellitus. The client reports feeling dizzy, lightheaded, and seeing "two of everything." What is the client likely experiencing? What interventions should the nurse perform?

CHAPTER 15: DIABETES MELLITUS

 Application Exercises Answer Key

1. A nurse is caring for a 7-year-old child who is newly diagnosed with type 1 diabetes mellitus. His mother expresses concern regarding the implications of the diabetes, which she does not fully understand. What information is important to share with the client?

> **The nurse should first acknowledge the mother's concerns and provide support. The mother should be informed that close monitoring and strict control of blood glucose levels in clients with diabetes mellitus can delay the onset and development of any long-term complications. Share the appropriate dietary guidelines for fat, protein, and carbohydrate consumption. Educate the client's mother regarding the signs, symptoms, and treatment of hypoglycemia and hyperglycemia. Lastly, the nurse should provide the mother with educational materials and resources (The American Diabetes Association, the American Dietetic Association, a local support group for parents of children with diabetes mellitus).**

 NCLEX® Connection: Health Promotion and Maintenance, Health Promotion /Disease Prevention

2. Which of the following symptoms suggest hypoglycemia in a client with diabetes mellitus? (Select all that apply.)

	Fruity odor to breath
X	**Confusion**
	Vomiting
X	**Shakiness**
X	**Sweating**

> **Signs of hypoglycemia include shakiness, sweating, and confusion. A fruity odor to breath and vomiting are signs of hyperglycemia.**

 NCLEX® Connection: Health Promotion and Maintenance, Health Promotion /Disease Prevention

3. A nurse is caring for a 53-year-old client with diabetes mellitus. The client reports feeling dizzy, lightheaded, and seeing "two of everything." What is the client likely experiencing? What interventions should the nurse perform?

> **The client is experiencing symptoms of hypoglycemia. The nurse should first perform a blood glucose test. Once hypoglycemia is confirmed, the nurse should instruct the client to take 15 g of readily absorbable glucose (two or three glucose tablets, five hard candies, ½ cup or 4 oz of juice, or 1 tbsp of honey or brown sugar). Recheck the client's blood glucose after 15 min. If it is above 80 mg/dL, follow with an additional 15 g if meal time is more than 1 hr away.**

 NCLEX® Connection: Health Promotion and Maintenance, Nutrition and Oral Hydration

UNIT 3	ALTERATIONS IN NUTRITION
Chapter 16	Cancer and Immunosuppression Disorders

@ Overview

- Nurses must gain an awareness of nutritional needs for clients with cancer and immunosuppression disorders. It is important to explore dietary needs with the client and recommend modifications in relationship to the disease process.

- Protein-calorie malnutrition and body wasting are common problems for clients who have cancer or immunosuppression disorders (HIV/AIDS). Nutritional deficits are a major cause of morbidity and mortality.

  ○ Major treatments for cancer include surgery, radiation, chemotherapy, immunotherapy, and bone marrow transplantation. Side effects of treatments compromise the nutritional status of affected clients, and more than one-third of all cancer deaths are related to nutritional complications.

  ○ Acquired Immune Deficiency Syndrome (AIDS) is a life-threatening disease that is caused by human immunodeficiency virus (HIV), a retrovirus that attacks T-cells and causes a severe depression of immune function.

- The goals of nutritional therapy are to: minimize the nutritional complications of disease, improve nutritional status, prevent muscle wasting, maintain weight, promote healing, reduce side effects, decrease morbidity and mortality, and enhance quality of life and the overall effectiveness of treatment therapies.

- Nutritional plans are individualized for client needs.

Assessment/Data Collection

- For clients who have cancer and/or immunosuppression disorders, nurses should:

  ○ Obtain baseline assessment data (weight, body mass index [BMI], height, nutritional habits, recent weight trends, disease history, food preferences, pertinent laboratory values [albumin, ferritin]), for future monitoring.

Nutritional Guidelines and Nursing Interventions

- Cancer

  ○ Preventative Nutrition

    ■ Adequate dietary fiber may lessen the risk of colon cancer.

    ■ Eliminate tobacco to reduce the risk of lung cancer.

- High intake of fruits and vegetables is linked to a lowered incidence of many types of cancer. Eat at least five servings daily.

- Consume whole grains rather than processed or refined grains and sugars.

- Meat preparation by smoking, pickling, charcoal grilling, and use of nitrate-containing chemicals may be carcinogenic.

- High intake of polyunsaturated and monounsaturated fats in fish and olive oils is presumed to be beneficial in lowering the risk of many types of cancer.

- High alcohol consumption is associated with liver, pancreatic, and biliary cancers.

- Excess body fat stimulates the production of estrogen and progesterone, which may intensify the growth of various cell types and may contribute to breast, gallbladder, colon, prostate, uterine, and kidney cancers.

- A calcium-rich diet is associated with a lower incidence of colon cancer as it binds free fatty acids and bile salts in the lower gastrointestinal tract.

○ Therapeutic Nutrition

- Cancer may cause anorexia, increased metabolism, and negative nitrogen balance.

- Systemic effects result in poor food intake, increased nutrient and energy needs, and catabolism of body tissues.

- Nutritional plans are individualized according to client needs.

- Nutritional needs for the client with cancer include:

  □ Increased caloric intake ranging from 25 to 35 cal/kg to maintain weight and 40 to 50 cal/kg to rebuild body stores.

  □ Protein needs are increased to 1.5 to 2.0 g/kg.

  □ Vitamin and mineral supplementation is based upon the client's needs.

- Encourage clients to eat more on days when **feeling better (on "good" days)**.

- Encourage intake of foods that have been modified to contain additional protein and calories. Foods choices include:

  □ Milk, cheese, milkshakes, and pudding.

  □ Fish.

  □ Eggs.

  □ Nuts.

- Nutritional supplements that are high in protein and/or calories should be encouraged.

  □ These supplements should be offered between meals and can be used as meal replacements if necessary.

- Increase protein and caloric content of foods by:
    - Substituting whole milk for water in recipes.
    - Adding cheese to dishes.
    - Using peanut butter as a spread for fruits.
    - Using yogurt as a topping for fruit.
    - Dipping meats in milk and bread crumbs before cooking.
- Complications associated with nutritional management

COMPLICATIONS	INTERVENTIONS
Early satiety	• Eat small amounts of high protein foods, loaded with calories and nutrient
Anorexia	• Eat small amounts of high protein foods, loaded with calories and nutrient • Try to consume food in the morning when appetite is best • Avoid food odors • Do not fill up on low calorie foods (broth, high roughage foods containing water)
Mouth ulcers and stomatitis	• Use a soft toothbrush to clean teeth after eating and at bedtime • Avoid mouth washes that contain alcohol • Omit spicy, dry, or coarse foods • Include cold or room temperature foods in the diet • Cut food into small bites • Try using straws • Be sure dentures fit well
Fatigue	• Eat a large, calorie-dense breakfast when energy level is the highest • Conserve energy by eating foods that are easy to prepare • Utilize a meal delivery service
Food aversions	• Avoid eating foods that are well-tolerated and liked prior to having treatments (chemotherapy, radiation).

COMPLICATIONS	INTERVENTIONS
Taste alterations and thick saliva	<ul><li>Try adding foods that are tart (citrus juices)</li><li>Include cold or room temperature foods in the diet</li><li>Try using sauces for added flavor</li><li>Use plastic utensils when cooking</li><li>Suck on mints, candy, or chew gum to remove bad taste in mouth.</li></ul>
Gastrointestinal problems (nausea, vomiting, diarrhea)	<ul><li>Nausea, vomiting<ul><li>Eat cold or room temperature foods</li><li>Try high carbohydrate, low fat foods</li><li>Avoid fried foods</li><li>Do not eat prior to chemotherapy or radiation</li><li>Take prescribed antiemetic medication at the direction of the provider</li></ul></li><li>Diarrhea<ul><li>Ensure adequate intake of liquids throughout the day to replace losses</li><li>Avoid foods that may exacerbate diarrhea (foods high in roughage)</li><li>Consume foods high in pectin to increase the bulk of the stool and to lengthen transition time in the colon</li></ul></li></ul>

- A client receiving immunosuppressant therapy may need to minimize exposure to microorganisms found on the outer layers of fresh fruits and vegetables. Peeling and thorough washing or cooking may be necessary. In some cases, fresh foods may increase the risk of infection.

- Nurses should teach clients with dysphagia to inhale, swallow, and then exhale and tilt. Tilting of the head may help with swallowing. Avoid sticky or lumpy food.

- Ongoing nursing interventions include:

  □ Monitoring baseline assessment parameters during the course of treatment.

  □ Providing education for the client regarding expected symptoms and side effects of treatments, and the effects on nutritional requirements and patterns.

  □ Educating the client and his or her support system regarding nutritional recommendations and the appropriate food choices.

  □ Assisting the client with establishing realistic nutritional goals and discuss ways to increase consumption.

  □ Providing support to the client and his or her support system.

- HIV/AIDS
  - Therapeutic Nutrition
    - The body's response to the inflammatory and immune processes associated with HIV increases nutrient requirements. Malnutrition is a common problem and is one cause of death in AIDS.
    - HIV infection, secondary infection, malignancies, and medication therapies can cause symptoms and side effects that impair intake and alter metabolism.
    - Overall, caloric needs are increased, generally ranging from 35 to 45 cal/kg.
    - A high-protein diet is recommended with amounts varying from 1.2 to 2.0 g/kg.
    - The intake of a multivitamin that meets 100% of the recommended daily servings is sufficient, unless a specific deficiency is identified.
    - Poor nutritional status leads to wasting and fever, further aggravating the susceptibility to secondary infections.
    - Wasting is distinguished by an unintended weight loss of 10% and concurrent problems that include diarrhea or chronic weakness and fever for at least 30 days.
    - Decreased nutrient intake occurs because of physical symptoms (anorexia, nausea, vomiting, diarrhea). Psychological symptoms may include depression and dementia.
    - Diarrhea and malabsorption are prominent clinical problems in clients with AIDS.
    - Liberal fluid intake is extremely important to prevent dehydration.
    - Nutritional warning signs in clients with HIV/AIDS include rapid weight loss, gastrointestinal problems, inadequate intake, increased nutrient needs, food aversions, fad diets, and supplements.
    - If the client with AIDS is unable to consume sufficient nutrients, calories, and fluid, enteral feedings may be needed.
    - Encourage the client to consume small, frequent meals that are composed of high-protein, high-calorie, and nutrient-dense foods.
    - Ongoing nursing interventions include:
      - Monitoring baseline assessment parameters during the course of treatment.
      - Providing education for the client regarding expected symptoms and side effects of treatments, nutritional requirements, and patterns.
      - Educating the client and his or her support system regarding nutritional recommendations and the appropriate food choices.
      - Assisting the client with establishing realistic nutritional goals and discuss ways to increase consumption.
      - Providing support to the client and his or her support system.

CHAPTER 16: CANCER AND IMMUNOSUPPRESSION DISORDERS

Ⓐ Application Exercises

Scenario: A nurse is caring for a 28-year-old female client diagnosed with Hodgkin's lymphoma. She undergoes chemotherapy every 2 weeks, and has had two treatments thus far.

1. The client reports that she rarely eats more than two meals per day. She states that she is too tired and nothing sounds good. What information regarding nutritional requirements is important to share with her?

2. After educating the client regarding appropriate food choices based on her body's needs, the nurse determines that the client understands the information when she chooses which of the following snacks? (Select all that apply.)

    _____ Peanut butter sandwich on whole wheat bread with 2% milk

    _____ Popcorn with soda

    _____ Yogurt topped with granola and a banana

    _____ Meat lasagna with buttered garlic bread

    _____ Plain baked potato

Scenario: A nurse is caring for a 41-year-old male client with AIDS. During the assessment, he reveals that he has suffered from nausea, vomiting, and diarrhea for the last 3 weeks. He states that he feels weak and no longer has energy to finish tasks.

3. What guidance should the nurse provide to the client regarding appropriate food choices to combat symptoms?

4. If the client's symptoms do not improve, what should the nurse expect as the next step?

CHAPTER 16: CANCER AND IMMUNOSUPPRESSION DISORDERS

(A) Application Exercises Answer Key

Scenario: A nurse is caring for a 28-year-old female client diagnosed with Hodgkin's lymphoma. She undergoes chemotherapy every 2 weeks, and has had two treatments thus far.

1. The client reports that she rarely eats more than two meals per day. She states that she is too tired and nothing sounds good. What information regarding nutritional requirements is important to share with her?

    The nurse should acknowledge the client's feelings and provide her with an opportunity to share frustrations. It is important to instruct the client that cancer and chemotherapy are placing demands on her body that require an increase in protein and caloric intake. Encourage her to eat more when she is feeling better (on "good" days). Assist the client in developing achievable nutritional intake goals. Instruct her on food sources that are high in protein and calories. Also, provide the client with methods for increasing her caloric intake with regular food choices (add cheese to meals, use higher fat milk, use peanut butter as a spread).

    (N) NCLEX® Connection: Basic Care and Comfort, Nutrition and Oral Hydration

2. After educating the client regarding appropriate food choices based on her body's needs, the nurse determines that the client understands the information when she chooses which of the following snacks? (Select all that apply.)

__X__	**Peanut butter sandwich on whole wheat bread with 2% milk**
_____	Popcorn with soda
__X__	**Yogurt topped with granola and a banana**
__X__	**Meat lasagna with buttered garlic bread**
_____	Plain baked potato

    The selected food sources above are high in protein and calories. Popcorn and a plain baked potato do not meet the needs of the client by increasing caloric intake.

    (N) NCLEX® Connection: Basic Care and Comfort, Nutrition and Oral Hydration

Scenario: A nurse is caring for a 41-year-old male client with AIDS. During the assessment, he reveals that he has suffered from nausea, vomiting, and diarrhea for the last 3 weeks. He states that he feels weak and no longer has energy to finish tasks.

3. What guidance should the nurse provide to the client regarding appropriate food choices to combat symptoms?

   The nurse should encourage the client to eat high-carbohydrate and low-fat foods as they may help with nausea. This includes toast or crackers, yogurt, bananas, canned fruits, and cooked cereals. The client should be instructed on the importance of replacing fluids. Broths, soups, sports drinks, and canned fruits provide the client with calories and valuable electrolytes. Nutritional supplements may be recommended if the client is able to tolerate them.

 NCLEX® Connection: Basic Care and Comfort, Nutrition and Oral Hydration

4. If the client's symptoms do not improve, what should the nurse expect as the next step?

   When clients with HIV/AIDS are unable to consume enough calories, enteral feedings may be indicated. This is also true of clients with cancer.

 NCLEX® Connection: Basic Care and Comfort, Nutrition and Oral Hydration

References

Dudek, S. G. (2010). *Nutrition essentials for nursing practice* (6th ed.). Philadelphia, PA: Lippincott Williams & Wilkins.

Grodner, M., Long, S., & Walkingshaw, B. C. (2007). *Foundations and clinical applications of nutrition: A nursing approach* (4th ed.). St. Louis, MO: Mosby.

Hockenberry, M. J., & Winkelstein M. L. (2009). *Wong's essentials of pediatric nursing* (8th ed.). St. Louis, MO: Mosby.

Ignatavicius, D. D., & Workman, M. L. (2010). *Medical-surgical nursing* (6th ed.). St. Louis, MO: Saunders.

Lowdermilk, D. L., & Perry, S. E. (2007). *Maternity & women's health care* (9th ed.). St. Louis, MO: Mosby.

Pillitteri, A. (2007). *Maternal and child health nursing: Care of the childbearing and childrearing family* (5th ed.). Philadelphia, PA: Lippincott Williams & Wilkins.